WHAT MAKES RACIAL DIVERSITY WORK

IN HIGHER EDUCATION

WHAT MAKES RACIAL DIVERSITY WORK IN HIGHER EDUCATION

Academic Leaders Present Successful Policies and Strategies

Edited by Frank W. Hale, Jr.

FOREWORD BY *Dr. William E. Kirwan*

STERLING, VIRGINIA

Published in 2004 by

Stylus Publishing, LLC
22883 Quicksilver Drive
Sterling, Virginia 20166

**Library of Congress
Cataloging-in-Publication-Data**
What makes racial diversity work in higher edu-
cation : academic leaders present successful poli-
cies and strategies / edited by Frank W. Hale, Jr. ;
foreword by William Kirwan.—1st ed.
    p. cm.
  Includes bibliographical references.
  ISBN 1-57922-066-5 (alk. paper)—
ISBN 1-57922-067-3 (pbk. : alk. paper)
1. Minorities—Education (Higher)—United
States. 2. Multicultural education—United
States. 3. Educational equalization—United
States.
First edition, 2003
  ISBN: hardcover 1-57922-066-5
  ISBN: paperback 1-57922-067-3

Printed in the United States of America
All first editions printed on acid-free paper

In memory and in recognition of those who
sacrificed themselves
for the good of others

IN MEMORY
of

Mr. and Mrs. Frank W. Hale, Sr.,—my parents
Mrs. Ruth Colleen Saddler Hale—my wife
Dr. Eva B. Dykes
Ms. Henrietta Emmanuel
Elder Calvin E. Moseley, Jr.
Elder Frank Loris Peterson
Dr. Charles H. Wesley
Ms. Luvada Lockhart White

IN RECOGNITION
of

Dr. William J. Holloway
Dr. William E. Kirwan
Dr. Jannith Lewis
Dr. Gaines R. Partridge
Dr. Arliss Roaden
Dr. Jon Robertson
Dr. Calvin B. Rock
Dr. Mervyn Warren

CONTENTS

ACKNOWLEDGMENTS

I owe my greatest debt to those whose positive attitudes and personal encouragement helped me to tackle the problems of race so prevalent and pervasive during my youth. My special gratitude goes to those teachers along the way who brought out the stirrings of my potential which enabled me as a black man to navigate the vagaries of American life with all its ambiguities. I salute all those pioneers who were of inestimable support: LaVada Lockhart, Donald Gleckler, Leroy Laase, Morgan Maxwell, Frank Loris Peterson, Eva B. Dykes, Earl Wiley, Arliss Roaden, Calvin E. Moseley, Jr., Winton H. Beaven, Edward H. Jennings, William Kirwan, William J. Holloway, William E. Nelson, Jr., Mac A. Stewart, Rose Wilson-Hill, and Minnie McGee.

Of special significance was the generous and sacrificing support of Trina Phillips, my office associate, who with patience and good humor provided stellar clerical assistance. Peg Levine's critical and careful reading has supplied valuable feedback on matters of substance, mechanics, and style, and she also served as an insightful sounding board through the entire process.

Kudos to John von Knorring, publisher of Stylus Publishing, L.L.C., who spontaneously responded to the initial proposal dealing with issues of diversity that had been percolating in my mind for a long time. The need to know the thoughts and experiences of those who have been a part of the diversity movement has made this book a valuable resource that will prove relevant and critical for those who deal with issues of diversity on a day-to-day basis.

Two of the essays in this book were published elsewhere. We are grateful to the authors for their permission to make use of the following essays: Carlos E. Cortés's "Limits to *Pluribus*, Limits to *Unum*:

Diversity and the Future of Higher Education,"* previously included in *The Making and Remaking of a Multiculturalist* by Carlos Cortés and published by Teachers College Press of Columbia University (2002), and Neil L. Rudenstein's "Diversity and Learning at Harvard" which appeared in *Pointing our Thoughts*, published by Harvard University (2001).

I have been particularly privileged to be associated with Ohio State University in various venues during the past three decades. William J. Holloway, William E. Nelson, Jr., Arliss Roaden, Edward H. Jennings, and William E. Kirwan have been particularly strengthening in their visions and support.

Mere words do little to express my gratitude for the love that I have received during the final stages of this work from the queenly lady, Ms. Mignon Scott Palmer Flack, who will very soon become my bride and joy.

Finally, genuine gratitude goes to my family: my children Ifeoma, Frank III, and Sherilyn for sacrificing their time during my sustained recesses in the preparation of this work and my deceased wife Ruth who, up until her passing in November 2001, helped to "keep the fires burning" with fresh ideas, food on the table, abounding love, and uncompromising spiritual guidance.

*Originally printed in *National Forum: The Phi Kappa Phi Journal*, Volume 74, Number 1 (Winter 1994). Copyright by Carlos Cortés. By permission of the publishers.

This book, *What Makes Racial Diversity Work in Higher Education*, has been inspired by a desire to move beyond the rhetoric of diversity and to capitalize on the perspectives of those who have been active thinkers and practicing programmers in this vital area. Some institutions have been willing to move beyond the conservative aspects of ethnicity into a more inclusive framework of promoting the positive efforts of diversity. I have selected scholars who have played critical roles in establishing and clarifying the rationale for diversity in a democratic society. This book of essays establishes the case for racial diversity; the challenges which diversity offers to the academic community as a whole; examples of how some institutions developed successful models of diversity; and to what effect the history of racial diversity in higher education has influenced aspects of diversity today. It is my hope that this collection will contribute to the understanding and skills of those whose concern it is to develop strategies that will neutralize and eliminate the practices that have subverted and supplanted democratic ideals and goals.

In the foreword, **Dr. William E. Kirwan** highlights the importance of "acting affirmatively to eliminate the present-day results of bias and prejudice." He underscores the point that those in positions of responsibility should not be satisfied with race- and gender- "neutral" policies and practices, because "neutrality alone cannot erase the efforts of centuries of discrimination." Kirwan highlights "three reasons why higher education must do better—significantly better—in our efforts to create more inclusive campus environments: (1) the correction of past and present inequities; (2) the development of the high-quality workforce our nation will need in the coming decades; and (3) the value added to the education of all students when they learn within a diverse community." He insists that the challenge is not only to prepare minority students for success, but also to prepare all students from all races and backgrounds to work effectively in a decidedly more diverse environment.

William E. Sedlacek suggests that most programs in support of students of color focus on advising, counseling, tutoring, admissions, and financial aid. He insists that research is vital, and that any effective program to meet the needs of students should be based on research. Sedlacek's premise is based on research in which he, his colleague, and students have been engaged for more than thirty-five years. He readily admits that research alone can not bring about change but believes that professionals are likely to be more successful in their efforts when "armed with good goals, good data, and guiding principles" that can make a difference.

Paul Kivel's essay, *"The Culture of Power,"* is about racism for and among white people. He provides intervening strategies to help people and institutions to deal with systemic racism. Kivel provides a candid assessment of how whites use their inside power to gain advantages, privileges, and resources not available to other people. In the final analysis he states "building a democratic, anti-racist, multicultural society is the only way to provide us with a deep level of security. Nothing less will do because only justice will put out the fire."

Carlos E. Cortés reviews the concept of *pluribus-unum* and its value to societal diversity. He presents a forceful challenge of the necessity and importance of balancing the two imperatives, "both deeply embedded in our nation's history and its constitution." He laments *pluribus* extremism and *unum* extremism. Cortés notes that *pluribus*, while allowing for differences of opinion, should not be guilty of rejecting personal values. On the other hand, he indicates that those who espouse *unum* should not consider racial diversity as a threat to society. He seems to imply that society is richer because of the singular contributions of each racial group. There is no doubt the involvement of each is for the benefit of all.

Raymond A. Winbush looks directly at the relevance of diversity and its importance for maintaining the United States' competitive edge in the workforce. He argues that the nation must come to grips with the challenges of diversity. Winbush exposes the hypocrisy of a nation that espouses diversity on one hand while undercutting "the very strategy, affirmative action, that could accelerate its growth."

Samuel Betances's essay clearly demonstrates the breadth of knowledge that educators can gain by expanding their multi-cultural knowledge base, by working to make tenured teams inclusive, by becoming bridges to student success rather than barriers, by valuing the potential intelligence and competence of all groups, and by selecting only those textbooks that are balanced in their treatment of different racial, ethnic, and cultural groups.

Neil Rudenstein presents a cogent historical view of *"Diversity and Learning at Harvard."* He indicates the educational importance and the singular benefits of diversity in the academic arena. He provides a provocative survey of Harvard's progress when dealing with the issue of diversity. He cites the impact of Charles William Eliot who became president of Harvard in 1869, and who "saw diversity along regional, social, economic, religious, and racial or ethnic lines—as a defining feature of American democracy." W. E. B. DuBois paid him a handsome tribute by stating that he [Eliot and others] "sought to make Harvard an expression of the United States." The concept of diversity expanded at Harvard as the years came and went. Rudenstein emphasized the fact that Harvard does not admit first-year students "atomistically" in isolation from other students. Rather it tries to "compose" a class that, in all its variety, has considerable power to "teach itself," so to speak, "through innumerable encounters, associations, and discussions among students of varied backgrounds and experiences."

Clarence G. Williams's essay, *"The MIT Experience: Personal Perspectives on Race in a Predominantly White University,"* unfolds and mirrors, in a fluid and autobiographical way, the role that Williams has played in addressing issues of diversity at Massachusetts Institute of Technology during the three decades that he has served in key administrative positions at the institution. Williams highlighted solid principles and strategies as indispensable in making diversity an essential component in the life and structure of any institution. The essay indicates that MIT has made an enormous commitment of its resources over the years to address the continuing existence of barriers to educational access. The determined efforts of Dr. Williams have provided the higher education community with a model that is workable when there are leaders who understand the breadth and benefits of diversity.

Antoinette Halsell Miranda's essay, *"Self-Discovery to Actualization: Charting a Course to Make a Difference,"* gives us an understanding that racial and cultural diversity challenges people of color to look within themselves. Reared in a predominantly white setting during her high school years, she felt considerable pressure to adapt. After Miranda, a major in school psychology, was exposed to the disparity between IQ test scores of blacks and their white counterparts, she became seriously committed to giving every child an equal chance to learn; thus, she began a journey on the highway of exploration on issues of cultural and racial diversity. Believing that all students can learn, she made the commitment of giving them what it takes to learn. Directing the school psychology program at Ohio State University, she provides training for future teachers who will be working with diverse student populations. Believing that teachers must be properly trained to nurture students from diverse backgrounds, Miranda transformed the school psychology program in such a way that school psychology majors begin to focus more on urban education by connecting with and working in the Columbus (Ohio) City Schools. The goal of this mandatory experience is to establish standards for teachers that will equip students of color with the skills they need to be competitive in the school setting and in later life.

Milton E. Turner discusses the primary reasons for the success of racial diversity at the University of Virginia. He details the role that the Office of African-American Affairs has had in increasing the presence, participation, and persistence of African-American students at the institution. It is obvious that the university has made a massive effort to both recruit and retain its black students as 87.2 percent or 1,256 students were graduated who entered in 1996. It is obvious that the selection process, the Peer Advisory Program, the Faculty-Student Mentoring Program, the Parents Advisory Association, and the Luther Porter Jackson Black Cultural Center all combined to demonstrate that caring relationships produce a harvest of positive results and yield a bountiful return to the institution that has made an enormous commitment to educational equity.

Lee Jones describes the historical development of the Office of Multicultural Student Services at Washington State University during his tenure as director of that office. Jones is very methodical in his documentation that students' needs must be the core of successful programs that both recruit and retain students. He agrees with Vincent Tinto "that education, not mere retention," should be the guiding principle of retention programs. The office focused on six functional areas: recruitment and community relations, retention services, counseling services, strategic planning and new program initiatives, operations, and evaluation and assessment. Once the office was reorganized, a Multicultural Center was established, and it became the home base for students of color. Within the center the following were created: the African-American Student Center, Asian/Pacific-American Student Center, Chicano/Latino Student Center, and the Native-American Student Center. Their outreach efforts to target racial and ethnic constituents was successful in attracting students to the university. The university also set in motion a comprehensive retention program, which also is beginning to pay rich dividends.

Mac A. Stewart goes right to the heart of identifying diversity programs that work at Ohio State University. Over the years the institution has embraced a number of successive and successful innovations that has placed it among the top public universities which have invested heavily in the recruitment, growth, and development of students of color. The university is continuing to recognize that it must focus on results rather than on rhetoric in helping students of color to achieve success in acquiring a good education and in establishing significant career profiles after they have graduated. Many institutions have, in some measure, begun approaches to minimize racial disparities at their institutions. A limited number have invested millions of dollars over an extended period to close the discrimination gap so obvious on numerous campuses. Stewart chronicles the impact of such initiatives at Ohio State including the Young Scholars Program, the Freshman Foundation Program, the Minority Scholars Program, the Graduate and Professional Schools Visitation Days Program, the Minority Continuing Education Program, and the President and Provost's Diversity Lecture Series Program, among others. Under the leadership of Dr. William E. Kirwan, Ohio State President from July 1998 through June 2002, the university developed a comprehensive Diversity Action Plan, which focuses on accountability in all areas of the campus.

JoAnn Moody's perceptive and provocative essay places the major responsibility for the retention and graduation of minority students on departmental units. While recognizing the important contributions of various student support services, she nevertheless insists that departments must look themselves in the eye and elevate the focus of their efforts in taking on the problems associated with institutional racism. They need to establish new ways of thinking and in confronting those policies, traditions, and structures that create racial disharmony and discourse. Research indicates that students who leave graduate school do so because they have become demoralized, not because, as some faculty invariably infer, the students can't do the intellectual work. The students' academic weakness is not the culprit but rather a department's "hostile or laissez-faire approach" according to Moody. She enumerates seventeen Good Practices that contribute to student successes. Moody proposes cross-cultural workshops for departmental faculty and mentors to examine those cognitive schema and stereotypes that impede healthy faculty–minority student relations.

Myra Gordon plunges us deep into the approaches that are used to search for and select minority faculty members. In a system where racial privilege is determined, for the most part, by white males, Gordon reminds us that new strategies must be implemented to neutralize those racial disparities that are so ingrained at institutions of higher education. She shares her personal experiences of effective faculty diversification while working at a major research institution. She insists "that no one knows what goes on in a search committee, and that it "is not so much a matter of confidentiality, but rather it is a matter of privilege that makes the process a closed one." Gordon speaks to those deeper issues of culture, practices, and allegiances which minimize the probability of closing the racial gaps that exist in the academy. On the other hand, her essay focuses on what she discovered was doable and effective when there is committed and capable leadership, accountability that works, a representative search committee, position descriptions that include both required and desired qualifications, serious searches for diverse applicants, well-planned and human campus visits, and hiring candidates based on shared partnerships among the faculty, dean, and department chairs. Search committees were asked to create profiles of excellence rather than ranking candidates; then, the dean and department chair person made the final hiring decision. Based on her involvement in directly working in the area of faculty diversification, Gordon demonstrates that in a racialized campus community, racial privilege can change.

Freeman A. Hrabowski, III has cited the troubling underrepresentation of minorities in science as a professional challenge to develop programs and strategies to expand the pool of minority students in science and engineering. Under his leadership at the University of Maryland, Baltimore County, the Meyerhoff Scholars Program was established. Hrabowski identifies thirteen components that "create an environment that continually challenges and supports students from their pre-freshman summer through graduation and beyond. It has been particularly helpful and effective in graduating African-American students who have done postgraduate study and pursued research careers in science and engineering.

Donald Brown identifies and puts in perspective the value of the AHANA (African-American, Hispanic, Asian, and Native-American) Student Programs at Boston College. He has brought together those initiatives and strategies that have provided academic support and assistance to students who were identified as being academically underprepared. More than 1,000 students have participated in the Options

Through Education—Transitional Summer Program. Based on a retention rate of 95 percent, nearly all of the OTE students "have become highly productive and contributing members of society." In applauding them, Brown says, "They have become doctors, lawyers, nurses, ministers, educators, bankers, and entrepreneurs." The six-week OTE program provides a substantial orientation that prepares students to be competitive in the academic years that follow. Academic advising, tutorial assistance, peer mentoring, performance monitoring, career counseling, financial-aid advising, scholars recognition programs, church attendance, and community involvement combined to reflect the tenor of what can constructively happen for students when there are collaborative partnership efforts throughout the institution.

Linda S. Greene and Margaret N. Harrigan charted the experience of the University of Wisconsin-Madison that in funding for faculty hiring over a twenty-year period (1982–83 to 2002–03), the university showed significant increase in the proportions of new faculty who were members of a minority group than when the Madison Plan was underway during the period, 1988–93. There were significantly fewer minority hires in the pre-Madison Plan period and the post-Madison Plan period, each with only limited central funds to encourage diversity. Based on twenty years of data, the authors concluded that the existence of central funding for minority hires has been associated with an overall increase in the level of minority faculty hiring.

Leslie N. Pollard is very clear on what this book on racial diversity seeks to do. He makes a focused presentation on what Loma Linda University has done to respond to the educational challenges that policies and programs for racial diversity must confront in a university setting. He identifies five foundation approaches that must be embedded in an institution's culture for it to experience success in addressing the issues of race and racial harmony. Centering on the steps which one institution has taken to engage all players within the circle of the campus, Pollard pinpoints those positive interventions that are of crucial importance in making racial diversity work.

The purpose of this volume of essays is to facilitate change and discussion of how to address issues of diversity on college and university campuses. It is our hope that this collection will generate the kind of response that will invite attention and determination to develop new approaches that will achieve relevant practices that will make diversity a significant value at our institutions. The success of so many of our students is dependent on the commitment, the desire, the determination, and the ability of the institution to make a positive difference.

William English "Brit" Kirwan

WILLIAM ENGLISH "BRIT" KIRWAN became the third chancellor of the University System of Maryland on August 1, 2002.

A widely respected academic leader, Dr. Kirwan served as president of Ohio State University from 1998 to 2002 and as president of the University of Maryland, College Park (UMCP) from 1989 to 1998. Before his UMCP presidency, he was a member of the university's faculty for 34 years.

Dr. Kirwan received his bachelor's degree in mathematics from the University of Kentucky and his master's and doctoral degrees in mathematics from Rutgers and the State University of New Jersey in 1962 and 1964. He is a member of several honorary and professional societies, including Phi Beta Kappa, Phi Kappa Phi, the American Mathematical Society, and the Mathematical Association of America. A prolific scholar, he is co-editor of the book *Advances in Complex Analysis,* and he has published numerous articles on mathematical research.

Dr. Kirwan serves on the boards of directors of the American Council on Education (ACE), the National Association of State Universities and Land-Grant Colleges (NASULGC), the Business–Higher Education Forum, the National Visiting Committee for the National Science Digital Library, and the Blue Ribbon Panel of the National Dialogue on Student Financial Aid. He is chair-elect of NASULGC'S Commission on International Affairs, chair of its Council of Presidents, and chair of the Commission on Human Resources and Social Change. He is also a member of the board of directors of the Business–Higher Education Forum and co-chair of that organization's Diversity Initiative Task Force.

In 2002, Dr. Kirwan was elected a Fellow of the American Academy of Arts and Sciences; received NASULGC'S Commission on Human Resources and Social Change Distinguished Service Award; and was appointed by President Bush to the Board of Advisors on Historically Black Colleges and Universities.

President Clinton appointed Dr. Kirwan to serve on the National Commission on Mathematics and Science Teaching for the 21st Century. He chaired the National Research Council's Commission on the Mathematical Sciences in the Year 2000, producing the report *Moving Beyond Myths: Revitalizing Undergraduate Mathematics,* National Academy Press (1991).

FOREWORD
Diversity in Higher Education:
Why It Matters

As my contribution to this volume, I have been asked to share some thoughts on why diversity matters in higher education. It's an assignment I relish.

For me, there are three basic reasons why we in higher education must do better—significantly better—in our efforts to create more inclusive campus environments: (1) the correction of past and present inequities; (2) the development of the high-quality workforce our nation will need in the coming decades; and (3) the value added to the education of *all* students when they learn within a diverse community.

The first of these reasons—correcting past and present inequities—regrettably is out of vogue today. Instead, a new orthodoxy is affecting, perhaps I should say *in*fecting, our colleges and universities. It holds that race and gender have no part in any of our decisions. Proponents of this view argue that our society has reached a point where race and gender should not matter. But the sad truth is that race and gender still do matter. They matter very much in ways that are disproportionately harmful to many women and minorities.

Consider salary equity. In a comparison of the salaries of white males and similarly situated minorities and women, based on ample empirical evidence I conjecture that most universities have *significant* salary inequities for minorities and women today. The exceptions are those few institutions that have had the courage to seriously review their salary equity issues and address the problems. Consider as well that minorities and women continue to pay significantly higher home-loan interest rates than do their white male counterparts with equivalent financial circumstances and credit ratings. Can anything explain this reality other than bias and prejudice? Can we in higher education assume that somehow we are exempt from such prejudices in our recruitment, admission, appointment, and promotion practices?

Those of us in positions of responsibility must not only recognize and acknowledge the inequities that exist in our society and on our campuses, we must *respond* to them. This requires more than race- and gender- "neutral" policies and practices; neutrality alone cannot erase the effects of centuries of discrimination. Unless we act affirmatively to eliminate the present-day results of bias and prejudice, we will never achieve the diversity goals that we all boldly espouse.

Achieving diversity does not require, or even suggest, the abandonment of standards for admission or performance. But it *does* require us to ensure that individual merit evaluations do not resemble the patterns in salary equity or mortgage loans. Achieving diversity requires us to evaluate individuals on their abilities to help advance our institutions in a society where, unfortunately, race and gender seem to matter in everything except the interpretation of our laws.

A second reason that diversity in higher education is so important is much more pragmatic. It has to do with our future economic well-being and our global competitiveness. One of a university's central purposes is to prepare students for citizenship and careers; today that preparation must take into account the growing diversity of peoples and cultures that comprise our pluralistic global society.

In America today, we see a striking increase in the internationalization of our economy, the global nature of policy issues, and the education level required of our labor force and citizenry. Are we preparing to face these challenges? Will we have adequate numbers of people with the skills and knowledge to compete successfully in this emerging national and global environment? Can we make real our national motto, *E pluribus unum*, in a nation with a degree of diversity unimagined by the Founding Fathers?

We are on the cusp of monumental demographic change. More than 80 percent of the new entrants to our labor force are women or minorities; moreover, given differential rates of birth and immigration, our Hispanic and Asian populations are increasing 10 times faster than the white population; while the African-American population is growing more than five times faster than the white population. By 2020, the number of U.S. residents who are Hispanic or non-white will have more than doubled while the *non*-Hispanic white population will not be increasing at all; in fact, it may decline. Just over fifty years from now, the average U.S. citizen—as defined by Census statistics—will be as likely to trace his or her ancestry to Africa, Asia, the Hispanic world, the Pacific Islands, and the Islamic world—as to trace it to Europe. At that point, diversity in the American workplace won't be a *goal;* it will be a *reality*.

Next, consider that by 2010, half of all jobs will require at least some college education. Also, as a result of retirements, the workforce will contain 10 percent fewer whites. Because there are fewer minorities in today's workforce, we will need a 30 percent increase in their numbers just to maintain the status quo.

Unless we dramatically increase the rates of participation of minorities and women in all fields—and most especially in those fields where they have been traditionally excluded—we simply will not have enough technically trained and culturally adaptable people to support a sophisticated, internationally competitive economy. Thus, the moral imperative for diversity in higher education is now united with social and economic necessity in a nation that, within a little more than one generation, will be without a racial or ethnic majority.

Our challenge is not just to prepare enough minority students for success in this new environment, however. The challenge is to prepare students from *all* races and backgrounds to work effectively in a decidedly more diverse workplace. This is the third reason why diversity is so vitally important in higher education today.

Recent research shows that cultural diversity and greater inclusiveness in higher education can enhance the learning environment of the entire university community, especially for those students who have lived mainly within a single cultural orbit. Thus, we are coming to understand that we can actually increase the learning of all students by subjecting everyone's provincialism to multiple perspectives.

As Justice Powell wrote in the *Baake* case, a university should be allowed to assemble a varied student body in order to create a more dynamic intellectual environment and a richer educational experience. This is what E. B. White called "the splendid fact of difference of opinion, the thud of ideas in collision."

A diverse environment fosters a plurality of perspectives. It creates the possibility of discourse and learning by talented people of various cultures, backgrounds, and experiences. It creates an opportunity for students to come together, challenge each other's ideas, learn new perspectives, and grow as individuals. It holds out hope that the next generation of leaders will understand that our differences are our strength, that our diversity can be the essence of our excellence.

In the following pages, Dr. Frank W. Hale, Jr., a distinguished academic leader and a lifelong champion of diversity, has assembled papers from some of the nation's leading thinkers on the subject of inclusion in higher education. It is my hope that many will learn from the wisdom in these papers and implement the ideas contained therein on their campuses. It is important that they do so, for nothing less than the future well-being of our nation is at stake.

Dr. William "Brit" Kirwan
Chancellor
University of Maryland Systems

WHAT MAKES RACIAL DIVERSITY WORK

IN HIGHER EDUCATION

Frank W. Hale

FRANK W. HALE, JR. is vice provost and professor emeritus at Ohio State University, where he served from 1971 to 1988. Prior to coming to Ohio State University, Dr. Hale served as President of Oakwood College in Huntsville, Alabama. He is a graduate of the University of Nebraska, where he earned a bachelor's and a master's degree in Communication, Political Science, and English. He received his doctorate in communication and political science from Ohio State University and was awarded a post-doctoral fellowship from the University of London.

Hale, who has served in the field of higher education for fifty years, has held full professorships at Central State University (Ohio), Oakwood College (Alabama) and Ohio State University. At Ohio State, he served as Associate Dean and Chairman of the Fellowship Committee of the Graduate School, Vice Provost for Minority Affairs and Assistant to the President. Currently he serves as a distinguished university representative and consultant. Following Hale's retirement in 1988, he served as Executive Assistant to the President at Kenyon College in Gambier, Ohio.

Dr. Hale has authored and edited eight books and more than fifty articles in professional journals. He has lectured at more than 250 colleges and universities and at fifty state and national conferences. His innumerable awards and citations include the Frederick Douglass Patterson Award, the United Negro College Fund's highest award, and the Distinguished Service Award for Human Rights and Social Change from the National Association of State Universities and Land-Grant Colleges (NASULGC).

As a scholar, researcher, author, teacher, administrator, consultant and civil rights crusader, Hale was the engineer of many new initiatives at Ohio State University. He founded the Graduate and Professional Scholars Visitation Days Program and the Ohio State Mu Xi Chapter of the Alpha Kappa Mu Honorary society. Through his efforts, nearly $15 million in graduate fellowship awards were granted to approximately 1,200 minority students. Eighty percent of these fellowship recipients earned masters and/or doctoral degrees. As a capstone to his illustrious career, Ohio State University Board of Trustees voted him Vice Provost and Professor Emeritus, naming in his honor the Frank W. Hale, Jr. Black Cultural Center and designated the building in which it is housed as Hale Hall. An endowed scholarship has also been established in his name.

INTRODUCTION

The Complications and Challenges in the Championing of Diversity

This book is about the struggles and some of the remedies for those struggles that people of color face on college and university campuses. Institutions of higher education are a part of a global culture that maintains the racial divide and highlights the constant clashes between the ideals America espouses and what Americans practice in fact.

While race-conscious inequities still persist in all areas of American life, progress has been made toward achieving equity and providing equal access for racial and ethnic constituencies in postsecondary education. Hopefully, some day our actions on matters of race will catch up with common sense. This book explores ways in which colleges and universities have consciously shaped their philosophies, policies, and programs to address the underrepresentation of people of color in all institutions of higher education. Special emphasis is placed on those areas of cooperation within institutions that have made a positive difference in the recruitment and retention of people of color. It is our dream that the goal and idea of a "just" and diverse community will be embraced by American society in general and higher education in particular. The latter has the duty and responsibility of preparing leaders of the future by responding to issues and crises that threaten racial harmony. The higher education community can be a significant leader by incorporating effective initiatives that promote the presence, participation, and persistence of people of color within the academy.

Stylus publisher John von Knorring has given us priceless support and has taken the risk of commissioning the book from tried and untried authors; it is an act of unspeakable trust. His insight, warmth, and encouragement have both buttressed and reassured us on our journey.

As the editor, I owe a debt of gratitude to all those individuals who gave so generously of their time, insight, and experience in measuring the distance between our successes and our failures as we confront the continuing existence of barriers to access and success that face people of color. We hope the book will provoke academics and interest all educators in what has been thought and done to design and establish programs that advance the quality of life for all constituents of color within the academy.

The essays are designed to cover real-world issues of racial diversity in higher education. They deal with every segment of racial diversity on college and university campuses—research, racial disparities among students, faculty, and administrators, as well as professional and historical considerations.

"Diversity" is a term I never heard while growing up. That fact is a disturbing reality because I grew up in a "Community of Walls" that were either black or white; school walls, theater walls, hospital walls, hotel walls, restaurant walls, water fountain walls, public park walls, church walls, and, yes, even cemetery walls. Everything was separated on the basis of race, and it was legal. Thank God for the *Brown vs. Topeka* decision and the role and courage of people of color. The advocates of freedom included black Americans: Rosa Parks, Martin Luther King, Jr., Daisy Bates and The Little Rock Nine, Vivian Malone, James Meredith, Hamilton Holmes, and Charlene Hunter; Native Americans: Jack Forbes, Dennis Banks, and Clyde Bellecourt; Hispanic Americans: Caesar Chavez, Rodolfo Gonzalez, Senator Joseph Montoya, Delores Huerto, and Angel Guitiérrez. So much of society with its opportunities and rewards had been closed to people of color until these heroes and heroines made a difference.

In those early days, it was easy to detect institutional racism because it was visible and intentional. All the machinery was obvious and designed to keep people of color "in their place." However academics have access to institutions that encourage ongoing studies of racial policies. Racial policies today are less visible and far more difficult to determine.

This book is an effort to bring into focus the extent to which universities have attempted to address the gulfs that have existed on campuses relative to the presence and participation of students and faculty of color and their white counterparts. The focus of this effort highlights the innovative approaches used to provide increases in enrollment, financial support, counseling, retention, mentoring, tenure, and promotion for those who have suffered from the predicament of historical and institutional racism.

There should be no question of the fact of white advantage; people of color must struggle to seize and keep hold of opportunities that whites expect at birth. Historical patterns of segregation and discrimination have plunged us into disruptive and controversial conflicts over how to reshape our society. I have lived and experienced the ebb and flow of higher education long enough to recall how higher education institutions imposed racial policies and practices on people of color who dared seek admission to their institutions. Universities used the forces of intimidation, imprisonment, and the support of government agencies to systematically keep blacks on the margins of education, shunted to the end of the line in their struggles for acceptance. Fortunately, polarization notwithstanding, the decision of *Brown vs. the Board of Education* and the Montgomery Bus Boycott gripped the imagination and spirit of black youth and some sympathetic whites. They refused to remain caged in the hardened history of America's neglect. They marched, they protested, and they occupied and confronted those in the hallowed halls of dehumanized learning with demands that began to make significant changes in coloring the landscape of universities.

The Historical Limits and Challenges of Diversity: Advocates and Adversaries

Racism is a disease ingrained in the fabric of American society. Racial prejudice becomes racism when one group has control over another group. Historically, blacks, Latinos, Asians, and Native Americans have been victimized by racism in the United States. Similarly, a small group of whites in South Africa promoted and perpetuated a policy of apartheid that used the whites' resources and power to deny rights and freedoms to the black majority, and when governmental powers are used to withhold education, a people's future is endangered; California's Proposition 209 has had a deleterious effect in recruiting students of color, and even some of its original supporters now admit that the results are unfortunate.

Since the decision of *Brown vs. Board of Education*, laws discriminating against blacks and other minorities have gradually been eliminated. It was assumed by many that when all people received equal treatment under the laws, equality of all racial groups would be assured; it didn't take long to discover the major defect in this optimistic reasoning. As a result of centuries of discrimination and institutional racism, blacks and other people of color comprised an infinitesimal percentage of trained professionals, entrepreneurs, politicians, the affluent, decision-makers, and leaders in general. It became obvious that the major institutions in the United States were racist not because of contemporary laws but because of embedded structures with long histories of discriminatory practices that subordinated particular groups of people. Faculty and students of color at universities were disappointed to find that they faced discrimination, neglect, disinterest, and emotional manipulation, commonplace for people of color outside the ivory tower.

Most educational institutions, companies, labor unions and political parties had leaders who were white. The criminal justice system, for example, was composed of judges, jurors, lawyers, police officials, and prison guards who were for the most part white. The racial imbalance of white majority control made it difficult for other racial groups to advance at even a snail's pace. For this reason affirmative action was introduced as a policy to address historical imbalances. In fact it was President John F. Kennedy in his Executive Order No. 10925 in 1961 who first used the term affirmative action.

Affirmative action was proposed as a hands-on approach to end racism; it was hoped that taking a positive and proactive stance would make a positive difference in employment, in the admission of students to colleges and universities, in the awarding of government contracts, and other initiatives. Affirmative action became a wonderful instrument for expanding diversity on college and university campuses as well as in every other area of American society. Race-conscious remedies were used as an antidote to race-conscious inequities. Nevertheless, its success was limited when it came to an environment that was favorable and nourishing to the minds and spirits of constituents of color.

The U.S. Supreme Court addressed the legality of affirmative action most directly in its 1978 *Bakke* decision. Allan Bakke sought admission to the medical school at the University of California at Davis. Bakke knew that 100 positions were available and that sixteen of those openings were reserved for minority students under the school's affirmative action policy. He sued the university for denying equal treatment regardless of race. The case made its way to the Supreme Court, which wrote a compromised position on a very complex issue. The ruling indicated that in certain circumstances race could be used as an element in judging students for admission to universities. The decision was an ambiguous one in that it did not say how racial equality is to be measured nor pursued. The court advised that institutions may "take race into consideration" in making policy, but they may not use race as the sole criteria for the measurement or remediation of inequality. In effect, the court inaugurated the idea of "reverse discrimination" as a legal force.[1]

The controversial nature of the court's decision made it easy for the adversaries of affirmative action to unleash furious attacks on measures designed to level the playing field for minorities. They managed to exploit the discomfort of the general public by pretending and professing to believe that racial discrimination in the United States had ended. It become even more apparent that institutions of higher education played no small part in serving the interests of a system that had been in place for centuries.

Obviously those who have been beneficiaries of white affirmative action over two centuries did not intend to share those extra benefits with people of color who were denied those same privileges. Adversaries of affirmative action have also had some success in blinding the millions of America white women whose opportunities had been enhanced by affirmative action policies. These benefits gave them muscle because of Title IX and a larger representation in the historical male dominated professions of law and medicine.

In institutions of higher education, policies of affirmative action, as set by trustees and key administrators, have been responsible for flexible admission policies, financial aid packages to meet the needs of underrepresented students, special support services, and programs for substantially improving the campus climate for people of color. Affirmative action policies have also encouraged aggressive hiring practices, mentoring programs for students and faculty of color, and curricula that reflect the contributions of people of color as a part of American historiography. All of these efforts were designed to close the gap in admission and graduation rates between people of color and their white counterparts. To be consistent and effective, these programs required substantial sums of money; it stands to reason that commitment without cash is counterfeit.

Meanwhile the opponents of affirmative action and diversity have directed their attacks against diversity, multiculturalism, and affirmative action. In a stinging and caustic attack on multiculturalism, Rush Limbaugh states that "multiculturalism is billed as a way to make Americans more sensitive to the diverse cultural backgrounds of people in this country. It's time we blew the whistle on that. What is being taught under the guise of multiculturalism is worse than historical revisionism; it's more than a distortion of facts; it's an elimination of facts." He pontificated further by saying, "I want everyone to be taught the things that are necessary for them to prosper as Americans, not black something or brown something or red something but as Americans."[2]

Allan Bloom disparaged those institutions during the 1960s that acquiesced to students' desire for equality in the academy. He chastened and demonstrated his contempt for these institutions in these words: "The American university in the '60s was experiencing the same dismantling of the structure of national inquiry as had the Germany university in the '30s. No longer believing in their higher vocation, both gave way to a highly ideologized student populace." Later he offered the following opinion:

> The fact that universities are no longer in convulsions does not mean they have regained their health. . . . The value crisis in philosophy made the university prey to whatever intense passion moved the masses . . . So far as universities are concerned, I know of nothing positive coming from that period; it was an unmitigated disaster for them. I hear that the good things were "greater openness," "less rigidity," "freedom from authority," etc.—but these have no content and express no view of what is wanted from a university education.[3]

Arthur Schlesinger in *The Disuniting of America* presents his position that children need to learn about their ethnicity and heritage from their families, churches, and communities. He insists that children do not need encouragement from the schools to learn about their ethnicity, their heritage, or their language. Schlesinger conveniently overlooks the fact that all children, not just those of a particular race or ethnicity, need to learn, appreciate, and celebrate the accomplishments of those unlike themselves. Students are taught most everything from a Euro-Western perspective so is it any wonder that their concept of justice and fair play is tainted by a schizophrenic approach to democracy that espouses liberty and equality on one hand and practices something quite different on the other.

The parade of bellicose anti-affirmative action proponents is unending. Wilmot Robertson accuses the American educational system of "force-feeding minority and majority students alike on a thin, curricular soup of one part liberal dogma, one part majority belittlement, and one part minority mythology, providing little educational nourishment for anyone." He insists that the great failure of a heterogeneous school is its inability to stress effectively the moral-building aspects of education. He asserts that such learning requires "centuries of common history and millennia of common ancestry." Robertson invokes a categorical attack on the state of education, declaring, "Desegregation kills it by robbing it of its principal ingredient—the homogeneity of teacher and pupil. The disappearance of this vital bond from the American classroom may prove to be the greatest educational tragedy of all."[4]

It is fairly easy to understand why there are profligate historians and propagandists who sidestep any serious consideration of believing in or supporting diversity. Many, like Robertson, insist on Negro inferiority. They claim that black enthusiasts are guilty of gilding their religious and historical past. Why would anyone want to support the dynamic of diversity if they thought of blacks as the most backward of races, the most violent, and the most racist? Presumptuously, boldly daring to be prophetic, Robertson insists that "the American Negro will soon be out of his private wilderness. He will either return to his Old World homeland or be assigned a new homeland in the New, or there will be no homeland for anyone, black or white, in urban America."[5] It is quite apparent that too many accept the inequities of society as a routine factor in the scheme of things or, worse still, they refuse to recognize or admit them at all.

It stands to reason that the need for diversity is ridiculed and rejected by many in the larger community; such ridicule has maimed the progress of diversity in the academy. It is an old, old story that the only way to be accepted by society on matters of race is to accept the higher status position of the dominant group; this is often referred to as "Mr. Charley's way" in the African-American community. On the surface it appears that those who are willing to eat "humble pie" and accept some form of self-humiliation by not raising their voices against institutional inequities gain favor and position by those in power. They gain certain positions of limited authority because they refuse to "rock the boat;" they sidestep and minimize their cultural heritage by adopting the manners of their benefactors. They assume swaggering insensitivity that gives them diminishing influence among their own people; they are partners in policies against the interest or conscience of those with little redress; they are against those who resist traditions and practices that dehumanize people of color.

The debate against affirmative action also includes so-called leaders of color as well, including Thomas Sowell, Shelby Steele, Dinesh D'Souza, and Linda Chavez, to name four of the most prominent. They make powerful arguments against using affirmative actions to address group membership, promote the rhetoric of "goals and timetables" and blur the distinction between equality of rights and results.

It's Decision Making Time

The concept of diversity in its broadest interpretation has been viewed by educators for well over a century. Bowen and Bok point out that diversity has been stressed as an educational value for years:

> Originally, diversity was thought of mainly in terms of differences in ideas or points of view, but those were rarely seen as disembodied abstractions. Direct association with dissimilar individuals was deemed essential to learning. The dimensions of diversity subsequently expanded to include geography, religion, nation of upbringing, wealth, gender, and race.[6]

While there are many competing definitions of diversity, this book, authored by numerous scholars, will emphasize racial diversity not as a singular percentage of people of color in the campus population, but as a network of values, policies, practices, traditions, resources, and sentiments used to provide coping mechanisms for students and faculty of color.

The inseparability of racial diversity and the changing demographics in our world bring to mind the discontent of those who perceive themselves as outside the system. Leslie Pollard expresses a sense of urgency in these words:

> The world is changing! Demographers say that the world of the 21st century will be more globally connected than at any other time in history. Communications, technology, media, immigration patterns, educational institutions, and travel are bringing diverse racial and ethnic groups into more intimate association. "Intimate diversity" is becoming the major descriptor of cross-cultural associations in our world. But intensity diversity is not taking place in a vacuum. In every interaction between groups there is a history—sometimes positive; often troubled, tortured; even painful between groups that makes cordial cooperation a challenge.[7]

Whereas civil rights was regarded as the nation's most important problem in 1964 and 1965, by the mid-1970s it had faded to the point of almost disappearing entirely. Whites commonly believe that the government has eliminated all the barriers and obstacles that stood in the way of black participation in American society. Feelings of racial resentment were encouraged by cultural conservatives such as George Wallace, David Duke, Pat Buchanan, and Rush Limbaugh. Such racial maneuvering was in stark contrast to Presidents Kennedy and Johnson who had challenged America to live up to its historical commitment to egalitarian ideals.[8] It also needs to be pointed out that certain scholars like William J. Bennett, Arthur Schlesinger, William Buckley, and Allan Bloom scorned the reactions of those who during the 1960s dared to express their discontent in non-Western tactics and threatening jargon. These scholars seem comfortable letting students remain in the unfriendly soil of intolerable circumstances on college and university campuses. By their testimony and stature as intellectuals, these scholars sought to give credibility to anti-affirmative action stances.

On university campuses after the assassination of Dr. Martin Luther King, Jr., there was a momentary surge of admitting black students to those institutional enclaves of "whiteness." Out of a sense of guilt, compromise, and self-interests, colleges and universities were prodded into admitting black students; they did so because of student protests and demonstrations rather than on the basis of conviction and commitment.

It is one thing to admit students, faculty, and administrators of color, it is quite another to "accept" them into a warming climate of inclusivity. So often lost in "an immense sea of whiteness," students and faculty of color often feel violated when they are expected to submerge their cultural identities in favor of that of the dominant group. Rather than respond favorably to the perspective of the dominant culture, people of color often organize themselves into a culture of resistance that speaks to their roots, their traditions, their interests, and their social comforts. Rather than ask what the institution has done to create such actions on the part of the students, the university administration seems so ready to eliminate or forestall protests.

Although there has been some modest improvement in the enrollment of some racial minorities, people of color are constantly being confronted by the harsh realities of those opposed to any pluralistic philosophy that allows for racial identities such as black and brown groupings or black and brown organizations. On occasions, even people of color shy away from anything associated with a common psychological pattern of their particular group. On the other hand, some fear being labeled as "acting white." There are those for whom identifying with their racial group provides mutual and reciprocal support in encountering alienation and isolation. They refuse to let society dismantle their connections with their aesthetic and cultural roots. Students of ethnic and racial groups cherish their cultural traditions; however, they still need to become involved in the overall activities of the institution and seek to establish meaningful relationships with students and faculty of the dominant group.

I am one who strongly believes that a diverse society should not require any person of color to be assimilated or culturally incorporated into the mainstream of society. "The existence of separate black institutions or a self-defined all-black community is not necessarily an impediment to interracial cooperation and multicultural dialogue."[9] In the larger community composed of a variety of different American cultures, it is not uncommon for these groups to establish homogeneous neighborhoods. This scenario is a pluralistic fact of life throughout America and the world. Thus people seek emotional support from people who share a common background.

There is ongoing evidence that college and university communities are a microcosm of their larger community. It is an illusion to believe that diversity in its genuine sense is alive and well in the academy. We need to face the stark fact of institutional hypocrisy on the issue of diversity. While teaching, research, and service have become the triangular slate by which professionals are judged in terms of their competency and their eligibility for promotion, no consistent set of rewards and sanctions has been encouraged as a means of holding people accountable in the area of diversity. Until sincere and serious efforts are made to encourage campus communities to make the cause of diversity their own and translate it into models that work and produce positive results, it is sheer nonsense to have high-minded expectations.

As the demands of the polity, the economy, and the world-at-large become more advanced, more complex, and more insistent, we need to concentrate our efforts on conducting programs that will take advantage of the potential available from African-American, Asian-American, Hispanic-American, and Native-American constituencies. We face the task of exploring and exploiting the potential, the values, the skills, and experiences of the untapped human potential that will enable all of us to live happily and productively in the modern world.[10]

Ernest L. Boyer, then president of the Carnegie Foundation for the Advancement of Teaching, challenged and reminded us in 1990 that "higher education has an important obligation not only to celebrate diversity but also to define larger, more inspired goals, and in so doing serve as a model for the nation and the world." The Carnegie Foundation released its report on *Campus Life: In Search of Community* that year and while focusing on its search for community, it made a compelling appeal for a "Just Community" where the sacredness of each person is honored and where diversity is aggressively pursued on a college or university campus.[11] The rate of African-American and Latino attrition among students and faculty of color speaks to the struggles that people of color experience in extremely prejudiced and hostile environments.

Some might ask, "Why is there ongoing discussion on the need for diversity?" It is difficult for some to understand that serious racial problems remain in our country. The dominant group reluctantly accedes to the reality that Oprah Winfrey, Bill Cosby, Colin Powell, Michael Jordan, Tiger Woods, Ronald Takaki, Jennifer Lopez, Edward James Olmos, and hundreds of other "successful" black, brown, red, and yellow Americans are not representatives of the "bottom-mired" people of color who are virtually lost in the desperate cycle of chaos. When *de jure* racial discrimination came to an end, many whites considered it an epoch-ending era. "Lifting the starting gate for blacks, long after virtually every other mixture of Americans had charged off over the horizon, was all that the national white political establishment was prepared with any resolve to do."[12]

But there is so much more to do, and what is so disturbing is that bold leadership is lacking. So much of what is espoused in the name of leadership appears tepid, measured, and without fire and fury. Those who have managed to momentarily side step the ire of their white counterparts seem to have lockjaw when it's time to speak up, stand up and be counted. I will never forget the historical impact of Frederick Douglass, Harriet Tubman, Marcus Garvey, Sojourner Truth, Demark Vesey, David Walker, Nat Turner, Martin Luther King, Jr., and Malcolm X. I'm also reminded of those heroic leaders, official and unofficial, like Rosa Parks, Crispus Attucks, Authurine Lucy, Daisy Bates, Elizabeth Eckford, Viola Liuzzo, James Reeb, Michael Schwerner, Angela Davis, Caesar Chavez, Paul Ongtooguk, Richard Rodriguez, David Mura, and Linda Brown who dared to challenge the status quo. They stood up for what they believed, and some sacrificed their lives in the process. There are thousands of unsung giants whose sacrifices paved the way for those of us who have experienced some measure of success because of their valiant efforts.

Leveling the Playing Field

The crisis of "haves" and "have-nots" has been as mismanaged in higher education as it has in all other American institutions. Civil rights advocates were marginally successful in forcing open closed doors; but they, at least, made themselves seen and heard. I was a participant in the spectacular 1963 March on Washington. Accompanied by a number of students from Central State University in Ohio, where I was Professor and Chairman of the Department of English, I reveled for a short time in what, on the surface, seemed a unifying and revitalizing concern that blacks should be included in the promises and benefits which were accorded to most other Americans.

After the civil rights initiatives of 1964, 1965, and 1968, Americans seemed more willing to close ranks, defy their upbringing, and venture into the untested waters of racial unification. Recognizing that profound adjustments needed to be made, institutions struggled to adapt to the sweep of concerns, and vast expectations were partially fulfilled. The federal government took some actions so racism would not continue to divide and distract America from fulfilling its jagged "commitment" that "all men are created equal and are endowed with certain inalienable rights and that among these are life, liberty, and the pursuit of happiness."

A more activist and demanding posture by youthful militants and adult supporters had driven institutions to change and to do more than they ever had before. Militants had targeted the low ratio of black students and faculty, limited financial aid, weak support services, curricular biases, negative campus environments, and the general attitude that black students and faculty were inherently academically and professionally inferior. For a few years, the time-worn traditions of exclusivity began to crumble.

The gains made during this period began to be challenged by the counterattacks of white conservatives, who desired to turn the civil rights clock back and thus began contemptuous appeals to the "dispossessed majority." The extremism of George Wallace, Ross Barnett, Lester Maddox, and others of their persuasion created a white backlash that contributed to a widening crevasse that once again separated whites and blacks. Institutions began to enroll a greater number of black and Hispanic students, and it became apparent that while many of these students were able scholars, still others were marginal; some institutions were either unable to meet their needs or were unwilling to take on the challenge of teaching students who were not considered to be college material. There were major forces at work, political and psychological, that enlivened the debate over the extent to which an institution should subscribe to an open door policy. Would a greater degree of openness strengthen an institution's mission in the area of diversity or would its image as a highly credible institution suffer?

The dilemma was real and confusing; consequently, a period of stagnation took hold. Affirmative action and diversity programs designed to offset a history of racial injustices in some instances were undercut by such negative perspectives as "lowering academic standards," "reverse discrimination," and "black nationalism." These discordant views were typical of those recurring cycles of limited improvement followed by the reassertion of traditional forms of dominance.

To give students and faculty of color a better chance, academic institutions introduced target efforts and remedies to neutralize past and current policies and practices that undermined America's commitment to equality of opportunity. Various strategies have been used to eliminate the gap between access and retention and to increase graduation rates of students of color in higher education. The most successful institutions (1) develop a recruiting plan; (2) inform students of the financial resources available to them on campus; (3) cooperate with secondary schools to create conditions that motivate students to achieve; (4) establish agreements with community colleges that encourage students to transfer to four-year institutions upon the completion of a two-year stint; (5) use corrective measures and supportive services to help students acquire the skills they need to succeed; and (6) create a warm and hospitable environment for students of color.

Ohio State University, Arizona State University, University of Michigan, University of Wisconsin–Madison, Wayne State University, Harvard University, University of California–Los Angeles, University of California–Berkeley, Georgia Tech University, Xavier University–New Orleans, and the University of Maryland, Baltimore County, have established intervention and uplift programs that have been arenas for intellectual achievement for students enrolled at their respective institutions. Ohio State's Graduate and Professional School Visitations Days Fellowship Program, established in 1971, has been highly successful in attracting nearly 300 scholars annually to visit the campus. This singular project has been responsible for awarding nearly 2,000 fellowships to students, 80 percent of whom have graduated with masters, doctoral, and professional degrees. Ellis Cose, in his book, *Color Blind,* suggests that the approaches of successful institutions focusing on diversity can be reduced to six simple steps: (1) find a group of young people motivated to learn and find a way to motivate them;

(2) convince them you believe in them; (3) teach them good study skills, including the art of studying in groups; (4) challenge them with difficult and practical material; (5) give them adequate support; and (6) demand that they perform.

It has been established that there is a symbiotic relationship between faculty of color and students of color. It should go without saying that teachers have a role modeling impact on students. In fact, many prospective students of color will not attend institutions or enroll in departments that are too white and have no faculty or advisors of color to support them. Strategies to recruit and retain faculty and administrators of color are well established. Some institutions have been successful in "growing their own"—identifying very able students and supporting them in their efforts to pursue advanced degrees. Others have been able to recruit faculty by attracting mature and competent persons from government, business, industry, social agencies, from historically black institutions of higher education, and from institutions with a high concentration of Hispanic students.

It is one thing to recruit faculty of color; it is quite another to create the kind of positive environment that contributes to their success and makes them want to remain at the institution. Faculty of color are inclined to connect with institutions that have (1) a welcoming campus climate; (2) mentorship opportunities with senior professors; (3) programs for ongoing professional development; (4) research funding; (5) serious research on minority-focused issues; and (6) minority focused journals especially for those who publish.

A number of institutions are known for their leadership in recruitment and professional development of junior faculty. Israel Tribble's Florida Endowment Program has received national acclaim for fellowships awarded annually to junior faculty to pursue academic interests as a means of enhancing their teaching and their tenure/promotion status at their home institutions. Similarly, the Carolina Minority Postdoctoral Scholars Program at the University of North Carolina at Chapel Hill, the Chancellor's Minority Postdoctoral Fellows Program at the University of Illinois at Champaign-Urbana, and the Gaines Charles Bolin Fellowship at William College have been successful in providing opportunity for minority scholars.

Where Do We Go from Here?

In the academic arena, the issue of diversity raises some basic questions about how people are recruited and admitted, how students and faculty are financially supported, how administrators establish diversity guidelines and require accountability in support of them, how people are selected for positions and promotions, how programs are developed to provide support services for students and professional development and mentoring services for faculty, and how ongoing efforts are made to evaluate and assess an institution's successes and failures.

After having worked in the area of minority affairs for nearly three decades, I am fully convinced that the academy is neither "colorblind" in policy or in practice. Policies are only as good as their enforcement. The larger reality is that both the country and the academy have made some gains in certain areas during the years since *Brown vs. Topeka*. The dramatic increase in the presence of students and faculty of color was heartening in the early 1970s, but the percentages of student and faculty of color have not experienced dramatic increases since that period. The presence of black college professors has barely changed. They represent less than 5 percent of all faculty positions, and only about 4 percent of all earned doctorates are awarded to black men and women. For years, the largest single field for black doctorates has been in education, while black and Hispanic candidates for Ph.D.s in engineering, physics, and chemistry are few.

Most black students are more successful at black colleges in terms of their retention and graduation. Hispanic students also seem to fare better in those institutions that have larger concentrations of Hispanic students and who have a significantly higher percentage of Hispanic faculty and administrators. Students do best at institutions that mirror themselves, their culture, and their interests. It is a fact of life that colleges and universities that remain faceless entities and respond to students and faculty of color in remote or impersonal ways are extraordinarily ineffective in the recruitment and retention of students and faculty of color. Such institutions are morally disarmed by not exemplifying the courage, insight, and resourcefulness available to them. They fail miserably when they do not use the advantage of their influence to promote awareness and policies that bridge gaps between people of color and the dominant group in almost every area of campus life. Any thoughtful person who opposes affirmative action must be aware that institutional policies, practices, and resources have favored whites since the birth of this nation. People of color did not invent affirmative action, which had been running full speed for whites long before the 1960s. Was it not "selective admissions" for whites for more than two centuries that kept black people out of white institutions of higher education?

Obviously access alone does not automatically lead to a successful education. Retention rates are low for black, brown, and red students. Educators are often surprised, even stunned, to discover that retention rates are often lowest in the so-called unselective institutions. While success cannot and should not be guaranteed, the institution has an obligation to provide useful and personally significant educational experiences that will lead to a student's success. Is it asking too much for faculty and administrators to be counted on to provide students with a perspective that motivates them to want to succeed?

The face of the academy has changed dramatically during the past three and a half decades. Ethnic and racial groups have sought to gain footholds in the educational arena which were not available to their parents in earlier generations. The new campus constituency springs from a variety of backgrounds in race, ethnicity, class, locality, occupational interests, socio-economic status, and cultural tastes. It is not enough for institutions "to go about business as usual" with traditional approaches to teaching and learning. Historically, higher education has been strikingly uniform, expecting students to be a reflection of the faculty who teach and mentor them; yet there has been a profound shift in the nature and composition of campus constituents since the assassination of Dr. Martin Luther King, Jr. The presence of new faces of color requires the institution to act on the difference between what has been and what should be.

Institutions need to free themselves from worn out forms of engagement. Commitments should be made which stretch beyond the overall educational mission and focus on programs and activities that meet the needs of particular campus populations. Such an approach requires time, creativity, and commitment. The university can ill afford to overlook the strengths and potential of those in whom they have wisely invested; the university must give students of color the support that a traditional student would receive as a matter of course.

The records at some institutions contradict the view that students of color are a greater risk than their white counterparts. Institutions such as the University of Virginia and Georgia Tech University have had superior successes in the retention and graduation of students of color. Their commitments to the ideas of diversity and minority access to higher education are buttressed by initiatives that help minorities' chances for equality of opportunity and success.

There are a number of institutions that have created programs to make participation in higher education compatible with the career interests of minorities. Some institutions have developed diversity models and practices that enhance the talents and aspirations of students and faculty of color. The unique role of higher education gives it extraordinary leverage to either help or hurt the chances of people of color for equality of opportunity. Institutions can play a positive role in neutralizing the ingrained negative assumptions and inhibitions of both students and faculty.

How can any institution of higher education, calling itself a university, be legitimate in its focus on liberal education unless it is committed to "universality"? True education should address the multiple and complex ways and contributions of various races and cultures in creative, credible, and authentic ways. It's impossible for an institution to be universal on one hand while being snobbishly exclusive on the other. Its very identity as a university should restrict any attempt on its part to deny the inclusive participation and advancement of people of color on any basis other than their limited capabilities. The challenge of inclusiveness is invaluable. The strength and quality of a university can be judged, in some measure, by the extent to which it is willing to acknowledge the quality, value, and integrity of the contributions of people of color as a part of American historiography, as well as their vital role in helping the nation achieve its democratic goals. We need to help all of our citizens know that each citizen is an important part of our pluralistic society.

This book will identify some of the institutions and their personnel who have developed concepts and models of diversity that have made a positive difference on their campuses. These perceptive approaches and conceptual frameworks have been developed to remove artificial barriers that unnecessarily stand in the way of people of color being able to achieve their educational and career goals. The problems of access and retention create barriers that are particularly difficult for people of color. The fact that these barriers exist speaks to the failure of institutions to analyze and understand the singular needs of students and faculty of color.

This volume includes intense expressions of commitment and creative activity on the part of some of the nation's finest scholars. It is designed to share the successes that some institutions have had in serving the educational needs of an expanding population of students and faculty of color. It offers the special insights of those who are deeply committed to their profession and to the educational needs of constituents of color in the academy. Sometimes their insights are autobiographical, recognizable in terms of their own experiences, and their views and perspectives develop from the crucible of their experiences as people of color.

We hope that this work will be widely used by academic institutions as a vehicle for discussion of the principles and strategies herein. We hope discussions become actions of institutions who better learn to value diversity. I am especially indebted to all who have offered their intelligent and fresh ideas to strengthen and extend our efforts to make diversity viable and meaningful.

Notes

1. Lorenzo Morris, *Elusive Equality* (Washington, D.C.: Howard University Press, 1979), p. 2.
2. Rush Limbaugh, *The Way Things Ought to Be* (New York: Simon & Schuster, 1992), pp. 204, 207.
3. Allen Bloom, *Closing of the American Mind* (New York: Simon & Schuster, 1987), pp. 113, 320.
4. Wilmot Robertson, *The Dispossessed Majority* (Cape Canaveral: Fly Howard Allen Enterprises, Inc., 1976), p. 289.
5. Robertson, pp. 212, 215–16, 222.
6. William G. Bowen and Derek Bok, *The Shape of the River* (Princeton, N.J.: Princeton University Press, 1998), pp. 218–19.
7. Leslie N. Pollard, "Leaders and Ethnicity: Temple or Vehicle?" in Leslie Pollard, ed., *Embracing Diversity* (Hagerstown, Md.: Review and Herald Publishing Association, 2000), p. 15.

8. Donald R. Kinder and Lynn M. Sauders, *Divided by Color* (Chicago: The University of Chicago Press, 1996), pp. 102, 104–5.

9. Manning Marable, "Staying on the Path to Racial Equality" in George E. Curry, ed., *The Affirmative Action Debate* (Reading, Mass.: Addison-Wesley Publishing Co., Inc., 1996), p. 6.

10. Lawrence A. Cremin, *Popular Education and Its Discontents* (New York: Harper & Row, Publishers, 1989), p. 124.

11. The Carnegie Foundation for the Advancement of Teaching, *Campus Life: In Search of Community* (Lawrenceville, N.J.: Princeton University Press, 1990), p. 25.

12. Randall Robinson, *Defending the Spirit* (New York: Penguin Putnam Inc., 1998), p. 59.

References

Allen, W. R. 1992. "The Color of Success: African-American College Student Outcomes at Predominantly White and Historically Black Public Colleges and Universities." *Harvard Educational Review.* 62, pp. 38–37.

American Council on Education. 1989. *Minorities on Campus,* ed. Madeline F. Green. Washington, D.C.

Banks, J. A. 1997. *Educating Citizens in a Multicultural Society.* New York and London: Teachers College, Columbia University.

Bennett, W. J. 1992. *The Devaluing of America.* New York: Summit Books.

Billings-Gloria, L. 1994. *The Dreamkeepers.* San Francisco: Jossey-Bass Publishers.

Bloom, A. 1987. *The Closing of the American Mind.* New York: Simon and Schuster.

Bowen, W. G., and D. Bok. 1998. *The Shape of the River.* Princeton, N.J.: Princeton University Press.

Cose, E. 1997. *Color-Blind: Seeing Beyond Race in a Race-Obsessed World.* New York: Harper Collins Publishers.

Curle, A. 1973. *Education for Liberation.* New York: John Wiley & Sons, Inc.

Davis, J. O., ed. 1944. *Coloring the Halls of Ivy.* Bolton, Mass: Anker Publishing Company, Inc.

D'Souza, D. 1992. *Liberal Education.* New York: Vantage Books, a Division of Random House, Inc.

Fleming, J. 1984. *Blacks in College.* San Francisco: Jossey-Bass Publishers.

Hacker, A. 1992. *Two Nations.* New York: Charles Scribner's Sons.

Hale, F. 2001. "Hale Inventory of Commitment to Multiculturalism." *Assessing Campus Diversity Initiative.* Washington, D.C.: Association of American College and Universities.

Hrabowski, F. H., III., K. I. Maton, and G. L. Greif. 1998. *Beating the Odds: Raising Academically Successful African American Males*. New York and Oxford: Oxford University Press.

Jones, L., ed. 2001. *Retaining African Americans in Higher Education*. Sterling Va.: Stylus.

Kivel, P. 1996. *Uprooting Racism: How White People Can Work for Racial Justice*. Gabriola Island, B.C.: New Society Publishers.

Limbaugh, R. 1992. *The Way Things Ought to Be*. New York: Pocket Books, a division of Simon & Schuster Inc.

Pollard, L., ed. 2000. *Embracing Diversity*. Hagerstown, Md.: Review and Herald Publishing Association.

Richardson, R. C., Jr. 1987. *Fostering Minority Access and Achievement in Higher Education*. San Francisco: Jossey-Bass.

Robertson, W. 1976. *The Dispossessed Majority*. Cape Canaveral: Howard Allen.

Rudenstien, N. L. 2001. *Pointing Our Thoughts*. Cambridge, Mass.: Harvard University.

Said, E. 1993. "The Politics of Knowledge." *Race Identity and Representation in Education*, ed. C. McCarthy and W. Crichlow. New York and London: Routledge.

Sedlecek, W., and D. W. Webster. 1998. "Admission and Retention of Minority Students in Large Universities." *Journal of College Student Personnel*.

Sowell, T. 1984. *Civil Rights: Rhetoric or Reality*. New York: William Morrow.

Thandeka. 1999. *Learning to Be White*. New York: Continuum.

Tinto, V. 1993. *Leaving College: Rethinking the Causes and Cures of Student Attrition*. Chicago and London: The University of Chicago Press.

Williams, C. G. 2001. *Technology and the Dream*. Cambridge, Mass. and London: The MIT Press.

Paul Kivel

Paul Kivel is a trainer, activist, writer, and a violence-prevention educator. His work gives adults and young people the understanding to become involved in social justice work and the tools to become more effective allies in community struggles to end racism. Kivel is the author of numerous books including *Uprooting Racism: How White People Can Work for Racial Justice,* which won the 1996 Gustavus Myers Award for best book on human rights, *Men's Work, Making the Peace, Helping Teens Stop Violence,* and most recently, *Boys Will Be Men: Raising Our Sons for Courage, Caring, and Community* and *I Can Make My World A Safer Place: A Kid's Book about Stopping Violence.* This chapter has been adapted by the author from *Uprooting Racism: How White People Can Work for Racial Justice* © Paul Kivel, 2001 (revised 2002). He can be contacted at pkivel@mindspring.com or through www.paulkivel.com.

I

THE CULTURE OF POWER

If you are a woman who has ever walked into a men's meeting, or a person of color who has walked into a white organization, or a child who has walked into the principal's office, or a Jew or Muslim who has entered a Christian space then you know what it is like to walk into a culture of power that is not your own. You may feel insecure, unsafe, disrespected, unseen or marginalized. You know you have to tread carefully.

Whenever one group of people accumulates more power than another group, the more powerful group creates an environment that places its members at the cultural center and other groups at the margins. People in the more powerful group (the "in" group) are accepted as the norm, so if you are in that group it can be very hard for you to see the benefits you receive.

Because I'm male and live in a culture in which men have more social, political, and economic power than women, I often don't notice that women are treated differently than I am. I'm inside a male culture of power. I expect to be treated with respect, to be listened to, and to have my opinions valued. I expect to be welcomed. I expect to see people like me in positions of authority. I expect to find books and newspapers that are written by people like me, that reflect my perspective, and that show me in central roles. I don't necessarily notice that the women around me are treated less respectfully, ignored, or silenced; that they are not visible in positions of authority nor welcomed in certain spaces; that they pay more for a variety of goods and services; and that they are not always safe in situations where I feel perfectly comfortable.

Remember when you were a young person entering a space that reflected an adult culture of power—a classroom, store, or office where adults were in charge? What let you know that you were on adult turf and that adults were at the center of power?

Some of the things I remember are that adults were in control. They made the decisions. They might have been considerate enough to ask me what I thought, but they did not have to take my concerns into account. I could be dismissed at any time, so I learned to be cautious. I could look around and see what was on the walls, what music was being played, what topics were being discussed, and, most important, who made those decisions, and I knew that it was an adult culture of power.

I felt I was under scrutiny. I had to change my behavior—how I dressed ("pull up your pants," "tuck in your shirt"), how I spoke ("speak up," "don't mumble"), even my posture ("sit up, don't slouch," "look me in the eye when I'm talking to you")—so that I would be accepted and heard. I couldn't be as smart as I was or I'd be considered a smart aleck. I had to learn the adults' code, talk about what they wanted to talk about, and find allies among them—adults who would speak up for my needs in my absence. Sometimes I had to cover up my family background and religion in order to be less at risk from adult disapproval. And if there was any disagreement or problem between an adult and myself, I had little credibility. The adult's word was almost always believed over mine.

The effects on young people of an adult culture of power are similar to the effects on people of color of a white culture of power or the effects on women of a male culture of power. As an adult I rarely notice that I am surrounded by an adult culture of power which often puts young people and their cultures at a severe disadvantage as they are judged, valued, and given credibility or not by adults on adult terms. Similarly, as a white person, when I'm driving on the freeway I am unlikely to notice that people of color are being pulled over based on skin color. Or when I am in a store I am unlikely to notice that people of color are being followed, not being served as well, or being charged more for the same items. I assume that everyone can vote as easily as I can and that everyone's vote counts. I am never asked where I am from (and this would be true even if I had stepped off the boat yesterday).

In a society that proclaims equal opportunity I may not even believe that other people are being paid less than I am for the same work or being turned away from jobs and housing because of the color of their skin. When I am in public spaces, the music played in the background, the art on the walls, the language spoken, the layout of the space, the design of the buildings are all things I might not even notice because, as a white person, I am comfortable with them; if I did notice them, I would probably consider them bland, culturally neutral items. Most of the time I am so much inside the white culture of power and it is so invisible to me that I have to rely on people of color to point out to me what it looks like, what it feels like, and what impact it has on them.

We can learn to notice the culture of power around us. Recently I was giving a talk at a large Midwestern university and was shown to my room in the hotel run by the university's hotel management department. After I had put my suitcase down and hung up my clothes, I looked around the room. There were two pictures on the wall. One was of a university baseball team from many years ago—twenty-two white men wearing their team uniforms. The other picture was of a science lab class—fourteen students, thirteen white men and one white woman dressed in lab coats and working at lab benches. In total I had thirty-five white men and one white woman on the walls of my room. "This clearly tells me who's in charge at this university," I said to myself; these pictures would probably send an unwelcoming, cautionary message to people of color and white women who stayed in that room that they could expect to be excluded from the culture of power in this institution. I mentioned the composition of the pictures to the hotel management and referred to it in my talk the next day.

A few years ago I would not have seen these pictures in terms of race and gender. The pictures themselves, of course, are only symbolic. But as I walked around the campus, talked with various officials, and heard about the racial issues being dealt with, I could see that these symbols were part of the construction of a culture of power from which people of color and most white women were typically excluded. I have learned that noticing how the culture of power works in any situation provides a lot of information about who has power and privilege and who is vulnerable to discrimination and exclusion; this institution of higher education was no exception.

The problem with a culture of power is that it reinforces the prevailing hierarchy. When we are inside a culture of power we expect to have things our way, the way with which we are most comfortable. We may go through life complacent in our monoculturalism, not even aware of the limits of our perspectives, the gaps in our knowledge, the inadequacy of our understanding. We remain unaware of the superior status and opportunities we have simply because we're white, or male, or able-bodied, or heterosexual. Of course a culture of power also dramatically limits the ability of those on the margins to participate in an event, a situation, or an organization. Those marginalized are only able to participate on unfavorable terms, at others' discretion, which puts them at a big disadvantage. They often must give up or hide much of who they are to participate in the dominant culture. And if there are any problems it becomes very easy to identify the people on the margins as the source of those problems and blame or attack them rather than the problems themselves.

Every organization has work to do to become more inclusive. I want to focus on some ways that groups often fail to include members of our country's most marginalized members — those marginalized by economic status, physical ability, and English language ability.

Often, when groups talk about diversity issues, they address those issues of race, gender, and sexual orientation that are most visible. Without an understanding of how class limits people's ability to participate in organizations a group may end up with a remarkably diverse group of middle class participants. Those who are homeless, poor, single parents, working two jobs, or poorly educated (and many people fall into more than one of these categories) often are unable to attend meetings or events because they cannot afford the time, the fees, the childcare, or the energy. When they do attend, they may feel unwelcome because they have not participated previously, because they do not speak the language (or the jargon) of the organizers, or because they are unfamiliar or uncomfortable with the middle-class values and styles of the group.

People with disabilities can be similarly excluded when meetings are held in rooms and buildings which are not accessible, when signing for the hearing impaired is not provided, when accessible public transportation is not available, or when the pace and organization of the meeting does not allow them to participate.

When English is not people's primary language, they may face comparable barriers to finding out about meetings, attending events, becoming part of the leadership of an organization, or simply participating as a member when interpretation is not provided. They are left out when non–English media and communication networks are not utilized or when the pace and style of the group does not allow for the slower pace that a multilingual process requires.

I am Jewish in a Christian culture. I am often aware of ways that the dominant culture of organizations I work with exclude me. When I get together with other Jews in a group I can feel so relieved that we are all Jewish that I fail to notice ways that parts of the Jewish community have been excluded. Because I am in the culture of power in terms of disability, I can overlook the fact that we may all be Jews in the group but we have scheduled a meeting or event in a place that is not accessible. We may all be Jewish but we may have failed to do outreach into the Jewish lesbian, gay, bisexual, and transgendered communities. Or because we are predominantly middle-class Jews, during our discussions we may be unaware of how we are excluding Jews who are poor or working class.

We each have ways that we are in the culture of power (for me, for example, as a white male) and ways that we are marginalized (for me as a Jew). Although we may be good at recognizing how we have been excluded, we are probably less adept at realizing how we exclude others because we do not see excluding others as a survival issue for us. We have to look to people from those excluded groups to provide leadership for us.

It is important that we learn to recognize the culture of power in our organizations so that we can challenge the hierarchy of power it represents and the confinement of some groups of people to its margins.

Assessing the Culture of Power in Your Organization

What does the culture of power look like in your organization? What does it look like in your office or area where you work? In your school or classroom? In your living room or living space? In your congregation? Where you shop for clothes? In agencies whose services you use?

The following questions can be used to identify cultures of power based on gender, class, sexual orientation, religion, age, race, language, physical ability, immigrant status, or education:

1. Who is in authority?

2. Who has credibility? Whose words and ideas are listened to with most attention and respect?

3. Who is treated with full respect?

4. Whose experience is valued?

5. Whose voices are heard?

6. Who has access to or is given important information?

7. Who talks most at meetings?

8. Whose ideas are given importance?

9. Who is assigned to or expected to take on background roles?

10. How is the space designed? Who has physical access?

11. What is on the walls?

12. What languages are used? Which are acceptable?

13. What music and food are available? Who provides them?

14. How much are different people paid? How are prices determined?

15. Who cleans up?

16. Who makes decisions?

Every person has the right to complete respect, equitable access, and full participation. Anything less limits the effectiveness of an organization by denying it the contributions—the experiences, insights and creative input—of those individuals and groups excluded or discriminated against.

Those inside the culture of power rarely notice it, while those excluded are often acutely sensitive to how they and others are being marginalized. Therefore leadership in efforts to eliminate the culture of power needs to come from those in excluded or marginalized groups. Unless they are in leadership positions with sufficient respect, status, and authority, the organization's efforts to change will be token, insufficient, and have limited effectiveness.

As they become better at identifying patterns of exclusion, people from within the culture of power can learn to take leadership in identifying marginalizing practices so the organization doesn't have to rely as much on people at the margins to do this work. Although groups will always need to look to the insights of people at the margins to completely identify how systems of oppression are currently operating, there is an important role for those inside the culture of power to take leadership as allies of those excluded. They can challenge the status quo and educate other "insiders" who are resistant to change. It is precisely because they have more credibility, status, and access that people on the inside make good allies. They can do this best not by speaking for or representing those marginalized, but by challenging the status quo and opening up opportunities for others to step forward and speak for themselves.

Every institution of higher education has a culture of power. Each department, division, school, program, and office within it has its own subculture of power. These may not be consistent or overlapping. The university may have an educated white male administration while the women's studies department has a middle-class white woman's culture of power which excludes poor and working-class white women and women of color of all classes. To be in opposition to the prevailing culture of power does not preclude us from creating subcultures of power that, in turn, exclude others who are even more marginalized than we are.

We have a responsibility, as people who have had access to educational opportunities, to not let the fact that we are on the inside of a culture of power deny educational opportunities to those who are on the outside. We need to fight for equal opportunity and full access and inclusion not just for those groups of which we are a part but also for groups to which we do not belong. For most of us that responsibility means listening to those on the margins, acknowledging our insider status compared with some other groups, and acknowledging our access to power, our resources, and our privileges. Then we can work with others to use our power, resources, and privileges to open up the educational structures to those who continue to knock on the doors.

One of our goals should be to create organizations and institutions that embrace an internal culture of full inclusion and whose members are trained to think critically about how the culture of power operates. We each have a role to play; we each have much to contribute to create such organizations; and we each must push every group we are a part of to move from a culture of power to a culture of inclusion.

Raymond A. Winbush

Raymond A. Winbush is the Director of the Institute for Urban Research at Morgan State University in Baltimore, Maryland. He is the former Benjamin Hooks Professor of Social Justice at Fisk University and Director of the University's Race Relations Institute. The Institute is the only institute of its kind housed at a historically black university and recently received a five-year $2.6 million grant from the Kellogg Foundation.

He also served as Assistant Provost and Director of the Johnson Black Cultural Center at Vanderbilt University, having previously taught at Oakwood College and Alabama A&M University in Huntsville. A native of Cleveland Ohio, Dr. Winbush is a product of public school education. In 1970, he graduated with honors in psychology from Oakwood College in Huntsville, Alabama, and during his undergraduate education there, won scholarships to both Harvard and Yale universities. After graduation he won a fellowship to the University of Chicago and received both his Masters and Ph.D. in psychology in 1973 and 1976, respectively.

His research interests include infusing African-American studies into school curricula, African-American adolescent development, black male and female relationships, and the influence of hip hop on contemporary American culture. He is the author of numerous articles on the "politics" of Afrocentricity and the resistance it encounters among scholars who wish to maintain existing intellectual paradigms. His book, *The Warrior Method: A Program for Rearing Healthy Black Boys,* is a comprehensive African-centered program for rearing black boys in a racist society. He is also editor of *Should America Pay?: Slavery and the Raging Debate over Reparations.* He is a member of the Advisory Board of the *Journal of Black Studies.* He travels widely to research the African influence on world culture. He can be reached at rwinbush@usit.net.

2

A BRIEF MEDITATION ON DIVERSITY AND "DUHVERSITY"

The term "diversity" as it relates to higher education became very popular after the publication of the 1987 Hudson Institute's seminal study *Workforce 2000*[1] in which Johnson and Packer outlined imperatives they thought necessary to maintain a competitive workforce during the twenty-first century. Written under commission by the Department of Labor during the Reagan administration, the core finding of the report was that continued U.S. dominance of labor and trade markets was directly dependent upon its ability to take advantage of the country's entire labor force. This U.S. dominance could only occur if those persons who had been historically marginalized in the labor and education sectors became full participants in the job and educational markets. The "Big Five" areas gender, race, age, disability, and sexual orientation were considered critical in terms of enlarging a workforce dominated historically by white males who would comprise fewer than 20 percent of new entrants to the workforce between 1987 and 2000.

Universities were seen by corporations and government as the "farm teams" for educating a diverse workforce, and many universities set as a priority the expanded inclusion of women, students of color, physically challenged individuals and non-traditional students, i.e., those older than thirty, in academic programs. Recruitment seminars, programs, discussions and in some cases conflict arose on campuses as diversity became a lightning rod for both supporters and detractors. It is a paradox that the recognition of diversity as important for maintaining the United States' competitive edge in the workforce occurred during a period when there was a simultaneous chilling affect plaguing the very strategy—affirmative action—that could accelerate its growth.

Throughout the Reagan administration and continuing into the first Bush administration, legal spikes were driven through the heart of programs seen as reverse discrimination by opponents of affirmative action. Universities, however, were remarkably firm in their determination to forge ahead with "diversifying their campuses" and despite legal setbacks maintained a steady pace to increase historically underrepresented groups on their campuses.

It is important to note that the nation's views of diversity became conflated relative to traditionally white institutions (TWIs) and historically black colleges and universities (HBCUs). In 1942, when Charles S. Johnson founded the Race Relations Institute at Fisk University, the "challenge of diversity" meant devising strategies on how blacks and whites could cooperate in desegregating the educational system of the United States, the armed forces, and the federal government. The success of these endeavors led to what is now known as the Civil Rights Movement and engendered legislation embodied in the human rights laws of the 1960s. The most notable of these laws was affirmative action, which included issues connected to gender, age, and later disability, but had at its core the goal of remedying past racial discrimination infecting this country since its beginning.

During the 1970s, the government approach began to include student enrollment into the affirmative action plans they required of universities. There was little doubt that they insisted on making race-conscious admissions, not merely an option, but obligatory. The legality of these admissions policies was challenged under Title VI of the Civil Right Act and reached the Supreme Court in 1978 when a white student claimed that he had been excluded from the University of California, Davis to make room for minority applicants with inferior academic records. The Court was sharply divided, four judges insisted that the racial quotas used by the medical school were discriminatory and violated Title VI. On the other hand, four judges supported the admissions procedure as essential to overcoming the effects of past discrimination. While Justice Lewis Powell decried the use of rigid quotas in admitting minority students, that at the same time, discriminated against particular persons, such as Bakke; he, nevertheless stated that admissions officers could "take race into account" as one of several factors in evaluating minority applicants in comparison with other candidates.

The Reagan-Bush years saw a chilling effect on affirmative action that remains with in today. Following the Bakke decision, the laws governing affirmative action were challenged in the courts; that case became the legal ancestor of *Hopwood v. Texas,* California's Proposition 209, and a host of other state initiatives still simmering on legislative platters. Affirmative action became two dirty words in a country that felt it had given its ex-slaves, women, and other protected groups enough time to get themselves together on issues of equality. A more palatable term would be necessary, so after the Hudson Institute's landmark study, we see the word "diversity" flexing its muscles as the term of choice when discussing affirmative action. Like a sedative slipped into the glass of an unsuspecting person, it lulled people into a dream-like sleep about affirmative action; it became the fashionable way to express the inevitable change that would take place on university campuses as well as the workplace over the next fifty years.

Truth be told, diversity *really* meant getting more persons of color to teach and matriculate at TWIs throughout the country. Even though the term was meant to include what I call the *GRADS categories* of gender, race, age, disability, and sexual orientation, it really meant recruiting African American, Latino/a and indigenous people to the campuses in positions where they had been historically underrepresented. Suddenly race became an unfashionable word in the lexicon of diversifiers. Phrases such as "we need more diversity" became the mantra of those wishing to darken their student bodies and faculties with persons of color. Joining diversity as the "in" term of the 1990s was "multicultural." Eventually affirmative action in both word and deed was relegated to obscurity.

But a funny thing happened when diversity was discussed at HBCUs. Black institutions simply did not *need* to recruit minority students but were *forced* to under a variety of court orders that sought to "desegregate" them. Alabama A&M, Tennessee and Jackson State universities, in a period of less than twenty years, were assaulted by a number of court orders that forced them to classify white students as minority, to offer them scholarships, and to establish goals and targets that would effectively deracinate these schools. In 2000, demonstrations occurred on Martin Luther King's birthday by students at Tennessee

State University against the court-imposed stipulations that said that TSU must be 50 percent white by 1993 a deadline that had been missed. Its graduate school has a student body population that is at present 63 percent white, a faculty that is 56 percent white, and an administration that is comprised primarily of majority—or should I say "minority" administrators. Bluefield State in West Virginia while still officially classified as an historically black college, has no black faculty, and its student body is 96 percent white; similar occurrences of the whitening of HBCUs have been noted in several publications.

So diversity at HBCUs meant something totally different from that of TWIs. It meant the wholesale elimination of indigenous African American culture and life. It meant court-ordered "duhversity" rather than *optional* diversity. Even though HBCUs have historically had the *most* diverse faculties among institutions of higher education, that has not been enough to satisfy federal courts, their legal aggression reflects a movement toward erasing the cultural heritage of HBCUs. Even private institutions have not been immune. Student demonstrations at Fisk University in Nashville in 2002 toward a black president who wished to diversify the campus were mounted because of her appointment of several white administrators in key positions and a "commitment" to aggressively recruit more non-black students to the campus.

I am amused when so-called white experts look for voices to speak about race in America; they look for puppets of color that echo conservative phrases about racism. Harvard's position that merit and diverse student bodies can be complementary goals has enjoyed a notoriety that rivals Booker T. Washington's "Tuskegee Machine" a century ago in Alabama when he was considered the "voice of Negro Americans," despite competing ideas from W. E. B. Du Bois. Now Thomas Sowell and Shelby Steele at the Hoover Institute, Walter Williams at George Mason, and Carol Swain of Vanderbilt are touted as courageous voices on issues of race when in fact they are minority voices among black scholars who write and comment about race.

In a 2000 speech at Fisk University, Archbishop Emeritus and Nobel Laureate Desmond Tutu called for a "Truth and Reconciliation Commission in the United States" similar to the one he chaired in South Africa after the fall of apartheid. He argued that the

United States has never told the truth about its racial past and that burying the past under pious platitudes of "brotherhood" and "patriotism" merely covers a gaping wound with a Band-Aid. We lie all too much about racism in the United States, and colleges and universities are some of the best liars. No TWI institution would tolerate a goal of 50 percent of its student body becoming black, Latino or Asian over a ten-year period; yet, as stated, such a stipulation is currently imposed on Tennessee State University. Universities need to discuss the truth about race on their campuses so that they can arrive at what Tutu calls "true racial reconciliation." Until such time, there will never be an honest dialogue about race, and duhversity experts will continue to do only what is necessary to maintain what they perceive as a level playing field for TWIs and HBCUs. Educator Michael Eric Dyson has said that when it comes to racism in this country we may well be referred to as the "United States of Amnesia." Coming to grips with the challenges of diversity is the only way the nation can become a place where diversity keeps house.

Note

1. Johnston, William B. and Arnold H. Packer 1987. *Workforce 2000: Work and Workers for the 21st Century.* Indianapolis, IN: Hudson Institute.

Carlos E. Cortés

Carlos E. Cortés is Professor Emeritus of History at the University of California, Riverside. Since 1990 he has served on the summer faculty of the Harvard Institutes for Higher Education and is also on the faculty of the Summer Institute for Intercultural Communication.

His two most recent books are *The Children Are Watching: How the Media Teach about Diversity* (2000) and *The Making—and Remaking—of a Multiculturalist* (2002). In 2001 Cortés received the National Association of Student Personnel Administrators' Outstanding Contribution to Higher Education Award. He currently serves as Cultural Consultant for Nickelodeon's pre-school series, "Dora The Explorer."

The recipient of two book awards, Cortés' publications include *Three Perspectives on Ethnicity, Gaucho Politics in Brazil,* and *Beyond Language: Social and Cultural Factors in Schooling Language Minority Students.* He has edited three major book series, totaling ninety-six volumes, on Latinos in the United States. He has also received his university's Distinguished Teaching Award and Faculty Public Service Award, the 1980 Distinguished California Humanist Award, the American Society for Training and Development's 1989 National Multicultural Trainer of the Year Award, the California Council for the Social Studies' 1995 Hilda Taba Award. He was also selected by the Smithsonian Institution to be a 1993–1994 Public Lecturer.

A consultant to many government agencies, school systems, universities, mass media, Private businesses, and other organizations, Cortés has lectured widely throughout the United States, Latin America, Europe, Asia, and Australia on the implications of diversity in education, government, and private business. He has also written film and television documentaries, has appeared as guest host on the PBS national television series, "Why in the World?" and is the featured presenter on the Video Journal of Education's training video, "Diversity in the Classroom."

3

LIMITS TO *PLURIBUS*, LIMITS TO *UNUM*:

UNITY, DIVERSITY, AND THE GREAT AMERICAN BALANCING ACT

Since its inception, the United States has engaged in a continuous, delicate balancing act involving varying and sometimes conflicting principles. One of those balancing acts has involved the alternatives posed by *pluribus* (pluralistic and individualistic) and *unum* (unifying and cohering) imperatives, both deeply embedded in our nation's history and its Constitution. Such *pluribus* values as freedom, individualism, and diversity live in constant and inevitable tension with such *unum* values as authority, conformity, and commonality.

However, this historical balancing act has involved more than values. Intersecting the *pluribus-unum* value tension has been the *pluribus-unum* tension of societal composition, because the United States began and has evolved not just as a nation of individuals, but also as a nation of groups—racial, ethnic, religious, and cultural groups, to name just a few.

Americans vary in their relative emphasis on *pluribus* and *unum*. Some emphasize *pluribus*, giving primacy to the defense of individual freedom and societal diversity. Others emphasize *unum*, arguing that the maintenance of societal unity reigns as the more essential value, often superseding the protection of *pluribus* rights, privileges, predispositions, and desires. While those who emphasize *pluribus* seek a capacious society that permits the maximum amount of socially benign diversity, those who emphasize *unum* focus their attention on upholding the societal core, not on preserving freedom for diversity.

Pluribus and *Unum* Extremism

Both *pluribus* and *unum* zealots sometimes become extremists—in support of their own particular versions of *pluribus* and *unum,* of course. Yet both *pluribus* and *unum* must have limits. *Pluribus* extremism can result in societal disintegration, particularly in light of our growing racial, ethnic, and cultural diversity. However, *unum* extremism can lead to the societal oppression of individual rights and group options.

pluribus extremism sometimes takes the form of the defense of all diversity, whatever the societal costs or threat to *unum*. Knee-jerk supporters of such *pluribus* extremism love diversity so much that they constantly preach tolerance of all differences, continuously celebrate all diversity, and proclaim non-judgmental acceptance of every group, regardless.

I believe deeply in diversity, but I also recognize my *pluribus* limits. I am not tolerant of bigotry, even if its roots are cultural—fortunately black and white abolitionists were not tolerant of the culture of slaveholding. I do not accept the restriction of opportunities for women simply because that restriction might be traditional within a particular culture. I do not celebrate the use of violence to resolve differences of opinion, although such problem-solving techniques might be endemic to some cultures. In other words, I do not subscribe to absolute *pluribus* because that necessitates a rejection of personal values, except tolerance, and an abdication of the right—better yet, the obligation—to make judgments. Such *pluribus* extremism, in short, becomes amorality.

At the opposite end of the ideological spectrum stand the *unum* extremists. Not only do they give primary to *unum*, but many of them also fear diversity—particularly racial and ethnic diversity—viewing it as a threat to the future of American society. So fearful are they that some even seek to punish others for their diversity.

Two Balancing-Act Issues

Since both *pluribus* and *unum* extremists are societally destructive, all Americans consciously or unconsciously grapple with two balancing-act questions. Whose *pluribus* should be limited? Whose versions of *unum* should triumph? To address these questions, I will briefly examine two balancing-act issues: language and ethnicity-based religion.

Language

The First Amendment to the Constitution guarantees freedom of speech and press without restriction on the language to be used.

Today, numerous American organizations are trying to eradicate or radically restrict the use of languages other than English within the United States. While such groups and their supporters sometimes issue pious statements about the right of individuals to speak other languages in their homes, they seek to banish it from schools, governmental services, and sometimes even private industry.

Moreover, they champion the establishment of English as our nation's official language, calling this a necessity for protecting *unum* and hyperbolically proclaiming that English is being threatened in our country.

Unquestionably, people in the United States should learn English, both because the nation functions better with a common language of public discourse and because individuals enjoy greater opportunities if they possess a solid facility in English. Immigrants realize this, which is why they flood into adult English-language classes, where they are turned away by the tens of thousands. But while the societal *unum* goal of a common language is laudable, many "official English" zealots appear to ignore the fact that this can be achieved without boiling out or punishing linguistic *pluribus*.

Making English the official language and establishing English-only rules in government or private business do not increase English fluency, but rather punish those who are in the process of learning English. Paradoxically, such mandates actually retard the achievement of *unum*—after all, you can study U.S. history, learn about American culture, and become a contributing part of American society using any language *while you are learning English*.

Moreover, English-only rules actually weaken some organizations and institutions by reducing effective communication among limited-English-speaking work crews and employees. In contrast, other institutions continuously draw upon the strengths of their multilingual employees by permitting or even encouraging workers to use their most effective languages when communicating with each other and when serving limited-English-speaking customers, as well as by posting vital information in various languages.

Religion

If language raises certain *pluribus-unum* tensions, religion raises others. This seems to be even more problematic where religions also reflect ethnic diversity.

The First and Fourteenth Amendments to the Constitution purportedly guarantee the *pluribus* right that governments "shall make no law respecting the establishment of religion." Yet two recent U.S. Supreme Court decisions, each involving an ethnicity-based religion, suggest the *pluribus-unum* complexities of the application of these amendments.

In April 1990, in the case of *Employment Division of Oregon* v. *Smith*, the Supreme Court, by a 5–4 vote, upheld the state's punitive action against a man named Al Smith for his sacramental use of peyote, even though it was a ritual of the Native American Church, of which he was a member. (I should mention that although the Eighteenth Amendment to the constitution banned the consumption of alcoholic beverages from 1919 until its repeal in 1933, the government nonetheless permitted an exception for the sacramental use of wine as part of religious services. Historical consistency, anyone?)

In the *Smith* decision, the Court ruled that religious groups were not exempt from "neutral laws." That decision dramatically altered the *pluribus-unum* constitutional balance by reversing more than a half century of *pluribus*-oriented First Amendment jurisprudence, which had maintained that the state had to demonstrate a "compelling state interest" in order to restrict religious practices. Under the *Smith* precedent, government need only demonstrate that laws are "neutral," even when those supposedly neutral *unum* laws encroach upon religious practices. As Mark Twain once asked when informed that someone was neutral on a critical social issue, "Then whom are you neutral against?"

Let's consider some possible ramifications of that decision. Could Amish children be forced to attend high school because "neutral" state laws require it? What about Jews who always wear yarmulkes, even in situations where "neutral" laws require other or no headgear? Or Laotian Hmongs who object to autopsies? Or Seventh Day Adventists whose religious convictions prevent them from working on Saturdays? Or Jehovah's Witnesses whose religious beliefs forbid them from saluting the United States flag? (Responding to the *Smith* decision, Congress passed the Religious Freedom Restoration Act in November re-establishing the compelling government-interest test.)

In June 1993, the U.S. Supreme Court again acted, this time protecting an ethnically based religion against a "non-neutral" law in the case of the *Church of Lukumi Babalu Ay* v. *Hialeah*. Faced with the growing practice of Santería, an Afro-Caribbean religion that blends Yoruba and Catholic traditions and sometimes includes animal sacrifice in its services, the city of Hialeah, Florida, prohibited animal sacrifice as part of religious ritual.

However, by a 9–0 vote, the Supreme Court voided this attempt to restrict *pluribus*. The Court did not approve animal sacrifice in religion, although some media pundits ravingly misinterpreted its actions. Rather, the Court ruled that Hialeah could not single out religion for such restrictions. The city would have to apply this prohibition neutrally if it so wished—meaning a total ban on the killing of animals within city limits, an action that Hialeah does not appear eager to take.

Challenge of the Future

The issues of language and ethnicity-based on religion merely illustrate the continuing saga of America's historical balancing act. With continuously increasing demographic diversity and inevitably increasing multicultural complexity, the American future will demand thoughtful, nuanced, and constructive ways both to protect and to set limits on *pluribus* and *unum*.

Alfred North Whitehead once argued, "The art of progress is to preserve order amid change and to preserve change amid order." One of America's great twenty-first century challenges will be to preserve *pluribus* amid *unum* and to preserve *unum* amid *pluribus*.

Dr. Samuel Betances

Samuel Betances is Senior Diversity Consultant at Souder, Betances and Associates, Inc., in Chicago. For the past twenty years of his academic career, he was a Professor of Sociology at Northeastern Illinois University. He now lectures and facilitates seminars for educational and corporate organizations worldwide on implementing diversity strategies as a mission-driven imperative. He is the author of the book: *Ten Steps to the Head of the Class: A Challenge for Students*. Dr. Betances may be contacted at info@betances.com.

4

HOW TO BECOME AN OUTSTANDING EDUCATOR OF HISPANIC AND AFRICAN-AMERICAN FIRST-GENERATION COLLEGE STUDENTS

There is a cultural shift that is taking place in higher education. For the first time in the history of colleges and universities, educators have to do what no previous generation of their peers had ever done before: educate learners who are members of the dominant society along with those who are not; educate those who view the institutions of the greater society as their friend, along with those who do not; educate those intelligent students who come with a middle-class college-learning framework and whose journey is enhanced by developed competencies for abstract thinking, theoretical ways of knowing and proficiency in written communication and formal discourse, along with those equally intelligent students who do not have those skills; educate those who are blessed with a vast network of supporters who provide resources to help them complete academic projects and who eagerly assist in removing sociopolitical/economic hurdles so they may climb to the top of their class, along with those who are not blessed with such support; educate those who come from well-to-do backgrounds and those who do not; educate those for whom completing post-secondary, higher educational requirements, and earning degrees form part of their rich family history, along with those for whom it does not; educate those whose cultural heritage/interest/racial group identities are positively affirmed in our racially stratified society, along with those whose are not; and educate those who are white, and those who are not.

The reason higher education must succeed in educating learners with and without all the pluses noted above has to do with demographic changes. Simply put, the demographic base available to colleges and universities to recruit and develop the talent for professional leadership needed by our public and private institutions has been altered forever.

Without inclusive and educated work teams at all levels of our organizations, our nation will not remain productive and competitive in the global economy. Therefore, differences in the fabric of our society must be embraced, not shunned. We must see differences as opportunities to grow in our collective purposes rather than to shrink from our collective expectations. We must practice deliberate inclusivity. We must implement diversity processes as a strategy to unleash the full potential of all the members in our diverse workforce. We must also recruit, retain, and grant degrees to students from all interest groups in order to be responsive to the changing demographics. Leading change in higher education requires that stakeholders also leverage diversity as a mission, bottom-line-driven imperative. This imperative is particularly significant for colleges and universities at the beginning of the 21st century.

The growth factor of students of color is the primary reason why racial diversity must work in higher education. Instead of referring to members of these interest groups as "minorities," they should be considered members of "emerging majority groups." The needs of these students should not be viewed as marginal on the educational agenda. Educational leaders must study the declining birth rates of whites, due in part to their success in the economy, and compare those numbers to the growth of emerging majority groups so as to implement inclusive strategies for all. For example, U.S. Census Bureau data indicate that the number of working-age Hispanics is projected to increase by 18 million while the white working-age population is projected to decrease by 5 million over the next twenty-five years. It ought to be crystal clear that as far as demographic changes go, the future is ahead of schedule. We must educate Hispanics and African Americans, not out of generosity, but out of necessity for all.

Hispanic and African-American first generation college students provide a series of unique challenges to leaders in higher education. These two groups are likely to feel the indignities of belonging to racially stigmatized groups. As a category of students, they may not have had the advantages of being socialized and nurtured into developing the competencies and framework for competitive learning in a middle-class place called college. Groups labeled "minorities" can experience as hostile the same institutional landscape that members of the dominant groups may view as friendly. The vast network of resources and support systems for completing challenging academic projects and for removing socio-political/economic hurdles is all too frequently not a part of their toolkit during the climb to the top of their class. Without allies in higher education willing to practice deliberate inclusiveness on their behalf, the negative situation impacting both of these interest groups will worsen, not get better, and the larger society will suffer as well.

This brief essay provides a series of recommendations to educators who, as willing learners, are eager to further develop their cultural competencies in order to unleash the learning potential of all students by making racial diversity work in higher education.

Expand Your Multicultural Knowledge Base

There is much that educators—particularly as members of the majority, dominant group—must teach themselves before they can become part of the force that will create a learning-teaching environment to ensure the success of first-generation college students from stigmatized groups. Namely, they must familiarize themselves with the ways students labeled "minorities" have been impacted by racism.

Dr. Jennifer James, after much reading on the subject and experiencing her own transformation, writes, "The majority consistently underestimates the depth of pain and anger endured by minorities and the enormous price—emotional and economic—paid by everyone" (James, *Thinking in the Future Tense*, 215). The books that have informed her journey are many and varied. She suggests books that members of the majority should read before they can ever hope to understand the issues and lead change strategies in the quest to achieve diversity goals. She writes with a sense of urgency and underscores the reason why we must be informed:

> Even in multicultural America, there remains a deep divide between black and white. Sanford Cloud, Jr., president of the National Conference of Christians and Jews, declared: "It's as though white

America is sleepwalking on the edge of a volcano of ethnic and racial differences." The O.J. Simpson verdict let us peer into the heart of that volcano. Several books by African Americans in the 1990s express deep resentment that discrimination persists. Brent Staples, in *Parallel Time: Growing Up in Black and White,* writes of the petty cruelties of whites and "the contained fury that grips even the most outwardly docile black man." *Makes Me Wanna Holler* by Nathan McCall chronicles the self-hatred of a young black male who rejects the society that has rejected him. *Rage of a Privileged Class* by Ellis Cose records the depth of anger of middle-class African Americans who have "made it" into mainstream America only to remain shut out of the actual power structure (James, 2, 16).

It was not until James dug deep into the literature of creative informants from the African-American experience that she was able to undergo her own paradigm shift, which led to her becoming an advocate for racial diversity.

Educators must become relentless readers. Teaching faculty must never stop learning. The challenge of becoming effective change agents in institutions of higher education and in the lives of first-generation college students requires passion. Passion persuades. Passion for social justice is driven by continuous acts of discovering new ways by which to confront power with truth!

No one really knows what they want until they know what options are available. Constant reading of the rich and growing body of multicultural literature by educators who are dissatisfied with the status quo inspires new, engaging, and revealing ways by which to provide options to students from poverty and the working class.

A true educator is an option provider. A true educator is a resource for universalizing the human spirit. A true educator strains every nerve to reach more than one class of student. To become a true educator requires familiarity, literacy with all kinds of analogies, stories, and case studies of the varied experiences, perspectives, wit, and social histories of our heterogeneous nation and world.

How do people survive in hostile environments? What lessons can be gleamed from survivors of concentration camps, slavery, segregation, abuse, harsh climates, and the many "isms" that create injury, perpetuate injustices, and then blame their victims? In what ways will reading those subjects help to increase the cultural competencies of educators genuinely interested in ensuring the success of all students?

Work to Make Tenured Teams Inclusive

There is nothing more pitiful to me than individuals with graduate degrees claiming to be professionals in higher education who seek and obtain tenure as a way of retreating from the challenge of acquiring and adding to the essential knowledge base by which to confront power with truth. All too frequently in post-secondary institutions, tenure is thought of solely by some educators as a type of union protection against being fired. Unquestionably, tenure is invaluable as a shield which protects true professionals who are engaged in research or the promotion of ideas and perspectives that may make colleagues and/or top administrators nervous or unhappy. Consider the fate of those without tenure who defend the interests of first-generation college students and wrestle resources for them against the keepers of the status quo in academe.

White faculty members with both tenure and informed passions can make a difference in helping to make higher education work teams inclusive. To do so, however, they must be bold in their stand against the hidden rules that exclude under-represented groups from their teams. Protecting privilege and preference for the familiar by some and a lack of boldness for justice on the part of others may keep members of protected classes from being considered for tenure.

A classic illustration of this practice is described by a courageous professor who confronted and exposed the hidden agenda in her university, one that sought to maintain an all-white tenured faculty. In her words, "When I was at the University of Washington in Seattle, professors being considered for tenure had to pass the 'lunch test': Would you want to eat lunch with this person for twenty years?" (James, 2, 20).

It is inconceivable that tenured faculty, who hold the view that no member of a "so-called unacceptable group" gets promoted, will want to ensure the success of Hispanic and African-American first-generation college students. Without people of goodwill willing to be in conflict with the practices that exclude and working inside the clubs and cliques of faculty members, racial diversity in higher education will not become a reality.

Professions exist to solve problems. The problem of ignorance can best be solved by mastery of knowledge. Tragically, we have become a very literate yet uninformed people. It is worse to be literate and uninformed than to be uninformed because of illiteracy. Educators must take steps to transform themselves before ever assuming that it is within their purview to attempt to create a transforming climate for anyone else. Students need less to be told what they need to do in order to succeed as much as they need to see positive change happening in the lives, worldviews, and behavior of their would-be models and mentors.

Don't Be an Obstacle, Become a Bridge

The act of failing first-generation college students for not knowing what they have not been taught constitutes one of the most flagrant acts of educational malpractice in higher education today. By becoming aware that they may not understand what needs to be done to stop inflicting pain on students that need to be educated rather than failed, educators can begin to battle their own ignorance. The transformation from being an obstacle to the success of non-traditional students to becoming a bridge requires open-mindedness and a total commitment.

The role of white faculty members in complicating the academic journey of African-American students in predominantly white colleges and universities has been documented by Joe E. Feagin and Melvin P. Sikes in their book, *Living With Racism: The Black Middle-Class Experience.* Through a series of interviews with students on college campuses throughout the nation, Feagin and Sikes reveal how white misconceptions about black competence tend to derail the progress pursued by some victims of stereotypes.

Several case studies illustrate the commonplace assumptions that may question black proficiency by white faculty members. Here is one:

> So, what happened one time in graduate school, I had this professor, and I didn't talk much in class, so when I did a paper, a final paper, he refused to accept the fact that I did the paper on my own ability. So, what he told me in essence, he would not accept the paper, and I wouldn't get another grade until I redid the paper, which I refused to do. I thought that was basically a discriminatory act. What he was saying was that black folks can't write this good. He didn't know my ability, what I was capable of. I didn't talk much in class, the class was

boring. [So, did you do the paper over?] No, I didn't. I took the incomplete. And I talked to the head of the department and I think he put a withdrawal on it. [So you didn't get any credit for the class?] No. I refused to do it. But, I didn't like that. I thought if it had been a white student who kept their mouth shut in class, and did a paper that was above what he thought, I'm quite sure that he wouldn't have challenged them (Feagin and Sikes, 110).

In an effort to maintain their dignity and self-respect, some students simply refuse to stay in required courses to complete a particular program of study. Such cultural incompetence on the part of educators should be measured in terms of wasted energies, time, and money that could otherwise be invested in preparing members of under-represented groups to increase their currency as valuable members of the professions.

Racist assumptions may very well fuel a lack of flexibility on the part of some faculty members. This kind of thinking derails any attempt to practice inclusiveness with some Latino students. Instead of attempting to implement strategies in higher education that promote ways to make instruction understood, some Hispanic students are simply punished. They are kept from cultural improvisations to achieve excellence in their studies. Instead of encouraging these students to do their best, some faculty members cast doubt on the motives of students who are eager to compete in a linguistically uneven playing field. A young Latina student explains how she met a wall of cultural resistance on the part of a professor who attacked her dignity and resolve to succeed with his faulty dysfunctional assumptions:

Evelyn moved to Chicago from Puerto Rico. Four months into her journey, she enrolled in the four-year commuter urban university close to her home. She wanted to take courses that would qualify her to enter dental school. She was smart but did not know English as well as her peers, who had been born in the United States. Her study strategy required that she read her work in English, make a mental translation into her native Spanish, and write her responses in English after she translated them mentally from Spanish. It was a slow process. Nonetheless, she was making progress.

By the time Evelyn took her mid-term biology examination, she was averaging a "B" grade. Not bad, considering the obstacles in her path related to language. She had only answered half of the questions on her biology examination when the exam period ended. She knew that her professor's office hours followed immediately after class. She requested permission to walk with her professor to his office and sit within close range of his vision and under his supervision so that she could finish her exam. Her problem was not that she could not answer the questions but that her strategy required double the time in view of her four-step bilingual approach.

Her professor became outraged at her request. He said, "No!" He explained in harsh tones that it was not his policy to give her an unfair advantage over the other students who had only the class period to complete their exam. "If you can't keep up at the regular pace, as everyone else," he advised, "drop the course, but don't expect special favors from me." She was distraught. She dropped the course. She felt she had no choice.

The two professors cited as obstacles and the countless others who practice exclusivity, hostility, or indifference to the needs of first-generation college students may never experience the joy of guiding students from poverty to the professions through a truly universalizing educational encounter.

Some years ago, I met a young man in one of the Introduction to Sociology classes that I taught. He handed in an essay response to a brief assignment. It was a brilliant piece of work. Instead of questioning his abilities, competency, or proficiency, I handed it back and said, "Do you know how well you are able to write? Keep it up. That is good work."

He visited me during office hours. We talked. He was hungry for an upbeat, respectful relationship with an adult. I desperately wanted to succeed as an urban educator with first-generation college students. We hit it off. So, my wife, who is also an educator, and I offered to mentor him. He has profoundly enriched our lives. I will now let him tell his story from his own vantage point:

From Average to Honors: Reflections by Carlos Jimenez Flores

> The family I was born into did not expect much from me academically. My father dropped out of school after the third grade. His father, in order to work and bring his share of money into the family, took him out of school. My mother did not enter school until a late age and graduated from high school at the age of twenty. All that was expected of me was a high school diploma.

Circumstances broke my family apart and I found myself alone in Chicago. My situation opened the door for me to connect with another family. This new family embraced me as one of their own. Their standards were much different than my previous family. They valued education. The people I was now looking up to as parental figures both had earned doctorates. Thus, the expectations of me were different. They were higher academically.

I was dissatisfied with the status quo. Being a part of this family opened my eyes to a middle-class world. Behaviors were different. Interactions were different. I was coming from a lower-class experience. I realized at that point that an education would be the way for me to make the transition from one class to the other.

I did not want to disappoint those who were now investing in me, so when I enrolled in a community college, I took being there very seriously. I knew I had to excel in order to succeed. My mentors could not stress enough how important it was to read. They provided me with the educational tools. All I had to do was apply them.

And apply them I did. I began noticing the difference between memorizing material just before class or the night before so you can pass an exam and learning the material by reading ahead of time, taking notes, highlighting important points, and studying them. My grades started to reflect this newfound understanding. Not long after, I began receiving invitations to join Phi Theta Kappa, the international honor society for two-year colleges.

The more I studied, the more I learned. The more I learned, the more I wanted to learn. I felt different. College was giving me a confidence I did not have before. I was proud of my grades, not because they were given to me but because I had earned them. I now viewed school as a place that can satisfy my hunger for knowledge.

I was seeing school in a different light. School used to be a negative for me growing up. I felt disconnected. I felt as if I was intruding in a place to which I did not belong. I was lost. School was not fun. Now, I could not imagine existing without school. School was now a positive.

I enjoy going to class. I utilize the syllabus to do assignments and projects ahead of time. I read all materials before class so that I can engage in class discussions and ask questions about what I did not understand. When I read, I highlight the important points. I take notes in class. I even highlight the important points in my notes. In the beginning of each semester, I trade phone numbers and e-mails with a couple of classmates in each class in order to create a study group. All these things are crucial to my success.

The rewards for being an honors student are many. I have received invitations and scholarships to attend universities across the United States. Being a member of Phi Theta Kappa has assisted me financially. I am also on the National Dean's List. My academic achievements have given me new incentives, motivation, and desire, which will ensure my success at the next level.

To become a bridge rather than an obstacle in the paths of first-generation college students as they sojourn through our institutions is most rewarding. But reading Carlos's testimony rewards my soul; Carlos has done more for me than I have done for him. When we, as educators, do justice for those students with fewest alternatives to survive except through education, we are not so much saving them we are really saving ourselves.

The Challenge for Educators

The path from high school to college is not clearly marked. At least it is not for those seeking a way out of poverty to the professions. Encounters between emerging majority urban students and their high school teachers explode into the agenda of those seeking to ensure the success of all students in higher education, as well.

The pessimism of educators and the pessimism of urban students from poverty are on a collision course in the public schools of America. Teachers are pessimistic about the intelligence and abilities of urban students to learn. Students are pessimistic about their teachers' compassion and competency to teach them. The clash between pessimism on both sides of the teaching-learning equation led an inclusive team of authors, an Hispanic female, and a white male, to conclude: "Working in an ER trauma center or air traffic control tower may seem like a dreamland compared to working inside an urban classroom" (Rodriguez and Bellanca, 2).

Authors Eleanor Renee Rodriguez and James Bellanca, in their essential textbook on how to improve urban education, invite readers to witness a clash between a teacher and student:

Andrea remembers the day it happened. "I was sitting in geography class. I was a sophomore. The day had started out really bad. My mother was on my case for my bad grades. My teacher was handing back our tests. When he got to me, he threw the test on the desk. All I saw were the red marks. 'Your kind,' he said, 'don't deserve a desk.' I didn't even hear what else he had to say. I snapped. Just snapped when I heard that 'your kind.' It was the last straw. I didn't say anything when he ignored my raised hand or all the times he pretended I wasn't there. When I snapped, I just glared and said in my meanest voice, 'Mr. Rossi, just what is it about me you can't teach?" (Rodriguez and Bellanca, 1).

Andrea's question inspired the title for their book. Those wishing to become outstanding educators of Hispanic and African-American first generation college students must also consider her profound query: What is it about me you can't teach?

Just what is it about first-generation students of color from poverty that is so tough to teach in a middle-class place called college? For beginners, mainstream educators may simply lack a framework for understanding and guiding students from poverty on how to succeed in middle-class places of learning. Students from poverty, on the other hand, tend to lack a framework for learning through middle-class ways of knowing. Andrea's clash with Mr. Rossi is a classic illustration of the disastrous consequences that may result when intelligent people without the framework to understand each other's potential or intentions come face to face in a classroom setting.

In her invaluable book, *A Framework for Understanding Poverty,* Dr. Ruby K. Payne discusses how the hidden rules that make one successful in poverty are dramatically different from those needed for success in the middle class. Without a mentor from the middle class to guide a willing learner from poverty through the hidden rules of the middle class, the transition from one class to the other cannot take place. Both educator and student must be willing to take steps to develop their respective frameworks to make the first-generation college experience a success.

Faculty members must read in order to become valuable resources to first-generation students from racially stigmatized groups, and they must get to know why it is so difficult for people to get out of poverty. They must learn how racism and discrimination impact the lives and communities from which Hispanic and African-American first-generation college students are likely to become. Also, they must resist the temptation to believe that it is primarily an issue of finances that keep the poor from escaping to the middle class. A lack of financial resources will keep people poor. But as Payne points out, "The ability to leave poverty is more dependent upon other resources than it is upon financial resources" (Payne, 17).

Payne provides a chart of resources, which she discusses in depth in her book, that are essential in the lives of people in order for them to escape from poverty:

Financial—Having the money to purchase goods.

Emotional—Being able to choose and control emotional responses, particularly to negative situations, without engaging in self-destructive behavior. This is an internal resource and shows itself through stamina, perseverance, and choices.

Mental—Having the mental abilities and acquired skills (reading, writing, computing) to deal with daily life.

Spiritual—Believing in divine purpose and guidance.

Physical—Having physical health and mobility.

Support Systems—Having friends, family, and backup resources available in times of need. These are external resources.

Relationships/Role Models—Having frequent access to adults who are appropriate, who are nurturing to the child, and who do not engage in self-destructive behavior.

Knowledge of Hidden Rules—Knowing the unspoken cues and habits of a group.

(Payne, 16)

First-generation college students often lack the support systems they need to succeed in higher education. In a recent article by Lucio Guerroro from the *Chicago Sun-Times* titled, "Many Latinos go to college, but few finish," Jorge Rendon, a business major at the University of Illinois at Chicago, was interviewed. He laments his lack of external resources: "When you are the first one in your family to go to college, there is added pressure, and you have to learn to deal with things on your own. If you are struggling with something, your parents don't understand. You don't have any brothers or sisters who went through the same thing. It's tough."

The literature is consistent in challenging educators to consider developing meaningful, respectful, personal, vibrant relationships with students from poverty if they really want them to succeed in college. In their book, *Beating the Odds: How the Poor Get to College,* authors Arthur Levine and Jana Nidiffer conclude, "Simply put, what mattered most to the students we studied was the intervention of at least one adult mentor at a crucial time in their lives. The mentors changed the odds" (Levine and Nidiffer, Preface xvii). Payne adds, "Educators have tremendous opportunities to influence some of the non-financial resources that make such a difference in students' lives. It costs nothing to be an appropriate role model, for example" (Payne, 60).

In a nutshell, it can be assumed that if one does not get to know one's students personally, it will be impossible to guide them as they navigate the uncharted waters of academia. To have credibility in the eyes of students who are not only poor but who have also suffered discrimination means that educators must change their belief systems about intelligence and the idea that some groups are more valuable than others.

Select Inclusive Reading Assignments for Students

Practice deliberate inclusiveness in your selection of textbooks and readings. Choose books that are written by authors who are powerful in their balanced inclusive approaches. Tap the wisdom of multicultural education scholars who have analyzed textbooks and curricula for their treatment of different racial, ethnic, and cultural groups. Determine whether there are books available for purchase that are authored, in whole or in part, by Hispanic or African-American scholars to enhance in the quest to achieve racial diversity goals.

Share syllabi with scholars in the same field, especially those with a reputation for social justice or who have critically analyzed the "isms" of exclusivity and request valuable feedback. Ask that they add value to the course readings by recommending books that they are familiar with not already on the reading lists.

Assigned textbooks and readings are powerful sources of authority to students. Hispanic and African-American students will appreciate knowing that, as a trusted guide in their journey through higher education, their professors thought about including them in the selection of readings, topics for discussion, and study tasks. Why should educators be trusted by students who may be suffering the indignities of racism and rejection outside of higher education? Why should students so often be confronted with the evidence of faculty incompetence or indifference inside their classrooms as they review selected course materials that also ignore or reject?

Educators stand to benefit the most by expanding their familiarity with the inclusive readings they select for their courses. By being inclusive in their choice of illustrations and case studies when doing their intellectual duty to clarify abstract principles, their status is enhanced by those who value fairness. By always valuing and reflecting diversity of thought, professors legitimize the goal of creating inclusive teams to achieve the mission of their institutions. Educators become invaluable as they teach by word and deed that the challenge of ensuring the success of all students in our multicultural society is not a destination but a journey.

Participate in a Diversity Reading/Discussion Group

Reading and discussing books on the subject will add value to the quest of developing a framework that is free of racist assumptions. To go through such a cultural shift is an enormous yet attainable task. The task requires partnerships for reading and discussing serious works on the topic as well as a desire to become freer, healthier, and an agent eager to create coalitions of interest instead of coalitions of color. It might help to team up with at least three other colleagues to form a diversity reading/discussion group.

Make the group inclusive. Encourage diversity of thought. Create a safe place for honest debate. Let passions and strong convictions shake away illusions as well as racist and ethnic myths. Allow opportunities for growth. Challenge each other to experience breakthroughs. Respect each other. Don't mug another person, but don't be afraid to conduct surgery either. Let freedom ring in higher education.

Select three books to begin with. Agree to meet once a month for at least three months of an academic year. Every member of the reading group must read the same book and meet to discuss it. A simple outline can be followed as a template to guide the discussion. Focus on the book's thesis, what qualifies the author(s) to write about the topic, and five important lessons learned. Finally each member of the reading group must share what action each is likely to take to continue to develop his or her respective framework. Each can propose an action step or a structural reform that each believes would help the institution succeed with first-generation college students. The idea is to develop among a critical mass of the faculty or administration some sort of common ground on the issue. The times and places to meet and what books to select can be worked out in concert with those interested in the challenge of change that membership in such a reading group would involve.

Reading and discussing books with peers, in and of itself, is hardly a panacea to the challenge of ensuring the success of first-generation college students from racially stigmatized groups. But learning about and then becoming grounded in the experiences of students is an integral part of the process of developing an essential framework. Action steps to introduce structural reforms must follow. As a preacher once said, "It is not important how many times you go through the Bible; the important thing is how many times the Bible goes through you."

Bibliography

Feagin, J. R., and P. S. Melvin. 1994. *Living with Racism: The Black Middle-Class Experience*. Boston, Mass.: Beacon Press.

Guerrero, L. "Many Latinos go to college, but few finish." *Chicago Sun-Times*, 8 September 2002.

James, J. 1996. *Thinking in the Future Tense: A Workout for the Mind*. New York: Touchstone.

Levine, A., and N. Jana. 1996. *Beating the Odds: How the Poor Get to College*. San Francisco, Calif.: Jossey-Bass Publishers, Inc.

Payne, R. K. 2001. *A Framework for Understanding Poverty*. Highlands, Tex.: AHA! Process, Inc.

Rodriguez, E. R., and B. James. 1996. *What Is It About Me You Can't Teach?: An Instructional Guide for the Urban Educator*. Arlington Heights, Ill.: Skylight Professional Development.

Neil L. Rudenstine

Neil L. Rudenstine is Chair of the Advisory Board for ArtSTOR, at the A.W. Mellon Foundation. Previously, he was President of Harvard University from 1991–2001. Before assuming this position in 1991, he served for three years as executive vice president of The Andrew W. Mellon Foundation. During the two preceding decades, Mr. Rudenstine was a faculty member and senior administrator at Princeton University, where he served as a professor of English, and as a dean of students (1968–72), dean of college (1972–77), and provost (1977–88). A scholar of Renaissance literature, Mr. Rudenstine is an honorary Fellow of New College, Oxford University, and Emmanuel College, Cambridge University, as well as a Fellow of the American Academy of Arts and Sciences. In addition, he is a member of the Council on Foreign Relations, the American Philosophical Society, the American Council on Education, and the Committee for Economic Development.

Mr. Rudenstine is married to Angelica Zander Rudenstine, an art historian. They have three children, Antonia, Nicholas, and Sonya.

5

DIVERSITY AND LEARNING AT HARVARD:

AN HISTORICAL VIEW

I would like to share with you some of the background of my present thinking on the subject of diversity in higher education. When I embarked on the research approximately two years ago, I found that there was little identifiable documentation of the history and certainly no historical study of the subject.

My goal was to try to define the case that might be made for college and university admissions programs that took the concept of diversity seriously: programs that made conscious efforts to reach out to identify and enroll selected students from under-represented minority groups—including groups that are usually classified as racial or ethnic in nature, such as African Americans, Native Americans, and Hispanic Americans.

I was pragmatic in my quest. You will recall that the Supreme Court had ruled—in the well-known *Bakke* case[1] of 1978—that there was likely to be only one possible rationale concerning this subject that might be acceptable to the Court. The opinions of the Court were unusually divided in the *Bakke* case. It was left to Justice Powell to expound the view that conscious efforts to achieve diversity—including racial and ethnic diversity—in university admissions were acceptable, but only when the goal was part of an articulated effort, with a carefully designed process, to enhance the educational benefits—the nature and quality of education itself—in a college or university.

In addition, Justice Powell stated that race and ethnicity could be taken into explicit account in the definition of diversity only if a college's or university's admissions policy and practice could withstand the difficult legal test of "strict scrutiny" by the courts.

Without leading you too far into the intricacies of the *Bakke* case, I hope I have said just enough to suggest which intellectual and historical questions might have intrigued me, and why.

My own thinking, I should add, coincided very much with Justice Powell's: that is, if a university were to make special efforts in outreach and admissions, then those efforts would have to be strongly linked to the university's central purpose: to the central activity of education and learning, and the development of leaders capable of making effective contributions to our society—a democratic, heterogeneous society of considerable complexity.

Because most people in the United States currently associate the concept of diversity with the idea of affirmative action and with the civil rights legislation of the 1960s, I was also interested in whether there was good evidence for a tradition of diversity that was distinct from affirmative action and that unequivocally predated the civil rights movement.

If one could show that educators, and major thinkers in other fields, had discussed the educational value of diversity long before the politics of the 1960s, it seemed to me that we would have a better chance of shifting the present debate from the charged political and legal arena where it is now lodged back to the educational arena where such matters properly belong.

When I began, however, I had no concrete evidence at hand, so I simply started out with a hope and a hypothesis. I began with the *Oxford English Dictionary,* looking up the word "diversity" to trace its different meanings over time. There were no dramatic discoveries, but there was one suggestive quotation from John Stuart Mill's *On Liberty,* published in 1859. I also happened to remember—because I had recently read through the annual reports of Harvard's presidents—that Presidents Hill and Felton had both, in the 1850s, discussed the need for Harvard to become a national, even international, university, and I began to wonder what had prompted them to propose that particular kind of expansion or outreach at just that time.

In other words, there were some early indicators pointing me toward the mid-nineteenth century, especially the 1850s, and I quickly added to my list of reference books *The Education of Henry Adams,* since Adams graduated from Harvard in 1858.

What was the net result of these initial probes?

First, it quickly became clear that, for President Felton at least, the prospect of a civil war was a precipitating event that led him to think explicitly about ways in which education could be helpful in avoiding regional and national friction, or actual conflict. Felton wanted to promote better understanding across the kinds of geographic, cultural, and social barriers that then existed in parts of the United States. He wrote, in 1860, that he wanted Harvard to have:

> Students from every State and Territory in the Union—without a single exception or secession, [because gathering students together] from different and distant States must tend powerfully to remove prejudices, by bringing [undergraduates] into friendly relations through the humanizing effect of liberal studies pursued in common, in the impressionable season of youth. Such influences are especially needed in the present disastrous condition of public affairs.[2]

That, in effect, was the early theory of the case: educate young, impressionable students from different parts of the country in one institution, and they will get to know one another, learn to understand one another, and overcome their prejudices through such contact. When they leave college, they will take their new forms of understanding with them back to their local communities. As they mature and become leaders, they will in time create a kind of national network, capable of bridging the great gaps that were so clearly emerging in mid-century American society. In short, student diversity—the gathering of different sorts of young people coming from different places, with different prejudices and points of view—could be a potentially powerful force in education and in the public life of the nation. That was the major reason Felton wanted to move Harvard from being a mainly regional institution to being a truly national one.

Was the idea plausible? Was there any evidence to suggest that education might really be enhanced if different sorts of students were in fact brought together in this way? When I looked at the chapter on Harvard in *The Education of Henry Adams*, I found Adams acknowledging that he, like most undergraduates in the Class of 1858, was from a well-established New England family. But, as he also wrote, "chance insisted on enlarging [Adams'] education by tossing a trio of Virginians" into the mix—a trio that included "Roony" Lee, the son of

Robert E. Lee. Adams and Lee became good friends, although Adams recognized "how thin an edge of friendship separated" him and the Virginians "from mortal enmity" on the brink of the Civil War.

This experience in diversity proved to be important. For the very first time in his life, Adams wrote, he was brought "in contact with new types [of people] and [was] taught . . . their values. He saw the New England type measure itself with another, and he was part of the process." Even though it was already too late for the students in the Harvard Class of 1858—the Civil War would soon be upon them—Adams remembered throughout his life that this "lesson in education was vital to these young men," and it clearly left a lasting impression on him.

We can see, in the 1850s, the beginnings of a theory of the educational benefits of diversity—in contrast to the view that students would generally be expected to come from the same geographical region, and more or less the same economic and social backgrounds, and very likely the same religious background. Even though neither President Felton nor Henry Adams actually used the word "diversity," the idea was clearly in the air, and at least two other important writers of the period did in fact use the term—and use it regularly.

John Stuart Mill, for instance, stressed the need for "diversity of opinion" in deliberative institutions and societies that were at least partly democratic in nature. He stressed the value of bringing "human beings in contact with persons who are dissimilar from themselves, and with modes of thought and action unlike those with which they are familiar."

Moreover, diversity in points of view—or modes of action—was not something that one should simply read or hear about; real contact with others was essential, because (as Mill said) it is important to hear "arguments" from

> persons who actually believe them, who defined them in earnest and do their very utmost for them. [One] must know [the arguments] in their most plausible and persuasive form [and] feel the whole force of the difficulty [that one's own arguments must encounter].[3]

In short, reading about points of view—or about other types of people, or actions and customs different from your own—is one important way of learning. But books do not talk back to you directly and do not respond to your arguments with the power and conviction of someone who can speak persuasively about what he or she believes and why. Contact, personal encounters, human associations, conversations, dialogue, and debate make a difference to the substance and texture of what one learns and how one learns it.

For Mill, as for Felton (and Adams), a critical aspect of education depends on being in the actual presence of people who are dissimilar from oneself in significant ways. In colleges and universities, the way to gain the particular educational values that come from various forms of dissimilarity is to have an admissions process that takes diversity explicitly into account as one of its important goals and that brings different kinds of students together in a residential community committed to learning in all its forms—outside the classroom, as well as inside.

Diversity can of course be defined in many ways, and few people tried to be more concrete in their definition than Charles William Eliot, who became president of Harvard just after the Civil War in 1869.

Much has been written about how Eliot transformed Harvard from a small college into a genuine university, how he ushered in the elective system, and so forth. But relatively little has been written about his ideas concerning student diversity and its importance to the process of education.

His views were complex, and I cannot do justice to them in this brief talk. But Eliot saw diversity—along regional, social, economic, religious, and racial or ethnic lines—as a defining feature of American democracy. And he brought an expanded conception of diversity to Harvard. He envisioned a university that would gather together students from a wide variety of "nations, states, schools, families, sects, [political] parties, and conditions of life." Harvard, he wrote, should welcome children of the "rich and poor" and of the "educated and uneducated," students "from North and South" and "from East and West," students belonging to "every religious communion, from the Roman Catholic to the Jew and the Japanese Buddhist." Bringing them together, he wrote, would allow them to experience "the wholesome influence that comes from observation and contact with" people different from themselves.

Eliot's conception of race was different from our own—especially in its emphasis on characteristics that we might today associate more with ethnicity, national origin, and immigrant status. But he specifically identified the "great diversity in the population of the United States as regards racial origin" as a crucial and positive element in American democratic society. He wanted to keep the races—whether Celtic, Teutonic, Mediterranean, Slavic, African, or otherwise—separate from one another, and he had his own Anglo-Saxon preferences. But he was able to entertain and embrace a vision that was considerably larger (and more inclusive) than his purely personal tastes, and he set about—quite consciously—opening Harvard's doors to at least some of the children of new immigrants, to members of religious minorities, and also (although in very small numbers) to African Americans.

Before Eliot's presidency, for instance, there were—as far as we know—zero black graduates of Harvard College. During his presidency, there were eight. They did not come accidentally or unnoticed: they were deliberately recruited, and they had an impact well beyond their numbers. Also, at the beginning of Eliot's presidency, there were just seven Roman Catholics and three Jews enrolled in the College—out of a total of 563 students. By the end of Eliot's tenure, 9 percent of the student body was Roman Catholic and 7 percent was Jewish, for a combined total of 16 percent, compared with less than 2 percent when Eliot started.

Interestingly, it was one of the African-American students, W. E. B. Du Bois, Harvard College Class of 1890, who would later affirm the significance of Eliot's broad vision. Harvard, Du Bois wrote, "was no longer simply a place where rich and learned New England gave the accolade to the social élite. It had broken its shell and reached out to the West and to the South, to yellow students and to black. . . . [Eliot and others] sought to make Harvard an expression of the United States."

It would be possible to cite testimony from other students if we had time—students such as John Reed, who was an undergraduate in the last years of Eliot's presidency. Reed wrote an interesting set of reflections on his Harvard experience, and he specifically mentioned the fact that he had once abandoned a close Jewish friend, when it became clear that the friend was becoming a social liability.

There was a later reconciliation, but the anecdote demonstrates that the lessons and the benefits of diversity are not always easy to discern, and that they are sometimes painful—even if the pain is subsequently transmuted into something valuable.

As things turned out, Reed came to appreciate and even revel in Harvard's diversity, and he saw the university as a place which brought together "characters, of every race and mind, poets, philosophers, [and] cranks of every twist," offering them all "anything [they] wanted" from the world's vast storehouse of learning.

Eliot himself was certainly no sentimentalist. He knew that diversity can cause friction and turbulence and can sometimes make the experience of being a student more difficult—and, at times, even alienating. But he insisted on the importance of a more open, diverse, and even disputatious university, where a "collision of views" would promote "thought on great themes," teach "candor" and "moral courage," and cultivate "forbearance and mutual respect." He saw that an inclusive vision of higher education not only would benefit individual students, but was also essential in a heterogeneous society whose citizens simply had to learn to live together if the nation's democratic institutions were to function effectively and if its ideals were to be fulfilled. He insisted, in other words, on the link between diversity in education and the requirements for citizenship and leadership in a diverse nation such as ours.

If we step back for a moment, we can take stock of the concept—and practice—of diversity at Harvard during the half century that passed between the late 1850s and the end of President Eliot's tenure in 1909.

First, we can see that the definition of diversity steadily expanded throughout this period. The early emphasis was primarily on diversity of ideas or points of view. But the most perceptive thinkers soon realized that those curious things that we call "ideas" are not disembodied phenomena or abstractions. They are complicated bundles of perceptions, intuitions, arguments, opinions, dispositions, convictions, feelings, attitudes, and rhetorical gestures that cohere—and also shift, mutate, and sometimes fail to cohere—in live human beings who constantly express, modify, reconsider, and reformulate what it is they think and feel, or what they *think* it is that they think and feel.

Moreover, these live human beings, in turn, are also not abstract phenomena, floating in a vacuum: they come from some specific place or places and have been affected by the customs, attitudes, and beliefs of their families and the culture of their points of origin. Each has a local habitation and a name that is partly regional, religious, racial or ethnic, economic, and social in nature.

That is why the effort to define diversity in college admissions almost always involves at least two major factors: first, a complex assessment of every individual as a unique human being; and, second, a thoughtful consideration of all those more general differentiating characteristics that can have a strong bearing on who we are and what we are—characteristics such as those enumerated by President Eliot when he said that Harvard should have students from different nations, states, schools, religious groups, political parties, and conditions of life.

There is no guarantee, of course, that a farm boy from Wisconsin will bring something substantially different to a university, compared with a student from a large high school in the Bronx, or one from a *lycée* in Paris. But it is a perfectly reasonable assumption, as a first approximation, and the assumption can then be tested in detail when admissions officers look carefully at individual applicants and their applications.

Similarly, there's no necessary reason that an African-American student from West Virginia should have ideas or perspectives or experiences or aesthetic tastes that are different from those of an Asian-American student from Los Angeles or a white student from Maine. But I think it would be odd if three such students did not turn out to be significantly different from one another in any number of interesting and stimulating ways, capable of expanding one another's horizons—and those of their fellow students.

In other words, it is not at all surprising, looking over the historical record, that educators like Felton and Eliot often talked in terms of broad categories—such as geography, economic background, religion, or race—when they wanted to identify important indicators of diversity. The categories are in fact extremely effective points of reference, and they have served many colleges and universities very well for at least a century. The critical issue, of course, is that we should not be trapped by these categories or use them mechanically as a substitute or shortcut for a thoughtful rounded assessment of each individual candidate.

If we care seriously about diversity, therefore, we will want to make sensible use of the relevant categories at our disposal, recognizing their limitations as well as their utility. I want to stress this point, because several recent proposals and judicial rulings—in California and Texas, for instance—have essentially banned the use of some well-established factors (specifically, race, ethnicity, and even gender) in college admissions, while allowing others to remain standing (such as socioeconomic background or regional place of origin). I, myself, believe that it is very difficult to identify a logically consistent set of reasons to justify these particular distinctions; and I also believe that, from an operational point of view, any excellent admissions process would find it essentially impossible to comply with prohibitions of the kind I just described. But these are policy considerations which—however important—deserve a much fuller discussion, on another day.

If we look briefly at developments during the major span of the 20th century, it is clear that the concept of diversity shifted meaning a number of times when applied to college and university admissions. There was no single, simple line of development but rather a series of changes and reversals.

The most important moment to focus upon—and it was a historical moment of the greatest significance—came in the years following World War II. Several things happened simultaneously: there was a massive expansion of the entire system of American higher education; there was substantially increased access to college on the part of different kinds of people, beginning notably with the GI Bill and moving through to the admission of more minority students, more foreign students, and, of course, the admission of women to previously all-male colleges. In addition, there was the rapid development of standardized testing—through the College Board and the Educational Testing Service—as a way of evaluating and sorting, on a national comparative basis, the huge number of students who were beginning to apply to college. And, finally, there was a major investment (by many, but not all, colleges) in the entire process of outreach and assessment in admissions, because admissions officers were faced for really the first time in history with the complicated task of selecting a very limited number of students from a large and expanding pool of candidates.

Given this situation, it became essential to develop much more explicit admissions criteria and guidelines, because it was no longer possible to enroll most of the people who wanted to matriculate. Not surprisingly, any set of admissions criteria could be, and came to be, openly challenged through discussion, debate, and even litigation.

The challenges have come in many forms, but the most visible—and divisive—have been legal cases in which white students have litigated against particular universities because the universities were said to have admitted African American or other minority students who had lower grade point averages and lower standardized test scores than the plaintiffs. The *Bakke* case in California, and the recent *Hopwood* case[4] in Texas are the two most conspicuous of these, but there have been others as well.

In very broad terms, we can see these legal conflicts as bringing to a head the clash between a particular "meritocratic" idea of educational quality—defined largely in terms of statistically measurable academic achievement—and an equally strong idea of education associated with the concept of diversity, including all the different forms of knowledge, the variety of human qualities and talents, and the multitude of perspectives on experience that are obviously not very measurable in statistical terms but are no less real for that.

Let us suppose, for a moment, that Harvard were to subscribe in a consistent way, to a statistical "meritocratic" view. What would happen, for example, if we were to take only those students with the very highest test scores and grade point averages, going mathematically from top to bottom, until an entire entering class was filled? The results would almost certainly be very curious. It is not at all clear, for example, how many of the students, chosen in this way, would be very talented in the arts, since certain creative abilities do not correlate at all strongly with SAT scores—or even with high grades in many subjects. It is not clear how many students with a capacity for leadership we would have in such a class—or individuals strongly committed to public service; or how many students who have exceptional and unusual abilities to understand other people; or to penetrate complex human and societal situations; or students who are good at ice hockey; or who are descended from our alumni.

Equally important, it is not clear that we would have assembled a group of students who were sufficiently dissimilar to learn very much from one another: about the varieties of human nature, about how people from different places, different social and economic backgrounds, different ethnic and racial backgrounds, different countries and religions and cultures experience the world, articulate their values, and indeed, live their lives.

In this respect, it is important to remember that when we *do* admit a class of first-year students to Harvard College, we do not do so "atomistically," looking at each candidate in isolation from all the others. Instead, we try to compose a class that, in all its variety, has considerable power to "teach itself," so to speak.

Of course, we want a very high level of academic achievement, measured in more or less traditional ways. But, we also want students to be able to achieve at college all those other dimensions of intellectual and human capacity—dimensions that are most likely to emerge in the actual dynamic process of education—through innumerable encounters, associations, and discussions among students as well as with faculty, day in and day out. Educational quality, as we know, has every bit as much to do with realizing potentialities still to be developed—in an environment designed to help such development—as it has to do with measuring prior achievement.

Perhaps I am wrong. But, I believe that very few of us—if any—would be very satisfied with a college admissions process that was mathematically driven by test scores and similar statistics; yet, it is just such scores and statistics that are being used as the chief evidence in the legal cases I have mentioned.

These statistical scores and grades are certainly useful and certainly important to take into account in any sensible admissions process. But when we try to describe why they are not wholly sufficient, I think we find ourselves mentioning criteria and qualities and characteristics that are mainly associated with the concept of diversity.

That, I believe, is why John Stuart Mill, President Felton, President Eliot, and students such as those I have cited, were driven to the conclusion more than a century ago that the concept of diversity or significant differences among people was central to any serious theory of education and learning. All of these individuals obviously valued academic excellence. But none of them thought that a narrow view of excellence was robust enough to capture anything like the full range of capabilities that we would want to include and help students to develop in a definition of education. Felton and Eliot and others sensed that their nation and the world were multifarious; that the needs and requirements of heterogeneous democratic societies were becoming complex beyond any imagining; and that one of the only effective ways to begin to understand and absorb some substantial part of that multi-fariousness and complexity was to encounter it directly, and come to know it through actual association, through having direct contact with a considerable variety of people, through diversity.

That recognition is every bit as important now—perhaps more important—as it was a century and a half ago. In closing, let me confess that I find it ironic—and inauspicious—that on a day when we can look back on President Eliot's clear-sighted determination to reach out consciously to enroll students of different immigrant groups and races, the State of California has recently passed a resolution prohibiting any consideration of ethnicity, race, or gender in college admissions.

Notes

1. *Regents of the University of California v. Bakke*, 438 U.S. 265 (1978).
2. Cornelius C. Felton. *Report of the President to the Board of Overseers, 1859–60*, p. 6.
3. John Stuart Mill. *On Liberty* (1859: reprint, London: Penguin Books, 1985), p. 99.
4. *Hopwood v. State of Texas*, 78 F.3d 932 (5th Cir. 1996).

Clarence G. Williams

Clarence G. Williams, an innovator in higher education for three decades, with a Ph.D. in Higher Education Administration and Counseling Psychology from the University of Connecticut (1972), is Special Assistant to the President and Professor of Urban Studies and Planning at the Massachusetts Institute of Technology, Cambridge, MA.

Dr. Williams received his M.A. degree from Hampton University in 1967, B.A. from North Carolina Central University in 1961, and he attended Harvard University and Cornell University, 1975 and 1965 respectively.

Dr. Williams joined the administration at MIT in 1972 as Assistant Dean of the Graduate School. He was promoted to Special Assistant to the President and Chancellor for Minority Affairs in 1974. From 1980 to 1982 he held the position of Acting Director of the Office of Minority Education, and in 1984 through 1997 he assumed additional responsibilities as Assistant Equal Opportunity Officer, along with a broader scope of the Special Assistant position, to serve the MIT community as an ombudsperson. Since 1992, he has been teaching a race relations and diversity course in the Department of Urban Studies and Planning.

He has initiated and coordinated several national conferences and has numerous publications, including *Reflections of the Dream 1975–1994: Twenty Years Celebrating the Life of Dr. Martin Luther King, Jr. at the Massachusetts Institute of Technology and Technology* and *the Dream: Reflections on the Black Experience at MIT, 1941–1999.* He is currently working on his third book.

Dr. Williams has lectured widely on the issues and challenges of our society, specifically on diversity and racial and cultural differences, in colleges, high schools, and national organizations. He stresses an all-inclusive environment as it relates to the nation's diversified population in the technological and scientific workforce in the 2000s.

He also maintains involvement with pre-college students and parents through participation as a member of numerous Boards in Boston and Cambridge schools, and through community organizations active in student achievement and success in the workforce in the twenty-first century.

6

THE MIT EXPERIENCE:

PERSONAL PERSPECTIVES ON RACE IN A PREDOMINANTLY WHITE UNIVERSITY

As I think back on my career in higher education, I realize that the path I have taken mirrors a number of familiar trends for blacks over the past half century: secondary and college education in black schools, 1950s to early 1960s; first teaching and administrative posts also in black schools and colleges, early to late 1960s; graduate work in predominantly white universities, mid-1960s to early 1970s; and administrative and teaching posts in a predominantly white university, early 1970s to the present. The path follows the general contours shaped by our post-*Brown v. Board of Education* ideals—away from a racially segregated environment toward a racially integrated one, yet involving a complex range of advantages, struggles, successes, pitfalls, opportunities, and limitations along the way.

Beginnings: Working with Black Youth in a Historically Black College

My first job in college administration was as assistant dean of students at Hampton Institute (now Hampton University). I was in charge of a residence hall of 257 men and stayed in that job four years, also teaching part-time in the School of Education. I learned a great deal from the Hampton dean of men, Tom Hawkins, a proud black Howard University graduate whose life was dedicated to showing young black men the key principles of life. Dean Hawkins was a powerful mentor and role model for me and others.

One of the things Dean Hawkins and I worked on together was developing educational programs that went beyond formal course offerings. We counseled and met with students on a regular basis. We organized forums at least once a week, where we would bring in speakers to provide not only guidance about careers and fields but also to motivate and inspire in a more general way. We produced exhibits and displays in the entrance of the residence hall, often about the accomplishments of blacks through history—a form of racial uplift, filling the gaps left or sometimes created by traditional texts and media. On one occasion I created a display featuring Hampton's president, Jerome Holland. It included photographs of him, a biography, news clippings, and other items and illustrations. Students were amazed to learn that he had been an All-American football player at Cornell in the 1930s, president of Delaware State College, and director of the New York Stock Exchange— an outstanding individual in every way; later, he became U.S. Ambassador to Sweden and an excellent example of the kind of person black students needed to see, emulate, and accept as one of their own.

The Hampton experience was valuable, introducing me through the living example of Dean Hawkins to the kind of service and dedication required to make an impact on higher education for people of color. All of this was happening, too, in the 1960s, when the nation was in a transitional phase—segregation in higher education (and education generally) was still the norm, but efforts were under way to integrate and diversify college campuses. In fact, I attended predominantly white institutions for my graduate work, earning a master's degree from Cornell (a joint program with Hampton that included summer classes at Cornell and regular-year classes at Hampton) and a doctorate from the University of Connecticut.

I actually wanted to go to Columbia for graduate work because I knew a number of blacks who had gone there. I applied and was accepted in 1967. But around this time, students were growing restless on the Hampton campus. It was the climax of the civil rights movement, a time of crisis on many college campuses. Several students wanted Hampton to take outspoken positions on civil rights issues. I think President Holland knew I was popular on campus among the men, so he didn't want me to go away for graduate work that year. He told me if I would wait a year, he would make sure that I got into a good school. He also said he did not think Columbia was the best choice, as there were too many blacks going there and other schools could benefit from an influx of blacks. He thought I should aim for a school where a friend of his, Homer Babbidge, was the president—and that is how I ended up at the University of Connecticut, Storrs.

Beyond Segregation: Racial Intersections in a White Institution

At U Conn, while working on my doctorate I also worked in the counseling and testing center, which played a major role in terms of my field of study. There were no other blacks in the graduate program I was in, although there were several by the time I left. The university had not recruited any black faculty members when I entered but, shortly afterwards, at least two were recruited from historically black institutions for the school of education. One was Dr. Floyd Bass from North Carolina Central, and the other was Dr. William Brazziel, who came from Norfolk State. I ended up working with Dr. Bass, who helped me develop a thesis topic and worked with me to complete my dissertation—an investigation of the affective dimensions of the black experience in higher education, essentially an instrument to test the knowledge of white folks regarding the black experience and black traditions in higher education.

The experience at U Conn started me thinking about racial intersections and relationships in higher education. While the original plan was for me to return to Hampton as vice president for student affairs, I kept my mind open to the possibility of other routes as well—the possibility, for example, of moving into an arena where there were opportunities for further exploring racial relationships and by extension increasing avenues of access for blacks to higher education. Also, by this time, President Holland had left Hampton to go overseas as U.S. ambassador to Sweden.

One day in the spring of 1972, while still at U Conn, I came across an interesting ad in *The Chronicle of Higher Education* seeking applications for the post of assistant dean of the MIT Graduate School, with special responsibility for increasing the number of minority graduate students. I was excited by the prospect. If I went to MIT, I could continue to pursue my interest in the education of minority youth and, in this case, develop strategies to expand opportunities beyond the traditional routes that blacks had been following in historically black colleges. Coincidentally, Dr. Holland happened to be a member of MIT's governing body, the Corporation, the first black so appointed; he encouraged me to apply for the job.

During the interview process, it was clear to me that the students—including Shirley Jackson (MIT, '68), now president of Rensselaer Polytechnic Institute and a life member of the MIT Corporation since 1992—were major actors who had persuaded the administration to create the post and who would be decisive voices in selecting a candidate. I learned that they had already worked hard with the administration, through MIT's Task Force on Educational Opportunity and other forums, to increase the number of minority graduate students from 16 in 1968 to 112 in the forthcoming academic year, 1972–73, and that the position for which I was applying had been created to ensure that this momentum would be sustained and, if possible, increased. The whole process seemed like a grass-roots initiative, an exercise in true democracy—something I would not have expected to find at an institution like MIT. I had never experienced anything like it.

As it turned out, I was the candidate selected. When I arrived, my charge was to increase the number of minority students in the graduate programs and to develop a retention program to ensure that, once here, these students did not fall through the cracks. I got to work on both tasks right away. I developed a strategy to identify and recruit outstanding black and other minority students who could benefit from the rigors of an MIT education.

In the summer of 1973, I coordinated a meeting of educators from predominantly black colleges in the South—members of the Thirteen College Curriculum Program (TCCP)—to explore ways in which MIT could attract more graduate students from Southern minority schools. Frederick Humphries, who went on to serve as president of Tennessee State University and later Florida A&M University, was the director of TCCP and vice president of its parent organization, the Institute for Services to Education. Also in the group were Elias Blake, then president of Clark College (now Clark Atlanta University) and head of the Institute for Services to Education, and a number of senior administrators from other historically black colleges and universities (HBCUs). At our meeting, when the first moonwalk was a recent memory, one of the college presidents wondered why, if we could put men on the moon, we could not get MIT to do something relatively simple like admitting black graduate students in greater numbers. Among the results that emerged was the Lincoln Laboratory Summer Minority Internship Program, bringing students in electrical engineering and physics from historically black colleges and universities to MIT's Lincoln Laboratory for ten weeks to introduce them to hands-on work and to MIT graduate programs in their respective fields.

In the fall of 1973, a year after my arrival, sixty new minority graduate students registered in various programs, bringing the total number at MIT to an all-time high of 136. I worked as assistant dean until January 1994, when I became "special assistant to the president and the chancellor for minority affairs."

Broadening Purview

My new duties covered not just minority graduate students but all matters relating to minorities at MIT, including advising senior officers on recruitment and retention of minority faculty, students, and staff; advocacy of the interests of minority members of the community; and addressing formal and informal complaints or concerns relating to treatment of minorities at the Institute. I was also the MIT representative on minority issues to the outside community. This included participation in urban affairs and affirmative action/equal opportunity conferences, boards, and other activities on the local and national levels. An analogous position to mine dealing with women's interests had been in place for about a year "as the special assistant for women and work." The new position I held advocating the interests of minorities had come about as a result of pressure from the black community at MIT. If there was to be an administrative position of such stature and prominence for women, they reasoned, there should be one for minorities too.

There were two areas, as I understood the job, that I would focus on: I would advise the president and other senior officers about minority issues and make suggestions about how to enhance programs relating to minorities, and I would develop new programs for minorities on campus. I served as the administration's eyes and ears, so to speak, on issues relating to minorities, with a broad mandate to develop ideas, strategies, and programs. While I couldn't always be certain that these proposals would be acted on favorably, I felt that the upper administration—Jerome Wiesner (president) and Paul Gray (chancellor)—would most likely support at least modifications of my ideas. I found them both to be sensitive and supportive on nearly all my concerns regarding race and race relations.

Early on, I met with Paul about once a month, but I had access to him more often if necessary. We didn't meet too often because I wanted the flexibility to generate ideas on my own and with others, and also to be considered someone with a level of independence. Paul and Jerry were comfortable with this; it helped inspire confidence that I was doing what I could possibly do to meet the needs of minorities. I did not want to be thought of as a mere attachment to the office of the president and chancellor, yet at the same time I needed to preserve access routes to Paul and Jerry. Achieving that balance wasn't always easy, but it helped that they agreed with my approach and were supportive.

Networking and Consciousness-Raising

During that first decade, 1974 into the mid-1980s, I think I did a reasonable job of improving communication between blacks on campus. As the faculty goes, so goes the institution; so if anything was to be achieved for minorities at MIT, senior faculty would have to become involved, flex their muscles, exercise their influence. With this in mind, I brought together black faculty and senior black administrators with the hope of creating a consensus on critical issues and, if possible, coming up with strategies for action. A group of us would meet to brainstorm, and we sometimes invited Chancellor Gray to dinner to share our thoughts.

In October 1975, I organized a day-long retreat for black faculty and administrators at the Endicott House, MIT's conference facility in Dedham, Massachusetts. We discussed issues, carved out strategies, explored ways to establish closer ties among the various segments of the black community at MIT, and developed specific objectives for follow-up. One faculty member wondered, half jokingly, whether Endicott House—"white man's territory"—was an appropriate venue for such a retreat, but we made good progress in our discussions nonetheless. Thirty-five faculty members and administrators were present. The group felt that priority should be given to consciousness-raising about racial bias at MIT, recruitment of black faculty, inclusion of blacks in decision-making at the highest level of the administration, and affirmative action efforts across all categories of personnel. Exactly how we would go about this ambitious program remained undecided, but suggestions included further meetings; liaison with the president, chancellor, and other officials; and a more proactive campaign on the part of black faculty and administrators.

By 1978, a core group of us—Wesley Harris, Willard Johnson, John Turner, Wade Kornegay, James Young, and myself—had come together semi-officially as "the Group of Six." At a meeting in Washington, D.C., in the spring of 1978, we tried to further define our goals. We decided to step up efforts to place blacks on key MIT policy committees and to prepare position papers on issues such as recruitment, academic performance, and financial aid. We then held a round of meetings with top-level administrators and, in September 1978, submitted a paper— "Blacks at MIT: The Challenge for Full Participation in the 1980s"—to the administration assessing the quality of academic life for black undergraduates, the status of graduate education for blacks, and the prospects for black faculty, administrators, and research staff. This effort was made to encourage the Institute to consider these concerns as it prepared to select its next president—which Paul Gray became in 1980.

In August 1981, a slightly expanded group—now including Frank Jones, Shirley McBay, Phyllis Wallace, and James Williams, in addition to the original members of "the Group of Six"—met at a retreat organized by John Turner and myself at the request of the group to discuss the objectives outlined in the 1978 position paper and to review progress on our recommendations. We spent a weekend in intense discussions on Shelter Island, off the east end of Long Island. Our sense of urgency was increased because of Institute-wide budget deficits that threatened not just our prospects for progress but also existing programs and personnel; we feared that retrenchment might diminish the Institute's commitment to minority issues.

Such occasional retreats created, I believe, a framework to mobilize the senior black faculty and administrators. However, while we opened up avenues of discussion, we were unable to sustain our momentum over the years or to come up with a consensus. The dynamic did not work out as well as I had hoped, but it did have an impact on the administration.

One difficult situation arose when Paul Gray took over the presidency from Jerry Wiesner in 1980. He met with senior black faculty members in an effort to persuade one of them to assume the directorship of the Office of Minority Education (OME). A replacement was needed for Wesley Harris, a black tenured associate professor of aeronautics and astronautics, who had served as the first OME director beginning in 1975 until he went on leave in 1979 as a program manager at NASA headquarters. Paul and the black faculty unanimously agreed that in order for OME to sustain its credibility, the directorship ought to continue to be held by someone not only with academic stature, but with affiliations in a quantitative field central to MIT's primary educational and research mission. Paul was deeply disappointed when black faculty members ideally suited to the job would not accept it because of the toll they thought it would take on their primary professional and scholarly pursuits. Meanwhile, in order to keep the office going, a supportive senior white faculty member, Arthur Smith, a professor in the Department of Electrical Engineering, served as acting director (1979–80); I succeeded him, also as acting director, in 1980. I served until 1982, and all my successors were black administrators without faculty status.

Also in 1980, Mary Rowe and I became "special assistants to the president," that is, without the title qualifiers "for women" and "for minority affairs." While both Mary and I retained our special functions—she in the area of women, I in the area of minorities—the idea was to broaden our reach. We were to be accessible as "shuttle diplomats" or mediators for all faculty and staff; we would be involved in facilitating communication between conflicting parties, complaint and grievance resolution, the flow of essential information to department heads and supervisors (a kind of early warning system in problem areas), and response to informal concerns, inquiries, suggestions, and problems. In short, Mary and I together maintained an ombudsperson's role.

In those early days, I was excited about the number of outstanding colleges and universities in the area and about the opportunity to develop relationships among black administrators and faculty outside MIT. In the early 1980s, I worked with a group of local black college administrators to organize the Greater Boston Inter-University Council (GBIUC), bringing together personnel from local colleges and universities to develop retention strategies for students of color. Among the original group were Ken Haskins, then co-director of the Principal Center, Harvard School of Education; James Cash, a professor at the Harvard Business School; Dexter Eure, then director of community relations at the Boston *Globe*; Kenneth Guscott, a prominent businessman; Bernard Fulp, then senior vice president of Bank of New England; and myself.

Our discussions began informally over breakfast once a month. We talked, for example, about the high dropout rate of black students at local colleges and universities, especially Northeastern University which had a dropout rate of about sixty percent at the time. The group asked me to come up with a program to address such issues in practical ways, and that is how the GBIUC concept got under way. I was selected as the first president, and the organization continues to carry on the work begun almost twenty years ago. At the inaugural GBIUC forum sponsored by the Boston *Globe* in June 1984, I delivered a position paper—"Retention of Black College Students: Where Should We Go During the 1980s?"—which provided a basis for GBIUC's future activities, including networking, professional development workshops, region-wide alliances, and efforts to evaluate institutional commitment in addition to strategies for student recruitment and retention.

During this period, the early to mid-1980s, I also became involved in one of the most satisfying and successful activities of my career—shaping the Association of Black Administrators at MIT and organizing two national conferences for which I was co-coordinator (the other co-coordinator was John Turner, associate dean of the Graduate School). While efforts to organize the black faculty never totally materialized, efforts to bring the black administrators together resulted in a supportive and successful group that met regularly to share information, ideas, and perspectives. I served as convenor of this group. However, in the mid-1990s the group gradually diminished, in my view, due to the lack of effective leadership transitions.

Two national conferences—the First and Second National Conferences on Issues Facing Black Administrators at Predominantly White Colleges and Universities, held in 1982 and 1984 respectively—were an outgrowth of our informal meetings and discussions in which John and I served as group leaders. The conferences attracted not only black administrators but also major black figures (a few key white ones as well) in public life—judges, elected officials, media personalities, national leaders in the struggle against racial discrimination—to explore the anxieties, stresses, and aspirations of black administrators within often hostile academic environments. Much was learned in those two conferences, and the published proceedings—*Proceedings: First National Conference on Issues Facing Black Administrators at Predominantly White Colleges and Universities* (Cambridge, Mass.: Association of Black Administrators, MIT, 1982) and *Proceedings: Second National Conference on Issues Facing Black Administrators at Predominantly White Colleges and Universities* (Cambridge, Mass.: Association of Black Administrators, MIT, 1984)—are an enduring source of insight. In summarizing the proceedings of the first conference, MIT president Paul Gray observed: "This conference is a bold, new step. The energy and ideas and associations which have been generated . . . have been extraordinary. And I trust that we leave here with strengthened resolve to building colleges and universities which truly serve an equitable and humane social order." Unfortunately, the motivation to continue our discussions and to organize further conferences did not last past the second conference, even though many of the issues that we explored remain today, real and unresolved.

As special assistant to the president and chancellor, I was also responsible for planning and coordinating the annual Martin Luther King, Jr. celebration at MIT, beginning in 1976. The event revolved around a breakfast or dinner meeting and a public address by an invited speaker, selected for his or her insight in the area of civil rights, race relations, and other issues dear to Dr. King's heart. I always thought it was important to emphasize local community leaders, following Dr. King's own preference for grass-roots activists as well as figures of national renown, although our program at MIT has since moved away from that philosophy in search of high-profile speakers. The text of addresses delivered during the first twenty years of the celebration appears in a book that I edited, *Reflections of the Dream, 1975–1994: Twenty Years Celebrating the Life of Dr. Martin Luther King, Jr. at the Massachusetts Institute of Technology* (Cambridge, Mass.: MIT Press, 1996). Each of the speakers helped educate and motivate our academic community, and reminded us of business left unfinished both at MIT and the society at large. Among the important outgrowths of the MLK celebration were the MLK Visiting Scholars program (established in 1988) and its successor, the MLK Visiting Professors program (established in 1995)—both of which brought minority academicians to MIT on term appointments to enrich the diversity of our curriculum and to provide our community with role models and other influences outside the white mainstream.

Equal Opportunity: An Uphill Battle

I would single out one area—monitoring and promoting equal opportunity, especially at the faculty level—as the most frustrating in my nearly three decades at MIT. The problem is partly structural, partly indifference or hostility on the part of non-black faculty, and partly insufficient pressure from the minority community on the leadership at the departmental and central administrative levels. For much of my career here, we had a white equal employment officer assisted by a succession of assistant equal employment officers, all black, who basically ran the operation and reported to the officer. He or she did all the procedural work, monitoring faculty and staff search processes as well as education, recruitment, and advising the chair of the Equal Opportunity Committee; responding to inquiries and reviews by the U.S. Department of Labor and the Office of Federal Contract Compliance Programs (OFCCP); investigating issues relating to employment discrimination; gathering data from the various schools and departments reflecting the Institute's progress (or lack thereof) with affirmative action; and compiling a detailed report of how many people had been hired, how many were minorities, how many were women, and so forth. The equal employment officer would then present the report to the Academic Council—the Institute's central decision-making body, comprised of all senior officers—and make policy decisions in consultation with them. This affirmative action report required by the OFCCP is used both inside and outside MIT to make public the Institute's efforts in affirmative action.

I took over the job of assistant equal employment officer in 1984. Although the job did not require it, I prepared an internal report at the end of my first year identifying some key areas where I thought we had made progress and others where I thought progress could be improved. Faculty recruitment efforts had not measured up to expectations, the proportion of minority graduate students had declined since 1974, the OFCCP had observed deficiencies that were later corrected, and a number of minority employees had complained about unfair treatment and poor work environments with possible racial overtones. I suggested measures for improvement, including seminars, social events, and visiting minority faculty who would provide a black presence until the number of minorities on the regular faculty increased.

The duties of the job were a good fit with my other responsibilities as special assistant to the president; racial discrimination, for example, arose frequently in the course of my work as ombudsperson. Yet the structure of the operation never seemed right to me—this idea of an assistant who happened to be black, with little if any authority, reporting to the vice president in the president's office. In my view, it was (and still is) a mistake not to have a black or other minority in a position to be heard directly at the highest level of the administration. A minority in charge, I believe, would have added legitimacy to the process. It was also clear from my contact with similar offices at other institutions in the area, especially the Ivy League colleges and universities, that we were understaffed relative to the complexity of our mission and to the demands placed on us to gather and review data, monitor compliance, and report to the regulatory bodies both within and outside MIT.

Almost a decade earlier, in May 1975, I had written a memo to senior administrative officers pointing out differences between the rhetoric of affirmative action and the results as illustrated by the number of blacks in certain categories at MIT (1.6% faculty, 1.4% sponsored research staff, 2.0% academic staff, and 4.5% administrative staff). I also suggested that the problem stemmed from "subtle attitudinal patterns of non-blacks who have been unable to accept full partnerships between blacks and non-blacks" at MIT, and that there would never be much improvement unless the administration brought pressure to bear on the faculty.

There was a note of administrative frustration in response to that memo, the reasons for which I did not fully understand at the time but which I later came to appreciate. After learning more about the ways of the Institute, it became clear to me that a president or chancellor has limited influence with tenured faculty and the directions taken by individual departments. Tactics of persuasion must be carefully thought through and, even then, there are no guarantees of success or even progress. Indeed, the proportion of black faculty in 2000 (2.5%), while better than in 1975 (1.6%), is still far too small.

The senior administration did try some things, such as financial incentives—fully funded positions along with extra cash—to encourage departments to hire minorities. But that made little difference. Few departments acted on the offer. The argument about the lack of minorities "in the pipeline" often became a convenient way for departments to sidestep racial attitudes or indifference within their own ranks. Other strategies could have been tried, but weren't—holding department heads accountable for results, for example, or publicly recognizing achievement in those rare instances where minorities were hired. But there were no assurances that these would have worked, either. MIT's culture is such that there is only so much the administration can do to exercise influence with a tenured, senior faculty that is brilliant, independent, and not always open to change or to new perspectives on issues such as race. One had to just accept that and move on—never forgetting, of course, how things could or should be in a better world.

In the mid-1980s, however, when obstacles were placed in the way of a couple of our most promising black junior faculty members, I became convinced that little serious change was likely to happen. I realized that those of us whose mission was to increase diversity among the faculty were fighting a battle that wasn't just uphill, it was up a mountain. I find unconvincing the argument by many senior white faculty members that such cases have nothing to do with race, and that two out of ten faculty members overall fail to proceed all the way through the system to the award of tenure. The fact that the two black professors in question were widely recognized as exceptional, talented scholars and educators, as candidates for at least the top fifth in any pool of faculty at MIT or elsewhere, raises questions about what else may have been at work in their rejection. While we at MIT may pride ourselves on the use of objective criteria in all our functions and activities—we are, after all, a premiere scientific and engineering institution—we are not always free of the conscious and unconscious prejudices common in our society at large.

My role in equal opportunity issues led me to a deeper understanding of how limited that process is—not just here at MIT, but at institutions nationwide. Essentially, the process allows institutions either to do very little or to obey only the letter of the law. The U.S. Department of Labor bureaucracy is cumbersome and ill-equipped to monitor progress in affirmative action: its compliance staff tends to be unfamiliar with the way a university operates and, therefore, makes unfounded judgments. Meanwhile, the mood of the country has been swinging slowly but steadily toward the notion that affirmative action is unfair and an example of government waste; it is a low priority at best, and there are complaints—even from some supporters—about how clumsy and impractical it has become. There is some truth to the observation that affirmative action compliance, both here and elsewhere, has generated mounds of paperwork to little or no effect, considering the original objective.

Beyond Numbers: Race, Culture, and Psychology

MIT is typical of many predominantly white institutions in that blacks and other minorities do not carry much weight in the balance of leadership. Concepts like diversity, recruitment, and inclusion are often expressed but not always or consistently acted on. While there have been positive changes during the past thirty years—especially in the larger number of minorities in the undergraduate student body—the Institute has not made as much progress as it could in minority recruitment within the faculty ranks, in promoting multiracial leadership, and in encouraging members of the MIT community, particularly students, to learn from each other's differences. In these areas, much remains to be done.

There are a number of reasons for this, cultural and psychological, that lie deeper than mere policy issues or surface numbers. First, the rhetoric of liberalism in universities has not translated into a consistent program of liberal action. So while many talk the talk, they don't walk the walk—they give off an appearance of concern unmatched by sustained follow-up action. Secondly, there is ongoing resistance to the idea of blacks and other minorities not only as equal colleagues but also as potential intellectual leaders. Non-minority faculty gravitate naturally to people who look like themselves. But even if they are able to rise above such prejudices, they still doubt whether a minority can fit in, become an integral part of the program, interact in an effective way socially as well as professionally, and end up a resource rather than a liability.

Various cultural intangibles—race, prejudice, and personal likes and dislikes—continue to influence the world of academia and career advancement beyond an individual's basic abilities and qualifications. So what can the academic world do to improve itself? We have done a reasonable job, as I said, of increasing educational opportunities, particularly at the undergraduate level. Growing numbers in all categories is the first important step, and the first important measure of success is how many minorities can be counted in a given environment compared to an earlier time. It is important, however, to recognize that increased numbers are just the beginning rather than the end of the process. Numbers tell only part of the story, and we cannot afford to congratulate ourselves and sit back on our laurels when the charts and graphs show an upward curve.

Once numbers increase, as they have in our case with minority undergraduate students at MIT, the next step is far more complex—to assess, shape, and monitor the qualitative aspects of minorities' inclusion in the process. There are deep psychological and cultural factors involved here that are often hard to measure empirically—factors about feelings, emotions, and other intangibles that reflect deeply on how well integration is working, how completely minorities have become part of a trend that includes not just acceptance but full participation.

That is why, beginning about ten years ago, I realized that we needed to get back to understanding some of the basics of human relationships—through reflection, modes of interaction, consciousness-raising. The way I chose to pursue this goal was by conducting life history interviews with a number of blacks—and with whites whose lives significantly intersected or impacted the lives of blacks—in the MIT context. Many of these interviews, over 200 in all conducted during a four-year period, are printed in my book, *Technology and the Dream: Reflections on the Black Experience at MIT, 1941–1999* (MIT Press,

2001). The experiences related by interviewees focus on a number of what I call "affective dimensions," defined broadly as qualitative measures of racial interaction. These dimensions are probed using oral history and psychological techniques—dimensions too complex for easy answers, yet too important to shy away from.

I tried to have everyone address the following topics: family background, early education, role models and mentors, racism and race-sensitive issues, choice of field and career, goals, adjustment to the MIT environment, best and worst experiences at MIT, assessment of support services, relationships among MIT students, faculty, and staff, and advice to current and future students and personnel. The result is a picture of blacks at MIT over time as a small, determined group that has reached for opportunities, seized them, and gone on to achieve much—sometimes with help, sometimes in the face of obstacles, always driven by deep motivation and both personal and community drive. *Technology and the Dream* conveys the personal perspectives of key players—both black and non-black, but with a focus on black students and faculty—about racial issues at MIT during the last half of the twentieth century.

In addition to the oral history interviews, I have been involved in three other efforts that provide further contexts I believe for qualitative study. One is a proposed book-length history of the role and experience of blacks at MIT, another is a course I am teaching, and the last is a concept I am developing that I call "bridge leadership."

The book-length history traces in greater detail the role and experience of blacks at MIT. That story begins in the late nineteenth and early twentieth centuries, when only a few black students were able to take advantage of educational opportunities here; it proceeds through the period between World War II and the mid-1960s, when the national emergency and growing civil rights activism created an environment in which blacks could participate more fully not only as students but as faculty and researchers; and the history concludes with the period since the late 1960s, which saw the formalization of minority recruitment programs and other incentives to enhance the participation of blacks and, more recently, a growing climate of uncertainty nationwide about the value and utility of affirmative action. The evolving historical narrative helps work through issues of race and also provides examples that are comparable to the exhibits and displays I worked on at Hampton Institute nearly 40 years ago, but go more deeply into how blacks perform at levels and in contexts not generally thought of as typical venues for them.

Second, I have been teaching a course on racial and cultural differences to undergraduate students at MIT for nearly a decade. We explore conflicts centered around race and culture in the workplace and society at large. To meet this challenge, I am convinced, leaders and ordinary citizens must learn to separate truth from myth with respect to race and culture. They must look beyond stereotypes and begin to use cultural differences as a valuable tool for social change rather than as a source of antagonism. Students in the course are encouraged to make use of their life experiences in our culturally rich and diversified population and to develop techniques for conflict resolution. The course challenges students to think about how these goals can be achieved. Our assigned readings are supplemented by films and interactive classroom exercises. To help students learn and develop insights about racial and cultural differences, I encourage them to broaden their focus beyond the classroom to include community outreach. By the end of the semester, nearly all class members have made a paradigm shift from their previous understanding of racial and cultural experience. As a part of a formal curriculum, such courses can do much to break down the fear, intolerance, and hatred that are still too prevalent in our society.

A key element in all these activities is acceptance rather than denial of cultural and racial differences (even biases) as part of the natural human makeup; yet we must recognize that the social contract requires coming to terms with differences and biases in the interest of social harmony, and secondly, that there is a practical need to maximize the contributions of each member of our society, regardless of race, ethnicity, religion, or national origin. In short, the larger social interest requires us to rise above prejudice, at the same time that we recognize that prejudice is an intrinsic part of the human condition.

So while numbers are a start—and we at MIT have made good progress with that, at least in terms of undergraduate admissions—the qualitative aspects of the inclusion process demand ongoing focus. These qualitative aspects are much more difficult to deal with; there are no quick fixes. In short, we must tackle not just statistics but issues relating to the inner self, conscious and unconscious bias, and psychological resistance to diversity. If we are to continue to make progress in accepting all human beings as our equal brothers and sisters—regardless of race, ethnicity, and other external factors, we must continue to work at coming to terms with these difficult but essential affective dimensions.

Principles and Strategies: A Summary

Raise awareness through exhibits, conferences, discussion groups, retreats, formal coursework, informal community interactions

Develop mentorship programs and role models such as the "bridge leadership" concept

Build support networks that are both inter-racial and intra-racial

Explore the complex values of racial integration, including both positive and negative implications

Work through difficult policies/situations patiently and systematically; accept reality that immediate results are out of the question, that strategies must be persistent and long-term

Recognize that growing numbers are only one measure of success; qualitative aspects—culture, human psychology, communication, interaction—need equal if not more attention

Antoinette Miranda

Antoinette Miranda is an Associate Professor and Director of the School Psychology Program at Ohio State University. Her research interests include effective interventions with at-risk preschool populations and urban youth, cultural diversity training, and urban education. Dr. Miranda completed her doctoral studies in school psychology at the University of Cincinnati. She has consulted with school districts in the area of diversity and has presented nationally on this topic. Dr. Miranda received the Alumni Award for Distinguished Teaching at Ohio State University.

7

SELF-DISCOVERY
TO ACTUALIZATION:
CHARTING A COURSE TO
MAKE A DIFFERENCE

Diversity is not a choice, but our
responses to it certainly are.
—*Gary Howard, 1999*

Self-Discovery

It is fairly well established that we are becoming an increasingly multi-cultural society. While this increase in diversity was accurately pre-dicted for the future as early as 1985 (Hodgkinson, 1985), it wasn't until the 1990s that serious attention was given to its potential impact, particularly in education. Many universities have developed successful diversity programs on their campuses. Yet, there are many individual efforts that are occurring on college campuses throughout the country that are making an impact, albeit on a smaller scale. It is this type of initiative that I wish to share.

My work in teaching and training in the area of cultural diversity has much to do with my development as a person of color. My high school years were spent in a predominately white Catholic high school. Issues of diversity were never raised, and I felt considerable pressure to adapt. My undergraduate years were a time of self-exploration and for the evolution of my own racial and ethnic identity. Being closed out of a three-hour class was the impetus for me to take my first black stud-ies class. It was the first time I was ever in a class where I was part of the majority. I was like a sponge, soaking up new knowledge about intelligent, innovative, and courageous black folk. But I also learned in a deeper way the tragedies, injustices, and travesties that were inflicted upon black people. Learning about W.E.B. DuBois, Carter G. Woodson, Langston Hughes, Ida Wells-Barnett, to name a few, was purely inspirational. I subsequently took three more black studies classes. My journey had begun.

Graduate school moved me from my own personal exploration as a person of color to broader professional issues concerning cultural diversity. One single incident started me on my professional journey. I chose school psychology as a major because I wanted to work with children. I did not know that one of the major job responsibilities of school psychologists is administering IQ tests for special education placement. It was during an assessment class that I first learned that blacks scored lower on IQ tests than whites. Fortunately, my professor also discussed how early research compared lower socioeconomic blacks with middle class whites, thereby not controlling for socioeconomic class. When one controls for class, there is no significant difference. We were trained to conduct non-biased assessments and to search for assessments that would be culturally fair to the extent they could be. My curiosity was piqued. I was smart in school and was never told I could not accomplish my goals academically. I knew I was, at least, of average intelligence. Yet, I began to realize, that might not be others' perceptions of black children. I recalled a conversation with a guidance counselor my senior year in high school. She said, "You have done well here for being a black girl." I knew she thought it was a compliment, but I remember feeling embarrassed by her comment and wondering what her expectations were of me as an African-American adolescent. My understanding of the impact of this difference in IQ scores began my quest. My journey went far beyond the IQ debate into a deeper and more complex world of cultural diversity.

While my program lacked diverse faculty and students, my faculty advisor, Dr. Dave Barnett, encouraged my exploration of cultural diversity. There was also an African-American male faculty member, Dr. Collins, and a white male faculty member, Dr. Camblin, both in Teacher Education, whose work revolved around diversity. I worked as a Graduate Teaching Associate for both of them and engaged in numerous conversations about the complex issue of "diversity." They provided validation for my interest and laid a path for my future development. I will always be grateful to Dr. Collins who prepared me for what it is like to be an African-American faculty member whose research interests are in the area of diversity. He encouraged me to move forward with this area of interest but also warned that many in the academy did not give legitimacy to this type of research. He encouraged me to place diversity as a foundation in a broader research agenda.

My work as a school psychologist in New York City public schools crystallized my commitment to working with culturally diverse populations. I asked myself, "What do I need to know and do to be an effective school psychologist with the children in this district who are black, Latino, and West Indian?" I used colleagues as "cultural mediators" before I knew that was what they were called. I read and went to workshops that dealt with diversity. But most importantly, I learned from the children and their families. New York was a training ground where I experienced diversity in all of its glorious colors. It was also where I personally witnessed the lack of commitment to bettering the lives of children by educational professionals, the grinding poverty that so devastatingly influenced almost every aspect of many children's lives, and families who struggled to give their children the social capital they needed to be successful in school. My graduate school studies and most importantly my experiences as a school psychologist in District 23, Brownsville, shaped who I was to become as a teacher, scholar, and psychologist and fueled my passion to make a difference.

Since coming to Ohio State University, I have been involved in a number of diversity initiatives. University-wide initiatives demonstrate the school's commitment to diversity. There are many small-scale initiatives that occur in the academy that are equally as important as the larger-scale programs. In this chapter, I will discuss three diversity related initiatives with which I have been personally involved. While they seem separate, in actuality they build on each other. These initiatives are a part of my commitment to make a difference by training future school psychologists and other education personnel to become cross-culturally competent in their work with culturally different children.

A Cultural Diversity Course in the Academy

I became an assistant professor at Ohio State University in the Fall of 1988. I was asked, as a part of my contract, to develop a multicultural education course. While I had no formal training in diversity, I did have my research, experience in New York City public schools, experience as chairwoman of the multicultural committee in the National Association of School Psychologists, and belief that education personnel need preparation for an increasingly diverse country. Using my own experience as a starting place, I developed a course that included elements I believed to be important in helping me become cross-culturally competent.

Cultural diversity course design. The goal of this course was to provide graduate students with an awareness and knowledge of cultural diversity and its impact in the United States. Cross-cultural competence involves the development of awareness, knowledge, and skill. Because this class was conceptualized as a service course that would not be discipline specific, skill was not a part of the agenda. It was a continually evolving course with changes made as a result of student input and feedback. It was not a teacher-directed, "textbook-based approach," which Grant and Sleeter (1985) defined as the most often used pedagogical approach. Instead, I viewed myself as more of a facilitator that helped empower students by engaging them in discussion and dialogue rather than engaging in the traditional teacher–student role that so often occurs in the college classroom (Freire, 1972). There were four factors in the course that I believe contributed to its success: (1) classroom climate, (2) course content, (3) meaningful assignments, and (4) readings and other media.

Classroom climate. The objective of the course was to focus on a broad and comprehensive view of multiculturalism, which would provide a context for students to expand their worldview and knowledge of cultural diversity. There was an attempt to establish a classroom context that invited all of the students to be equitably involved in all phases of the total learning process, whether it was through discussion or writings (Scott and Miranda, 1995). At the beginning of the course, ground rules were established for discussion. They included (1) sharing the air time, (2) maintaining confidentiality regarding personal statements and experiences shared, (3) speaking from one's own experience, and (4) encouraging participants to respect their classmates.

The goal was to develop a community of learners who respected what others said while recognizing that we all have some ethnocentric viewpoints and that one person's past reality does not necessarily define anyone else's. Students, even at the graduate level, come to the class with differing attitudes, ideas, and beliefs, based on their life experiences. For many students, engaging in discussion about issues of race and culture was not part of their cultural repertoire. Students often reported in their journal entries that they were afraid to speak up for fear they would be perceived as "racist."

The professor, as facilitator, became very important in setting the tone of the class. I provided information and facilitated discussions that encouraged students to think critically about what they read and heard. I challenged ideas but in a respectful way. Often, readings challenged previously held notions about cultural groups. Reading about and being presented with concepts of "white privilege," "racism," "oppression," to name a few can be overwhelming for students. As one student wrote in her journal, "I don't know how to deal with all the emotions these articles have stirred in me. I never realized my 'white advantage' until I read McIntosh's article *White Privilege and Male Privilege.*"

I attempted to convey my passion for the subject matter. My role was not to make white people feel bad (95% of my class consisted of white students) or for them to perceive themselves as racist. I mention this because, too often, white students expressed that they disliked diversity workshops or classes because they were made to feel guilty and were told they were racist. My goals were to have students keep an open mind throughout the course, make the class interesting, challenge their belief systems with not just one perspective but multiple perspectives, and engage them in self-reflection.

The format of the course was one of lecture/discussion. Discussion or dialogue was an integral part of the class, and over the years I have come to view this as one of the most critical components of cultural diversity training. Several years ago, I conducted a survey of past class participants. The discussion portion of the class was ranked as the number-one teaching strategy with lecture a close second. Participants have continually said they view this component of the class as one of the more powerful strategies in terms of its impact on their learning experience. As one white student stated, "I think the most valuable part of the course was the class discussions. The viewpoints and impressions expressed by the minority students served as a window into a world that I can never fully know because of the color of my skin." This is an opportunity for many students to engage, for the first time, in discussions around previously taboo subjects such as race. I have found, however, that the size of the class greatly influences the amount of participation. I experienced the most participation from classes that have fewer than 20 students. When class size is between 25 and 40, only one-fourth of the class participates on a regular basis. In sessions this large, students routinely write in their journals that they feel uncomfortable speaking during class. Thus, the journal assignment becomes important; I will discuss the journal in detail later.

Course content. The focus was on developing a multicultural awareness, self-awareness, and building a strong knowledge base about the identified cultural/racial groups, concepts associated with cultural diversity, as well as issues centered around oppression (e.g. class, race, etc.). Arguably, one of the most difficult areas to explore was centered around issues of power that have the effect of marginalizing the structures and experiences of specific racial groups. It is the exploration of these complex issues that often forces students to unlearn negative attitudes as they relate to issues of diversity and develop a more positive outlook and ultimately to look at the world differently. It can be difficult because students often struggle with information that challenges their belief system.

The beliefs and experiences of different cultural populations in our society were constantly explored. There was an attempt not only to explore the axiology of different cultural groups but their ethos and epistemology. The social and historical forces that have impacted these cultures were also discussed at length. In my opinion, it is important for participants to understand the influence society has had on many special populations in American society. Because there is a limited amount of time, particularly in a quarter system (10 weeks), only five ethnic minority groups are examined. These are African Americans, Asians, Native Americans, Latinos, and Appalachian populations. In addition, socioeconomic class, gender, and gay/lesbian/bisexual, and transgender issues were examined.

Assignments. A strong emphasis was placed on the personal growth of students and on students' ability to examine themselves critically.

This involved self-exploration which "challenged them to look inside themselves for the answers" (Moore, 1999, p. 174). In other words, the class was a personal journey or growth experience. Assignments were, therefore, designed to help students develop a better understanding of who they were, how they perceived people who were different from them, how issues centered on oppression impacted their everyday lives, and how their beliefs and values influenced how they viewed people who were culturally different.

Students wrote five reflection journal entries throughout the ten-week quarter. The journal reflections allowed many of the students to share their viewpoints, disagreement with readings, fears, and confusion in a safe format. What they felt they couldn't say or ask in class, they were able to express in their journals. A cultural heritage paper was one assignment that encouraged the students' self-exploration. White students often told me that this was one of the most difficult assignments as they felt they did not have a culture. An example of this was a comment in a journal entry: "When I saw that I had to write a cultural heritage paper that was at least five pages long, I didn't know how I was going to find that much to say. It was hard for me to see myself as others see me." This paper helped students to think broadly about culture and to investigate how it shaped their socialization in general and with minority and majority peoples in particular. Other assignments included a cultural immersion experience and interviews with two people culturally different from themselves.

Readings and videotapes. A variety of reading material was chosen to expand students' state of consciousness. Such readings focused on different cultural populations including their histories, cultures, interactions with other groups and current issues as well as issues of racism, sexism, prejudice, oppression, cultural pluralism, and culturally diverse groups and the educational system. In the past three years, I have included readings by whites that discuss their own journeys toward recognizing their privilege and working toward the goal of becoming cross culturally competent. These have been particularly helpful to the white students who often have an overwhelming feeling of guilt. These readings allow them to see that their feelings are quite typical and provide them with a model for the evolvement of white racial identity.

Videotapes have also been particularly valuable to the course. One that has had a significant impact is *The Color of Fear.* This is a very powerful video that addresses difficult issues of racism, prejudice, and oppression. Because my students are overwhelmingly white, this video allows students to hear about these issues from a diverse group of men. Other videos used were *Ethnic Notions, Tale of O, A Class Divided, True Colors,* and *In the Image of the White Man.*

Diversity as a Requirement. After fourteen years, this course has evolved as I have evolved in integrating my teaching and research. At the preservice level of training, there continues to be the long-debated question of whether diversity should be a single course or infused throughout the curriculum. I have actually advocated that both should occur. The single course provides for the development of an awareness: "Awareness is viewed as a critical component of multicultural development" (Miranda and Andrews, 1994, p. 528). I believe the course is important in establishing a foundation for the development of a multicultural framework. Whether the emphasis is on a single course, infusion, or both, the area of cultural diversity as a curriculum component is less than aggressively pursued and implemented in the academy.

It is interesting to note that while I was asked to develop and teach a multicultural course, students in the school psychology program were not required to take it. It was presented as an option to fulfill the multicultural requirement. At the time, another course was used to meet two requirements of which multicultural was one, despite the fact that the course did not focus on diversity. It was a disturbing first lesson about how critical it is to establish policies, programs, and practices that create models of progress in multiculturalism. During my fourth year as a faculty member, it was decided that my diversity course would be a requirement, in large part because we were critically cited by our learned society for not fulfilling the diversity requirement. Unfortunately, many programs in school psychology have been slow to add this type of course as a requirement. Only through the efforts of our learned society has this requirement been taken seriously and presented in the form of National Association of School Psychology standards.

Having the course as a requirement in our program was a step forward. As I evaluated the content of our core courses and examined the major issues effecting educational systems, I was more convinced than ever that as administrators of academic programs and academicians, we have a commitment to prepare our students to be prepared for the twenty-first century.

Professional associations such as The National Council for the Accreditation of Teacher Education (NCATE) and the American Association of Colleges for Teacher Education (AACTE) were among the first to include a multicultural requirement in their standards. As a result, this requirement gave impetus to the single course addition in many programs. During this time, I began to ask myself the following question: "How do we know that our multicultural training is effective or makes a difference?" Unfortunately, I also began to realize that it is not easily discernible. I knew I had made a difference when former students returned to tell me that the course made a difference; the studentsx would provide me with a scenario of how they approached situations. They often spoke of how it opened their eyes and made them think differently about multicultural issues. But I also realized for many students that after completion of the class, they weren't quite sure how to take this "new" knowledge and apply it to their professional lives, such as being school psychologists.

I have learned that most students come to the course with little, if any, experience in the area of diversity. As a result, they tend to personalize the information first. By that I mean, they engage in self-exploration and spend time adjusting their previous attitudes about their perceptions of diversity. Figuring out how to apply the knowledge professionally takes time.

At one time, I thought just getting a diversity course into the curriculum was enough. However, I later realized that simply adding a diversity course and/or infusing supplementary material dealing with diversity into other courses was not enough. There was a need to be deeper and broader.

The Training Grant

Writing and obtaining a Personnel Preparation Training Grant from the Office of Special Education Programs at the federal level allowed me to have a forum in which I implemented the ideals I so strongly believed. The focus of the grant was on developing specialized skills in the areas of assessment, consultation, and intervention with early childhood populations for school psychologists (Miranda and Andrews, 1994). The grant had a strong emphasis on training students to work with culturally diverse children. Thus, a major component of the training grant was identifying those areas that would help students understand the culture of many of the children with whom they would be working (Miranda and Andrews, 1994).

This grant provided me with the opportunity to put into place what I envisioned as ideal for diversity training. I had determined that it was not enough to have academic learning in the area of cultural diversity; there also needed to be an experiential component. Thus, our major site for training was a large Head Start agency. Out of this grant developed the University-Head Start partnership. After the four-year grant ended, we continued the partnership in which school psychology students work as mental health consultants in the Head Start agency.

The field-based training was considered an extremely important piece of the grant and a significant move in expanding what it meant to have training in the area of diversity. Issues of cultural diversity were integrated throughout the training experience. Instead of highlighting and singling out an issue as "multicultural," diversity became a natural part of the varied components of the training grant (Miranda and Andrews, 1994).

What was most encouraging was that students appreciated and valued the training they received with the diversity emphasis. Many of them expressed commitments to working in culturally diverse environments after graduation and actually found jobs in such settings. For example, one student worked as a mental health consultant for two years, had practicum experiences in an urban school district but did her internship in a suburban, upper-middle-income district. When it was time to look for a job, she made the decision to work in a diverse district because, as she says, "her internship left her unfulfilled." I felt I was making a difference. What more could I ask for?

Transforming a Program

Based on my experience of training school psychologists for a diverse world, interviewing people who had transformed school psychology programs, and reviewing the literature on diversity, I came to believe that there were a number of elements that had to be in place to assure that a program would be culturally relevant, promote cultural competence, and have a sociopolitical consciousness. While I was able to realize some of this through my diversity course, training grant, and subsequently through the University-Head Start partnership, I believed it would be more powerful to have a commitment to training students in diversity at a program level.

The school psychology program is housed in Ohio State's College of Education. Much of my early collaboration was with teachers and teacher educators. There were many wonderful people who equally shared my passion about the importance of training educators for increasingly diverse student populations. Fortunately for me, there was ongoing dialogue about issues of diversity in the college during the 1990s. So while the school psychology program did not have an emphasis on diversity, there was support and belief from other colleagues that my journey was purposeful and had meaning.

I had begun to develop a vision for training. It started with the multicultural class and continued with the training grant. I strongly believed that there was a need and that if the program was created, students would attend. My beliefs were reinforced every time a student personally sought me out to thank me for the training I provided in diversity. However, I became concerned from an ethical point of view that we were training future school psychologists who were not prepared for what awaited them. Research consistently demonstrated that school psychologists lacked training in working with diverse populations, yet this population of children was increasing significantly.

While I was committed to these ideals, it was apparent that I was the only one in my program area. In the field of school psychology, there were discussions about diversity but not at the level I believed the discussions should be. In a review of the diversity literature published in school psychology journals during the 1990s, it was found that there was very little research in this area (Miranda and Gutter, 2002). The lack of a diversity presence could be seen at our national conference, which often had no major workshops devoted to the issue. In fact, during a discussion with a colleague at another university who also writes about multicultural school psychology, we determined that we could identify only ten people in our field who published in this area, and of those only five were minorities. As in the field of education, people of color were underrepresented in school psychology. My goal became the transformation of the school psychology program.

In the past five years, several factors allowed my vision to come to fruition. First, the new president of the university in 1996, Dr. "Brit" Kirwan, saw diversity as one of his top priorities. This provided a forum for further discussions of diversity in the university community. As a result, one of the initiatives was a mandate that each college submit a diversity plan. Second, the university initiated a plan to connect with Ohio's public schools. This initiative was called the P-12 Project. Its mission was to help improve Ohio's schools, particularly in districts that serve children and youths from lower socio-economic families. During the 1990s, the College of Education began to focus more on urban education by connecting with the Columbus City Schools. The P-12 project was one way that the college aligned itself with the urban public schools. Third, at the administrative level, from the dean to the director, there was encouragement to focus on urban education at a program level as it supported the mission of the college and aligned with the university's priorities. This type of support provided the encouragement to go forth with such an agenda. And finally, all senior faculty in the program who helped develop it had either left the university or retired. This was significant in that issues of diversity were not a priority on their agendas. These system-level events made it possible to restructure a program and allow it to have an urban specialty focus which encompasses diversity issues.

Ladson-Billings (2000) suggested that programs that choose to have a multicultural focus should not only have a broad and comprehensive view of diversity but should provide experiences where students could recognize and appreciate various forms of diversity in their environments. Cultural diversity must be viewed as both a comprehensive educational reform and basic education for all students (Banks, 2001). It is a process that moves both educators and students from being monocultural to being multicultural; the process must focus on the building of a multicultural knowledge base that promotes understanding, appreciation, and affirmation of other cultural groups.

To successfully train students to be cross-culturally competent in their practice requires that issues of diversity be pervasively present throughout the program. For this to occur, it was believed that the following areas needed to explicitly incorporate diversity: mission statement, curriculum, field-based experiences, and research.

Mission Statement. In restructuring the school psychology program, a new mission statement was developed that had as a cornerstone an urban specialty focus. At the same time, we were in the midst of a faculty search, and this mission became important because having experience and/or commitment working with culturally diverse and/or urban populations was a desired characteristic for the candidate. Over the years, I have learned that programs that seek to focus on diversity MUST have a critical mass of faculty that are passionate and committed to the ideals. Stating explicitly in our mission statement that we will address diversity and urban issues was the first and foremost demonstration that we were committed to these ideals.

Redesigning the curriculum. The restructuring of the program gave us the freedom to essentially start over. All courses were evaluated and significant changes were made to the content which reflected the mission statement and program philosophy. This provided the opportunity to infuse issues of diversity throughout the core courses. As a faculty, we engaged in discussions regarding important issues or concepts. It should be noted that faculty may be engaged at different commitment levels regarding diversity. For example, it is necessary for all faculty to have a shared mission, but I do not believe all faculty need to have these issues as part of their scholarship. However, at least a majority of the faculty need to have issues of diversity as a part of their knowledge base in order for them to infuse it throughout their courses.

Field-based experiences. This was viewed as essential to the program. To prepare students to work with diverse children it was believed that they needed to have urban-based experiences. Thus, the year-long practicum in the students' second year occurred totally in Columbus City Schools. It should be noted that students had the opportunity to do field-based work in suburban and rural school districts as well. A mandatory experience in an urban setting was another indication of the commitment.

Research. Several faculty are conducting research in diversity and urban issues. While this is not viewed as necessary for the program to be successful, it is one significant way that the program can gain a national presence while simultaneously adding much needed scholarly work in the area of diversity. We have also encouraged students to conduct research for theses and/or dissertations with diverse populations or in an urban setting. To facilitate this, we have developed an urban research team that involves both faculty and students. The research team allows the students to develop research skills in a developmental fashion and models a collaborative process in the design and implementation of research. Students have the opportunity to assist with projects in which faculty are engaged that are related to diversity and urban issues. Becoming involved in diversity and urban research allows the student to learn about diversity and urban issues in a more in depth fashion. It assists in establishing a knowledge base that translates into practice and clearly helps students have a broader understanding of these issues across the board.

Final Thoughts

What are the indications of success? The program is only in its second year of restructuring, yet changes have occurred. While we always had a strong applicant pool, our applications increased 25 percent the first year of the restructuring. Of the students we admitted, 30 percent were students of color. This number equals the total number of students of color we admitted to the program during the past thirteen years I've been at Ohio State! In addition, 75 percent of those admitted to the program applied because of the urban specialty focus. Of even greater significance is the social justice consciousness that is being fostered in the current students. The students early on see their work in urban environments as more meaningful and more openly express a desire to work in these areas. They also have a deeper and more comprehensive understanding of the complex issues involved in working in diverse and urban environments and with culturally different people. These ideas are demonstrated through reflection papers, conversations, and feedback from practicum supervisors.

I know my journey has not ended. My commitment to personally making a difference still drives me. I have learned that I, as an individual, can make a difference. I was able to create experiences for students in the area of diversity that transformed their practices. There are many individuals in the academy doing great things at an individual level that often go unrecognized. I do what I do because it is the right thing. For those wishing to implement their own projects, I provide the following strategies or suggestions:

1. Have passion for what you do. There are times you will be going it alone and obstacles will be placed in your path. It is at these times that you need to persevere.

2. Find a support group, even if it is in a different discipline. A group helps validate your work and keeps you committed.

3. Strike while the iron is hot. Because issues of diversity were on the radar screen, it was easier for me to implement my initiatives. For example, at the time I wrote my grant, there were initiatives related to diversity in the Call for Proposals. If you included these issues, you received extra points in your overall total.

4. Demonstrate your commitment to diversity by acknowledging it in your program philosophy. For those disciplines that work directly with people (e.g., teaching, counseling, psychology), it is important to include experiences with diverse populations. It is also much easier to make change if you have a critical mass of faculty who are committed to those issues.

As I was completing this chapter, I received an e-mail from one of my doctoral candidates who had recently taken a job in Maryland as a school psychologist. Reading it again gave me resolve that my work has purpose and meaning. I end this chapter with her refreshing and rewarding comments:

> I wanted to let you know that an issue of culture came up in one of my initial cases at the middle school. The school is primarily white and a black student—who enrolled late last year due to placement with a new foster family—got referred for an initial MFE (*multifac- tored evaluation*) at the end of last year for "learning and behavior problems." Upon evaluation, no cognitive or academic achievement issues were apparent whatsoever—but behavioral issues were/are a major concern. So, I raised the issue of culture in the MFE meeting and it was pretty well received. The assistant principal took me aside afterwards and told me that she was relieved that someone wasn't afraid to use the word "culture" when talking about students. She also e-mailed my supervisor. I am so thankful for our training—in

both your MC (*multicultural*) class and in your practicum—when considering issues of culture. I remember well the scenarios you had us go through in practicum class—where we read students' profiles and hypothesized reasons for their struggles. I just wanted to thank you for that foundation.

References

Banks, J. (2001). "Multicultural education: Characteristics and goals." J. Banks and C. A. McGee Banks, eds., *Multicultural Education: Issues and Perspectives,* pp. 3–30. New York: John Wiley & Sons.

Freire, P. 1972. *Pedagogy of the oppressed.* New York: Herder and Herder.

Grant, C. A. and C. E. Sleeter 1985. "The literature on multicultural education: Review and analysis." *Educational Review,* 37(2), 97–118.

Hodgkinson, H. L. 1985. *All one system: Demographics of education—kindergarten through graduate school.* Washington, D.C.: Institute for Educational Leadership.

Ladson-Billings, G. 2001. *Crossing over to Canaan: The journey of new teachers in diverse classrooms.* New York: John Wiley & Sons.

Miranda, A. H., and P. Gutter. 2002. "Diversity and equity research in school psychology: 1990–1999." *Psychology in the Schools,* 39(5).

Miranda, A. H., and T. J. Andrews. 1994. "Preservice preparation of school psychologists for providing related services in early childhood intervention: A university–preschool partnership." *Topics in Early Childhood Special Education,* 14(4).

Moore, E. 1999. "The challenges of difference and diversity: preparing Iowa for black, brown, and international." L. Jones, ed., *Brothers of the Academy,* pp. 169–78. Sterling, Va.: Stylus Publishing, LLC.

Scott, J., and A. H. Miranda. "Designing a multicultural class: Promoting cultural awareness, curriculum/instructional change, and social action." *Multicultural Education* (Winter 1995).

M. Rick Turner, Ph.D.

M. Rick Turner has served as Dean of the University of Virginia's Office of African-American Affairs since August 1988. Since his arrival, the university has boosted its African-American graduation rate to 87 percent, among the highest of any other public institution in the nation. Prior to coming to UVA, Dr. Turner served in various student affairs positions of leadership at institutions across the nation, including the University of Connecticut, University of California-Irvine, and Stanford University.

In addition to his role as Dean, Dr. Turner also serves as adjunct faculty of the University of Virginia's Department of Sociology, teaching courses on "Sociology of the African-American Community" as well as multicultural education. He has served as a consultant and speaker for numerous education foundations, higher education institutions, public and private schools, community organizations, and municipal and federal agencies. He has also spoken and written extensively about African-American academic achievement; affirmative action; and the recruitment, retention, admission, and graduation of African-American students, other students of color, and student athletes. Dr. Turner is the founder of the Saturday Academy, an educational enrichment program for families. He is active in community affairs, working closely with parents and children.

For his work, Dr. Turner has received numerous awards, including the Crispus Attucks Award for Higher Education Leadership, the Ron Brown Award for successfully educating African-American youth and other students of color, the Parents Advisory Association Warrior Award for his student advocacy, NAACP Award for his commitment to the needs of the community, and Outstanding Black Faculty/Staff Award for his devotion to his students. During the spring 2001 convocation exercises, Dean Turner was awarded the prestigious Algernon Sydney Sullivan Award, given in recognition of excellence of character and service to humanity.

Dr. Turner's inspirational life was featured in the fall 1999 issue of *Albemarle*. More recently, *Black Issues of Higher Education* spotlighted Dr. Turner and his family in "Family Matters," documenting their success in extending "traditions of athletic and scholarly excellence." He is presently writing a book, *A Ball and a Book: Raising African-American Student Athletes*.

8

THE OFFICE OF AFRICAN-AMERICAN AFFAIRS:

A CELEBRATION OF SUCCESS

During the past decade, few issues have aroused more debate than that of racial diversity in higher education. Contrary to popular belief, diversity on college campuses did not magically emerge in the 1960s. Rather, it had its beginnings in the nineteenth century. The issue was no less volatile in American life then than it is today (Rudenstine, 2000).

In 1976, the University of Virginia created an Office of African-American Affairs (OAAA) and gave it a specific mission of assisting the university in providing a welcoming and nurturing environment for black students. Because of the times, it was not an easy task to fulfill, nor was it expected to be. It was a journey of advocacy, in the sense of supporting the presence of African-American students at an institution their ancestors helped build but could not attend. My predecessors, previous OAAA deans, set the tone and laid the foundation in developing goals and objectives that continue to guide and to inspire us for over a quarter of a century.

One of the primary reasons for the success of racial diversity at the University of Virginia is the Office of African-American Affairs. A recent article in the *UVa Alumni News* states:

> The University of Virginia is one of the nation's premier schools in retaining black students. For the class that entered in 1996, the most recent year that statistics are available, the university graduated 87.2 percent of its black students, good enough to place it in the top 15 nationally, behind most of the Ivies and Stanford and Georgetown. But a closer look at the numbers reveals how exceptional the university truly is. Among schools with black graduation rates over 70 percent,

the university graduated the most black students—256—which shows
[that no university] is better at the dual task of recruiting large classes
of black students and retaining them. (Le, 2002)

Since 1988, when I arrived to assume the dean's position, the
office's programs have changed to reflect both old and new challenges of the 20th and 21st centuries. Some challenges are ongoing;
others are deceptively new and hiding under the guise of words like
"multiculturalism." My first objective was to look at collaborations;
it became important to look more comprehensively at what the university does and the kind of environment it creates. I began to cultivate relationships within the university community, building partnerships with a wide range of faculty and administrators in academic
and non-academic departments. I especially sought out those who
seemingly had a strong appreciation for an understanding of the
OAAA mission.

The second clear objective was to work with our first-year students,
starting early to introduce them to OAAA programs and services.
Having the opportunity to hire new staff members who could develop
and create new programs along with building upon existing ones was
a bonus I valued. Together we developed and worked toward making
our goals realities.

Specifically, the Office of African-American Affairs' goals are:

- To provide a supportive environment through direct contact with
  African-American students

- To enhance the sensitivity of the larger community by ensuring
  that academic components and social programs are reflective of
  African-American culture

- To provide information and support to the parents and guardians
  of African-American students by strengthening the Parents
  Advisory Association

- To monitor and assess the university's climate and ensure full
  participation of African-American students in the life of the
  university

- To enhance relationships in the Charlottesville/Albemarle
  communities through civic involvement and activities

In the pages that follow, I will discuss the role the Office of African-American Affairs has had in making diversity work at the University of Virginia, especially as it relates to the retention and graduation of black students.

Introduction

The University has integrated key components of a successful retention model: a Peer Advisor Program, a Faculty–Student Mentoring Program, and a Parent Advisory Program. In addition, students have the Luther Porter Jackson House as their home away from home. Here at our institution, students learn immediately the reason the university has one of the best reputations nationwide for graduating African-American students (*Journal of Blacks in Higher Education,* 1994).

The Peer Advisor Program

Knowing the importance of the freshman year on the college experience and its impact upon retention and graduation, the OAAA created the Peer Advisor Program in 1984. It works with entering students (first-year and transfer) to ease their college transitions. To show how the office helps implement the program, Associate Dean Sylvia V. Terry gives the following example of her role in the Peer Advisor Program:

> Earlier this week in making Peer Advisor Program telephone spot checks, I talked with a student who was abrupt and seemed out of sorts. Thus, I pressed her to find out if this was something related to the Peer Advisor Program or something else that was going on with her. As it turned out, she was feeling overwhelmed. She is an athlete in a pre-med track taking courses in chemistry, calculus, composition, African-American studies and psychology—heavy-duty classes. She had shut herself off from her Peer Advisor and had only talked with her faculty advisor once. Sadly, in this case, he had encouraged her to take this load without possibly considering the demands of track and overall first-year adjustment issues for a first-year student. I talked to her about her courses, including the "withdrawal" option, to ease the burden. I referred her to the Athletic Advising Office (since she had not used the office as a resource) and set up a follow-up appointment with her in my office. Even though our conversation on the telephone

was extensive, I wanted her to come to the Office of African-American Affairs (OAAA), to see me, and the other OAAA deans. I might add here that this instance is not unusual. When I make telephone spot checks, it is as much about getting feedback about my Peer Advisors as it is about checking on each advisee's welfare as well. Thus, I frequently end up doing telephone counseling or simply celebrating students' excitement about college life.

Dean Terry's story provides an excellent example of the implementation of the Peer Advisor Program goals, which are:

- To provide sensitive, personalized support to African-American first-year and entering transfer students. "Retention studies reveal that students of color who have at least one strong person in place are more likely "to get through" the sometimes difficult adjustments that they face at predominately white institutions."

- To promote academic excellence

- To inform students about the services and resources available at the University of Virginia

- To encourage involvement in university organizations and extracurricular activities

- To foster ownership of and pride in the university

- To increase retention

The program provides immediate support that begins soon after students have accepted their offers of admission. Peer Advisors communicate with their advisees during the summer. Throughout this time, they respond to wide-ranging academic and non-academic issues. In addition, throughout the year Peer Advisors provide individual support, group activities, and program-wide events (ranging from orientation to academic recognition). What our entering students find in a Peer Advisor is a knowledgeable resource, an encourager, a friend and role model. Consequently, the advisees become more quickly adjusted to college life and are able to find support and guidance as they adapt to University of Virginia's challenges. The program's motto, "Lending a Helping Hand: Academically, Psychologically and Socially," sums up the broad scope of what UVa Peer Advisors do.

Faculty–Student Mentoring Program

Building upon the successes of the Peer Advisor Program in supporting first-year students, the OAAA launched a Faculty–Student Mentoring Program to provide upper-class students with expanded support for intellectual and personal success. It is designed to promote and facilitate interactions between faculty and upper-class students of color. During the 2001–02 academic year, the program received thirty-five new faculty applications and more than 100 new student applications. Seventy-eight pairs were matched. In addition, thirty-four pairs that were matched in the previous years are still functioning this year.

Program goals include:

- To provide students of color a structured approach in developing a meaningful relationship with university faculty, administrators, or graduate students

- To help students of color to continue to form a more positive identification with the university community

- To motivate and to inspire students of color through moral, intellectual, academic and social support that will contribute to their success through graduation and career development

- To promote cross-cultural understanding in the university community

Program evaluations demonstrated that both faculty and students felt satisfied with their involvement in the program. A majority of the participants (90%) would like to continue being part of the program, and most participants (91%) would recommend the program to others. Participants have made such comments as, "I applaud the program and the OAAA. All academic administrators should find this kind of experience or others to keep in touch regularly with undergrads"; "I felt that the program was extremely worthwhile. I met my mentee normally once a week where we discussed all aspects—school, career, activities and personal life. For me, my job as mentor was easy since my mentee was so great. I was able to help by encouraging her and setting up opportunities for her to meet with people in the area she wants to pursue as a postgraduate"; and "My mentor is very helpful in many ways:

personal issues as well as academic aspects. Any time I have a problem or anything, I never hesitate to come to talk to or e-mail him. I think he's the nicest professor I've ever met. One more thing I'd like to mention is why I appreciate his help so much. I'm a transfer student, so things are not as easy for me as for many students who start here as freshmen. He is very busy but he doesn't mind spending time to give me some ideas on my senior thesis. Sometimes he also sends me an e-mail to ask how I am and how my classes are. That touched my heart very much."

Parents Advisory Association

Another important component of the Office of African-American Affairs and its work in issues of diversity is its Parents Advisory Association (PAA). More than fifteen years ago, the Office of African-American Affairs formed a relationship with black parents by creating the PAA. Its mission is to work with the staff of the OAAA to improve the academic, cultural, and social life of African-American students. We want parents to be strong advocates for both students and faculty while voicing their concerns, wishes, goals, and interests. The PAA model was born out of a need to assist the OAAA in maintaining its autonomy in the delivery of academic support services to African-American students. The program is based on the premise that parents and family are the most powerful of all human attachments.

The goals of the Parents Advisory Association are as follows:

- To provide creative opportunities to share our cultural heritage with students
- To establish strategies for fund-raising to support scholarships, emergency loans, and special services provided by the OAAA
- To work with the staff of the OAAA and the University of Virginia on the effectiveness of its programs and services to African-American students
- To establish working relationships with the University of Virginia student organizations and black alumni
- To provide outlets for parents to exchange information and ideas

As one former president of the PAA noted:

Many people, including parents, believe that direct parental involvement in a college-bound child's education should cease once she has been dropped at the gates of some institution. I differ in this belief and have been fortunate to have found comrades who not only share, but practice the philosophy of continued parental involvement for college-age students. We must affirm and support our college-age children and the staff of the Office of African-American Affairs, who are our children's advocates.

The Parents Advisory Association chapters meet quarterly throughout the year to organize various activities both in their home areas and at the university. For example, the PAA organizes a picnic each year for new students and parents in their respective areas. This event gives incoming parents and students an opportunity to meet and get acquainted with each other and with the OAAA staff before classes start. Meeting parents at this early date gives us an opportunity to provide a mini-orientation and to address their questions. Parents and students also meet current black students and alumni at these picnics. Many of the students who attend the picnics are Peer Advisors who work in the OAAA. So even before they arrive on campus to start classes, many new students have the opportunity to familiarize themselves with other university students, faculty and staff. This activity sponsored by the PAA also gives the association an opportunity to recruit new members.

The Luther Porter Jackson Black Cultural Center (LPJCC)

The LPJCC embraces our students' cultural sensitivities, awareness, and knowledge. Among other things, it preserves and disseminates information and ideas about the rich cultural heritage of African Americans and African people all over the world. The center has at its heart the belief that culture is a catalyst for excellence and for human understanding. It provides this through activities designed to enhance the cultural life of students at the university.

The Cultural Center's goals are:

- To offer forums, lectures, performances, celebrations and recognitions which provide students with cultural exposure and education, as well as an outlet for African-American cultural expression. These annual programs include a Kwanzaa Fest, Dr. Martin Luther King, Jr., Commemoration and Black History Month events.

- To organize programs and events throughout the year that create meaningful opportunities for cross-cultural interaction and understanding that attack racial intolerance at its core

- To provides students with a comprehensive understanding of the history, struggles and diversity of the African-American community

- To encourages students to become actively involved in educational and cultural activities within and outside the community

- To maintain a library collection of books, periodicals and videos focused on African-American history, culture and literature

- To maintain the Harris-Bland Computer Lab to provide the university community with software programs and Internet access that will provide information about the African and African-American historical and cultural experiences

The center helps establish a strong sense of community. African-American students need to have that sense of community to truly excel. Diversity contributes to the psychological comfort of black students, especially if diversity is welcomed and accepted in the community. It is also important to have a critical mass of black students so that they do not feel alienated, have self-doubt, or feel an overwhelming pressure to represent "the race." While having a strong community of black students may be seen as self-segregation to some, it actually strengthens black students and gives them the confidence and desire to share themselves with the larger community. Black organizations such as Black Voices, Brothers United Celebrating Knowledge and Success, and even the Black Student Alliance all sponsor programming that educates the larger community about black culture, issues of race, etc. Their organizations are not exclusive to blacks and they are very open and welcome the participation of non-black students. Therefore, having a strong black community at a predominately white campus provides a great opportunity for non-black students to learn and grow if they choose to do so. The programming that we offer often serves as a way to create this sense of community, unify black students, and reaffirm them culturally. Our annual programs, Kwanzaa, MLK Celebration and Black History Celebration, all foster community and celebrate culture. Our new initiative, the Black Leadership Institute, convenes black student leaders to work together to strengthen community and cooperation.

Our programming is open to all students. Our aim is to educate the university community about the culture and experience of African Americans. A forum on affirmative action, racial profiling, a Kwanzaa celebration, and lecture on the life of Malcolm X are important for all students, not just black students. It is even more important for non-blacks to participate in these kinds of events so that dialogue can begin on race relations and how we perceive and relate to each other. Integration is a two-way street. Non-black students have a great opportunity to learn and share their perspectives, thus improving relations between black and non-black students. (Levy, 2002)

Conclusion

The Office of African-American Affairs' service to the University of Virginia's black students is all about caring. This caring and the relationships that we establish with students, and the relationships that they establish with each other cannot be legislated. It is precisely because of such relationships that programs to support and assist black students on predominately white campuses must continue (Haniff, 1991).

At the OAAA's recent twenty-fifth anniversary celebration, an African-American student stated:

> The presence of the OAAA and its advocacy for the African-American population at UVa is an attempt to make students feel at home at an institution that has historically been someone else's house. Programs such as the Peer Advisor Program, the Faculty–Student Mentoring Program, and the Luther Porter Jackson Cultural Center (just to name a few) create a support group for black students and is a refuge for what can sometimes be an overwhelming experience in a predominately white setting. Being a black person in a predominately white environment can be psychologically taxing and draining at times. It's important that we have people with whom we can identify and share ideas and concerns. The OAAA is a place where we can go to regroup, reconnect, and (most importantly) be reassured. This is why the Office of African-American Affairs exists at the University of Virginia. (Visions, 2002)

The progress the university has made in the recruitment, enrollment, and graduation rates of African-American students during these past 25 years is notable. However, recent attacks on affirmative action have resulted in a decline of African-American students offered admission during the past three years. Nevertheless, we will continue to offer the highest quality services to our students—that will not decline. We are encouraged by the university's proactive stances on its commitment to ensuring that the university environment will continue to be welcoming and supportive for African-American students and other students of color. It is a foregone conclusion that in the future the university will continue to face pressure to change the affirmative action programs it has implemented. I am reminded of a recent statement that Neil Rudenstine, the former president of Harvard University, made: "Twenty-five years of improved access to higher education is a very brief time span. It is scarcely one generation—barely long enough for gradu-ates of the late 1960s to raise children who are now reaching college age." The OAAA must remain steadfast in the light of the changing social, political, economic and educational landscape. We must continue as a vibrant and viable organization if African-American students are to succeed at the university and in their lives after the university.

Bibliography

Hariff, N., ed. 1991. *College in Black and White: African-American Students in Predominately White and Historically Black Public Universities.* Albany: State University of New York.

Le, S. 2002. *A Home Away From Home. Alumni News Magazine*–U.Va. Alumni Association.

Levy, L. 2002. *The Luther Porter Jackson Black Cultural Center.* Charlottesville: Office of African-American Affairs.

Orfield, G. and M. Kirdaender. (2001). *Diversity Challenged: Evidences on the Impact of Affirmative Action.* Cambridge: Harvard Education Publishing Group.

Rudenstine, N. 2001. *Student Diversity and Higher Learning.* Cambridge: Harvard Publishing Group.

Terry, S. 2002. *Peer Advisor Program.* Charlottesville: Office of African-American Affairs.

Turner, M. R. 2002. *The State of African-American Affairs.* Charlottesville: Office of African-American Affairs.

Yu, P. 2002. *Faculty-Student Mentoring Program.* Charlottesville: Office of African-American Affairs.

Lee Jones

Lee Jones is the Associate Dean for Academic Affairs and Instruction in the College of Education and Associate Professor of Educational Leadership and Policy Studies at Florida State University. He is a member of the Dean's Administrative Team. Dr. Jones is responsible for coordinating many functions within the College of Education, including the Offices of Clinical Partnerships, Academic Services, Learning Resource Center, Curriculum Resource Center, Living Learning Center, and Student Access, Recruitment, and Retention. In addition to his academic and administrative responsibilities, Dr. Jones finds the time to produce and host a TV talk show that reaches more than one million viewers throughout the state of Florida and parts of southern Alabama and Georgia.

Dr. Jones has received more than 175 awards and citations including the Alumnus of the Year award from Delaware State University and the Graduate School Leadership award from Ohio State University. He has M.A.s in higher education administration and in business and administration, and a Ph.D. in organizational development from Ohio State University.

Dr. Jones is in great demand as a speaker throughout the country and abroad. He is a member of Kappa Alpha Psi Fraternity, Inc., National Association for Equal Opportunity, Association for the Study of Higher Education, American Association for Higher Education, Academy of Human Resource Development, and a host of other civic and professional organizations.

He is the editor of three books, *Brothers of the Academy: Up and Coming Black Scholars Earning Our Way in Higher Education* (2000), *Retaining African Americans in Higher Education: Challenging Paradigms for Retaining Students, Faculty and Administrators* (2001), and *Making It on Broken Promises: Leading Black Male Scholars Confront the Culture of Higher Education* (2002); and co-editor of *The Majority in the Minority: Expanding the Representation of Latina/o Faculty, Administrators and Students in Higher Education* (2003).

9

THE DEVELOPMENT
OF A MULTICULTURAL
STUDENT SERVICES
OFFICE AND RETENTION
STRATEGY FOR
MINORITY STUDENTS:

STILL MILES TO GO!

As we have witnessed in previous chapters there are a plethora of models and success stories throughout this important and timely book. I am personally and professionally very excited to have been invited to submit a chapter alongside the wonderful work of scholars who have been in the trenches for a long time. The focus of this essay is to highlight the development of a Multicultural Office on the campus of Washington State University. The essay aims to provide a historical overview of the history of the Office of Multicultural Student Services, review the development of a structure that aimed to addressing the specific needs of each underrepresented group (African American, "Hispanic," Native American, and Asian Pacific American), and discuss a series of examples highlighting what led to the development of the Office of Multicultural Student Services. I begin this chapter by operationally defining terms that take on different meanings for readers and by offering a review of the literature relative to retention issues for minority students in higher education.

An unavoidable dilemma when dealing with multicultural issues is that of the terminology used to conceptualize them. It is evident that there is no consensus in the use of terms, particularly in the area of "labels for specific groups." In the development of a university's retention strategy, as is the case throughout the literature, there is bound to be some inconsistencies in the way some people use terminology. To assist the readers, selected words have been defined for the purpose of this chapter. Other definitions are also included in an attempt to make the reader aware of the diversity that exists within specific racial/ethnic groups. Common questions that exemplify the complexity of these situations include inquiries such as who are multicultural students, students of color, minority students? Who are Asian-Pacific Americans, Native Americans, African Americans, Chicano/Latino, Hispanic, and Mexican Americans? The development of the definitions was perhaps the most difficult part of planning a campus-wide retention strategy (Figure 1).

Researchers suggest that successful minority programs or retention programs are vehicles for bonding (Noel and others, 1985). Institutions can play a part in providing individuals with the social and intellectual communities of the university that will allow them to become congruent and integrated. Successful institutions are, according to Tinto (1987), like healthy communities and families, collectivities whose

---

Terms defined for the purpose of this document:

- **Culture:** The ideations, symbols, behaviors, values, customs, and beliefs that are shared by a human group. Culture is transmitted through language, material objects, ritual institutions, and from one generation to the next.

- **Diversity:** Recognition and acknowledgment of differences that are unique to each group that is part of the multicultural community.

- **Multicultural Students:** The four under-represented racial/ethnic groups: African American, Asian-Pacific American, Chicano/Latino, and Native American.

- **Race:** A socially and historically defined human grouping hereditarily assigned but not biologically defined. Refers to very large human groups comprised of diverse populations and ethnic groups.

- **Recruitment:** The process of identifying and informing African American, Asian-Pacific American, Chicano/Latino and Native American populations in order to provide them with support systems that will facilitate improved and enhanced access to the university with the expectation of increasing enrollment of multicultural students.

- **Retention:** The continuous process to create, maintain, and support ongoing strategies for meeting the personal, academic, social and financial needs of multicultural students to ensure academic success and graduation.

- **The university:** The main campus of the home institution and any branches, which may comprise a multi-campus system.

Figure 1 Definition of Terms.

members reach out to one another in order to establish the social and intellectual bonds so important to community membership.

It has been suggested that institutions can strive to be systematic in their actions for student retention, particularly tose that address the needs and concerns of minority students (Tinto, 1987). Because student leaving often mirrors individual experiences in the total system of the institution, formal and informal, institutional actions must address the full range of student experiences in the social and intellectual areas of the institution. Moreover, Tinto suggests that they do so in a manner which recognizes the multiple ways in which experiences in one segment of the institution, formal and/or informal, academic and/or social, impact upon experiences in other segments of the institution.

Researchers, who continue to study the phenomenon of retaining students whether they are majority or minority, suggest that actions should be initiated earlier rather than later in the students' careers. Tinto asserts that because the process of student membership and student leaving is characterized by different stages, institutional actions must be sensitive to the varying times at which different actions can effectively address the changing needs of students. In this regard, successful programs begin to address student needs as early as possible so that potential problems and concerns do not become actual problems later in the students' careers.

Lastly, researchers suggest that successful minority or retention programs are invariably student-centered (Noel, 1985). They take as their primary obligation the serving of student needs and interests even when those needs and interests appear to run counter to those of the institution. In this very important respect, Tinto asserts that successful programs and institutions exhibit a deeply embedded commitment to serve the students they admit. The long-term benefit is that it is commitment, more than anything else, which underlies the actions of successful programs. Consequently, institutional commitment to students, demonstrated in the daily actions of institutional members, will ultimately be the source of the development of student commitment to the institution (Tinto, 1987).

Researchers also suggest that education, not mere retention, be the guiding principle of retention programs, particularly those programs that address the needs and concerns of minority students on large university campuses (Tinto, 1987). Programs are thus designed to provide each and every person with continued opportunity to grow both socially and intellectually, while in college. Institutions should be doing much more than simply acting to ensure the continued presence of students on campus. Institutions should come to view the success of retention programs not only by the increased numbers of persons who stay until degree completion, but also and more importantly by the character and quality of the living and learning which takes place during that period (Tinto, 1987). Furthermore, institutions are urged to provide individuals with the resources to acquire the skills needed for college work and with interactional opportunities for the establishment of community membership, but also to ensure that those skills and communities are such as to promote the social and intellectual growth of its members.

Minority Student Departure

Although research on the departure of different types of students in different types of institutions is still quite limited, researchers are beginning to see a number of significant differences both in the sources and the frequency of different forms of student leaving (Tinto, 1987). The most noticeable are those which occur among students of different sex, age, race, and social class, and among institutions of different level, size, and residential character.

In describing these differences, Tinto suggests taking care to avoid the tendency to attribute to each and every member of a group of individuals or institutions the characteristics which may serve to describe the group generally. It would be a serious mistake to assume that all group members are alike in their experience of higher education or that all institutions, however similar in structure, exhibit similar patterns of students leaving. We must consider the extent that we can talk of aggregate differences in patterns of departure between groups of students and types of institutions as well as the discussion of the interactive character of the forces which shape the experience of different individuals in varying institutional settings (Tinto, 1987). By such a consideration, both theory formulation of institutional departure and policy development are sensitive to the needs of minority students and institutional differences, can be further understood.

Studies of departure among students of different races and social class have, until recently, focused almost entirely on black and white students. These studies support the contention that departure among disadvantaged black students is more a reflection of academic difficulties than it is leaving among white students (Donovan, 1984). Donovan's multi-institution study of low-income black students finds that their departure is primarily determined by the nature of their on-campus academic behaviors, especially those pertaining to the meeting of the formal demands of the academic system.

Studies by Tracey and Sedlacek (1985) share Tinto's view of the role of academic integration in the persistence of disadvantaged black students. They note that the ability of students to meet academic standards is related not only to academic skills but also to positive academic self-concept, institutional environment, academic support, and familiarity with the academic requirements and demands of the institution.

Tinto suggests that minority students also face particularly severe problems in gaining access to the mainstream of social and intellectual life in largely white institutions (Loo and Rolison, 1986). For minority, as much as for majority students, social and intellectual involvement and positive faculty contact are essential to continued persistence (Alien, 1985). However, the types of involvement, activities, and interpersonal relationships which lead to effective social integration of minority and majority students may not be the same. Nonetheless, involvement, particularly in leadership roles, may enhance self-confidence, leadership abilities and interpersonal skills for minorities attending large white universities (Pascarella and Terenzini, 1991).

Tinto asserts that beyond the existence of possible discrimination, minority students generally and black students in particular may find it especially difficult to become a member of a supportive community within the university. Sharing a common racial origin (or any other single attribute for that matter) is no guarantee for the sharing of common interests and dispositions. Though it is obviously the case that differences in racial origins do not preclude commonality of interests and dispositions, it is the case that on all but the very largest campuses minority students have relatively fewer options as to the types of communities in which to establish membership than do white students. In such situations, Tinto suggests minority students are more likely to experience a sense of isolation and/or of incongruence than are white students generally.

Minority Student Programs

Universities, with varying degrees of commitment, employ support services such as counseling centers in order to sustain and nurture students of color. These support systems are designed to bridge the gap between the college or university's academic and social cultures. Scholars substantiate the claim that college holds an importance for students that transcends the curriculum. For example, Weingartner (1993) asserts that "learning academic subjects is not all that students should be doing in college; those four years must contribute to the preparation for life in all of its facets. The job of college is to develop the whole person" (p. 119). A minority student services office is just one example of the ways universities may aid in that holistic development for students of color—by providing them with role models and guidance.

There are several types of programs which offer support of retention for students of color at large university campuses, and these sources begin with pre-collegiate, early intervention programs. One such program, proposed by Taylor (1986), suggests that minority student services be provided from matriculation to graduation. Such services include student orientation, academic advising, and career placement. For example, among many of the existing programs offered to students of color is a mentoring program, such as the one currently in place at the University of Texas. This program pairs faculty members with incoming students of color. Another program to address the needs of students of color, currently being applied at Kutztown University is a peer counseling program which offers "student to student counseling in such areas as academic advising and personal concerns" (Taylor, 1986, p. 95). Other programs and activities involve the entire campus in retention efforts. Taylor's model takes into consideration social factors such as institutional racism, cultural conflicts, alienation which may effect the retention of students of color. Taylor suggests that "programs addressing social factors, student anxieties and frustrations, and environmental issues have a positive effect on retention" (p. 212). According to the research of this scholar and others, special services aimed specifically at minority students are more effective at increasing retention and graduation rates for students of color than services designed for all students. Strategies that include outreach efforts, strong support services, and sensitive faculty have a positive effect on retention.

Vaz (1987) suggests that students of color need a retention system that would afford opportunities for networking with minority scholars on other campuses, providing mentor relationships and encouraging faculty involvement with students of color. The system would also take advantage of the friend-kin network by encouraging students of color to challenge each other academically and support each other socially. In addition, a retention system for students of color should have the same programmatic goals as those of other students in general. These goals include the development of their potential and the reinforcement of academic and creative striving.

It is therefore concluded that support systems, such as minority student services, include major elements of mentoring type relationships with counselors and knowledgeable staff, student culture learning with more advanced peers, academic and financial counseling with culturally sensitive faculty, and special programs/seminars. It has been shown that support services have direct implications for easing minority student adjustment to college life, as well as increasing the probability of their successful matriculation (Moore and Carpenter, 1985).

Throughout this book you have been presented with myriad major recruitment and retention initiatives that have been implemented in different types of institutions. In the next section I will provide a brief history of the development of a Multicultural Center, which led to the development of a five-year retention model for a mid-size northwestern university.

History of the Multicultural Center

The Multicultural Center of Washington State University and its host community are nestled among wheat fields in an agricultural area in the Pacific Northwest. Students come to Washington State University from various cities and towns throughout the state.

The Multicultural Center at Washington State University is probably the most sophisticated, highly structured, well-equipped (i.e., fiscal, financial, human, and physical resources) program that serves the needs of ethnic minority students at any predominantly white college or university.

As provided by the Office of Multicultural Student Services (1996), on March 19, 1986, the Provost proposed that the following action be taken concerning the creation of a Division of Minority Affairs at Washington State University:

1. Formal creation of the Division of Minority Affairs as a separate budgeting unit within Student Affairs. Existing budgeted units which were to be moved entirely under the new division would include, initially, the four ethnic minority counseling programs, the Historical House, and the Science Supportive Services.

2. Identification of internal leadership of the new division in advance of launching a national search for a director.

3. Establishment of a Minority Affairs Advisory Committee with representation, at the level of director or chair, from Comparative American Cultures, Admissions, Financial Aid, Student Affairs, Academic Development program, and possibly the external community.

4. Realignment of budgets and personnel in Admissions and Financial Aid pertinent to the recruitment and admission of minority students. Joint appointments with well-defined responsibilities and reporting relationships appear the most likely mechanism.

5. Designation of specific individual(s) within the Academic Development Program (jointly budgeted with the Division of Minority Affairs) to assume primary responsibility for retention difficulties associated with academic performance.

Soon thereafter was the appointment of an Interim Director of the newly structured Division of Minority Affairs. At that time, there were four ethnic minority counselors—one for each protected group: African American, Asian Pacific American, Chicano/Latino, and Native American. In addition, there were two recruitment coordinators for students of color who had a joint appointment either in Admissions or Financial Aid and the Division of Minority Affairs. The original focus of the division was, and remains, to increase the enrollment of students of color and to provide counseling (academic, personal, financial, and social) and other support services to reduce the attrition of students of color.

In 1990, funds were provided to hire a Native American and Chicano/Latino recruitment coordinator, bringing the total number of full-time permanent recruitment professionals to four. All joint appointments were abolished so that reporting lines go directly to the Director of Minority Affairs. Funds were also provided to hire an Associate Director of Minority Affairs.

In 1992, the name for this unit was changed to the Division of Multicultural Student Services and was placed under the supervision of the Vice Provost for Human Relations and Resources. At the same time, the unit was relocated to the Multicultural Center. This brought the administrative area, recruitment and the student centers (with the exception of the Chicano/Latino Student Center which remained in its old location) all under one roof.

During the summer of 1995, the Office of Multicultural Student Services embarked on a plan to reorganize the department to better serve multicultural students at Washington State University. A new director was hired to provide strategic direction for the office and plan the reorganization. The first phase of the reorganization was to review the department's mission and current structure. The director, in consultation with the Vice Provost for Human Relations and Resources and representatives from the office of Human Resources Services, presented six functional areas for the department. They were recruitment and community relations, retention services, counseling services, strategic planning, and new program initiatives, operations, and evaluation and assessment.

Organization of the Multicultural Center

Phase I of reorganization included personnel promotions and a restructuring of the organizational chart. The appointment of a university-wide Council for Multicultural Student Retention and a Council for Multicultural Student Recruitment was included in the Phase I reorganization. Both of these councils are designed to provide a strategic approach on how to recruit and retain students of color at Washington State University.

Additional space was anticipated during the 1995–96 school year. As of July 1996, the administrative and the recruitment units were moved to the new student service building. Three of the four students centers will remain in the Multicultural Center along with the newly organized Retention Services Center. However, the Chicano/Latino Student Center will continue to be housed in its present location. Additionally, the Historical House will be managed through the African-

American Student Center and be located in a new site within walking distance.

The newly focused Multicultural Student Service's primary purpose is to provide services and programs that help students of color apply to the university, meet new friends, succeed in classes, and graduate. Other goals are to expand cultural awareness, to celebrate differences and similarities in an atmosphere of appreciation of both their individuality and common origins, and to heighten the appreciation of cultural diversity within the university and the community.

It is this Multicultural Center at Washington State University's campus that students of color consider a "home away from home." Furthermore, the center identifies marks of culture where heritage and traditions flourish and lifetime friendships form. Within the Multicultural Center are the administrative office, the division of multicultural recruitment staff, the African-American Student Center, Asian/Pacific-American Student Center, Chicano/Latino Student Center, and the Native-American Student Center (See Organizational Chart, Appendix A).

The administrative office consists of (1) the director, (2) associate director, (3) secretary supervisor, (4) program assistant, and (5) office assistant. Multicultural student recruitment and community relations staff consist of (1) the associate director, (2) coordinators for each of the four respective ethnic centers, and (3) a recruitment secretary. The division's multicultural recruitment staff travels extensively to meet with Asian Pacific Islander, African American, Chicano/Latino, American Indian, and Alaskan Native students in high schools and community colleges. The multicultural recruitment coordinators present information about Washington State University and guide students through the admissions process.

Lastly, there is one counselor for each of the four student centers that represent that cultural background or ethnicity. Once a student is enrolled at Washington State University, the multicultural counselors continue to assist and advocate for students of color. They can do academic advising, give help in problem solving, direct programs, conduct workshops, and help locate internships.

The centers are set up to offer a number of services such as social support, academic advising, referral to other departments and services on campus and cultural programs as well as information on scholarships, summer internships, and career or graduate programs. Furthermore, the centers are also gathering and working places for the various student organizations.

The mission of each of the four student centers is to assist with recruitment and retention of students of color. Yet, each center orients itself in a distinctive way, described here mainly from the perspective of the coordinators of each center. In addition, numerous student organizations on campus provide opportunities for other developmental, leadership, and organizational skills. These organizations include the following:

- African American Association *
- Black Women's Caucus *
- National Society of Black Engineers
- Asian Pacific American Student Committee *
- Association of Pacific and Asian Women *
- Cambodian Students Club
- Filipino American Students Association
- Hui Hauoli o' Hawaii *
- Vietnamese Student Organization
- Movimiento Estudiantil Chicano de Aztlan *
- Mujeres Unidas *
- Organization of Latin American Students
- Society of Hispanic Professional Engineers
- Student Association of Bilingual Educators
- Ku-Au-Mah *
- Native American Women's Association *
- American Indian Science and Engineering Society
- Native American Alliance

With a new well-defined structure of the Office of Multicultural Student Services in place, the university, under the direction of the director of the office, began to develop a five year retention strategy for clearly defined underrepresented students. This next section provides an overview of the retention strategy developed for the office.

To assist the university in its ongoing initiatives to retain and ultimately graduate large numbers of multicultural students, it is important to develop a comprehensive strategy; this strategy will guide the university and all of its units in developing and maintaining a climate that is conducive and reflective of the type of students enrolling at institutions of higher education. The strategy proposed is not intended to provide all the answers to a very complex issue; rather, the intent of the university's development of a recruitment and retention strategy is to provide a document that is treated as a "work in progress." Although a strategy should be developed to cover a minimum of five years, it is beneficial to make yearly revisions to its specific objectives and strategies. Ideally, the president, and the senior vice presidents will need to work with a "multicultural taskforce" to ensure that appropriate accountability structures are in place that will ensure responsible and timely implementation of this important initiative. In short, this retention strategy will be a living document for the university.

Given the multi-dimensional character of minority retention problems for most predominately white institutions, the retention strategy will need to use several different approaches. Four major objectives help define the tasks for developing this retention strategy: (1) the first objective is to review actual retention and graduation data of the university and then compare this data with selected peer institutions; (2) the second objective is to assess the various aspects of the university environment to determine factors that may lead to the attrition of culturally diverse learners; (3) the third objective is to ascertain what specific multicultural retention initiatives are available; (4) and the fourth objective is to develop a specific retention plan and time lines with built-in accountability structures designed to increase the retention and ultimate graduation of multicultural students.

While the retention strategy will not necessarily identify cause and effect relationships between variables, it should offer the following: (1) a view of the latest retention literature; (2) a statement of the problem; (3) national recruitment, retention, and graduation data by ethnic group; and (4) operational definitions. When adopting a retention plan, it will also be necessary to include: (1) an extensive audit of retention initiatives occurring throughout the university; (2) a synopsis of the university's recruitment history and retention graduation data; (3) the university's athletic retention and graduation data; and (4) retention and graduation data of selected peer institutions.

A comprehensive retention strategy, by definition, must focus on the complete student, intellectually, socially, spiritually, physically, and culturally. While there are some strategies that are generalizable to all underrepresented groups, it is important to recognize that the strategies that follow are meant to look at each underrepresented group as a separate entity.

There are many strategies that can be incorporated to develop an effective retention model. Of these strategies, models should (1) have the support of administration by incorporating retention diversity into the strategic plan of the university; (2) recruit faculty for participation; (3) provide motivational lectures; (4) provide proactive financial aid counseling; (5) get students involved with programming activities; (6) maintain up-to-date knowledge on retention issues; (7) regularly assess program effectiveness; (8) incorporate early assessment and intervention; (9) develop faculty mentoring; (10) develop leadership seminars; (11) and develop and maintain a caring and competent staff (Carreathers, Beekman, Coatie, and Nelson, 1996).

Carreathers et al. (1996) highlight some or all of these characteristics in Texas A&M's Department of Multicultural Services, the University of Louisville's Center for Academic Achievement's "Thriving and Surviving" program, and the University of Texas at Austin's Preview Program. These three models were initiated and are supported by the leadership of their respective university and/or a governing body. Texas A&M's Department of Multicultural Services was initiated by the institution's Division of Student Services. The University of Louisville's Thriving and Surviving Program was mandated the U.S. Office of Civil Rights. Lastly, the Preview Program at the University of Texas at Austin is a part of the Office of the Dean of Students. Parker (1997) and Madison (1993) both indicate the crucial need for an institutional leader to support such efforts.

Suggestions for retention models are infinite; however, other notable strategies include mentoring, peer advising, student leadership conferences, student skills workshops, and cultural events (Carreathers et al., 1996). Mallinckrodt and Sedlacek (1987) suggest policies to maximize use of athletic facilities and campus gyms; more union programming for specific groups; and that the use of areas such as libraries and career and counseling centers also help retention. Lastly, Parker (1997) and Tinto (1987) provide suggestions which discuss retention from a systems perspective. Parker suggests (1) the creation of positions dedicated to handling retention activities; (2) the recognition of the need for additional funding sources; (3) the establishment of mentoring programs for minority students, such programs have exposed minorities to successful staff and students who can show them a path to success and give them the confidence and support they need; (4) the reorganization of faculty/staff duties and responsibilities to assist in retention activities, especially for institutions with limited resources; (5) the development of a reporting system for identification and tracking so that institutions can have accurate data and data processing capabilities on the different facets of their programs; the development of faculty/staff training to help them better understand minority populations (Parker, 1997, p. 120). Tinto (1987) indicates that (1) institutions should ensure that the new students enter with or have the opportunity to acquire skills needed for academic success; (2) institutions should reach out to become more personal with students beyond the formal domain of academic life; (3) institutional retention actions should be systematic in character; (4) institutions should start as early as possible to retain students; (5) the primary commitment of institutions should be to their students; (6) education, not retention, should be the goal of institutional retention programs.

Once the data have been collected and compared with a university's sister institutions and national retention data, and frequently used terms have been operationally defined for the campus, as well as a review of the retention literature has been obtained, it is then time to begin the most important part of the retention plan: The Strategy. Following is an outline of a Five-Year Multicultural Retention Strategy. While I do not propose that the retention strategy following has all the answers, it could provide a good start for those institutions that are serious about institutionalizing efforts to retain underrepresented students.

Vision for Retention Strategy

The university should seek to develop a university-wide approach whose ultimate goal is to increase the retention and graduation rates of multicultural students so that they equal or exceed that of majority students at the university.

Statement of Values

In the process of developing and implementing a strategy that aims at increasing the retention and graduation rates of multicultural students, the following principles must permeate all actions taken. First, an institutional commitment that communicates respect, inclusion, trust, a challenge for growth, and understanding of and positive regard for multicultural students is imperative. Second, students must be made aware of the importance of their individual responsibilities, their freedom to grow and gain self-confidence and a sense of their own authorship of their destiny. Third, to meet multicultural students' needs holistically, student services and support should be based on a spirit of collaboration and cooperation across the university community.

Mission Statement

The university is committed to developing, implementing, and assessing a five-year plan to improve the retention and graduation rates of multicultural students.

At the practical level, it will provide guidance to administrators in higher education, specifically at predominantly white institutions, in understanding and delivering a more comprehensive perspective in educational program planning, university and faculty development, cultural and diversity issues, and the needs and development of students of color.

The Multicultural Retention Strategy (see Appendix) is designed to provide structure. Further, in recognizing the university's strong commitment to recruiting multicultural students, it is imperative that each academic department and academic support unit play a significant and ongoing role in formulating, implementing, and maintaining coordinated retention strategies and plans.

Reviews of the characteristics of effective retention models demonstrate that there is no shortage in concepts or ideas to assist universities in retaining minority students. While many retention strategies have assisted with the retention of minority students, many of these students leave higher education without accomplishing degrees, which is cause for concern by the higher education community. The next decade will present many new challenges for higher education, particularly regarding issues such as diversity, quality, accountability, and productivity. Minority populations will continue to increase, while calls for accountability and productivity and the need to do more with less continue to haunt institutions. The pressing issues outlined in this essay and certainly throughout this book suggest that is imperative that institutions consider new, or maybe not so new, alternatives to address these concerns.

Appendix

Goals, Objectives, and Strategies

I. To create an inclusive university climate that supports and enhances the well-being and the total educational experience and ultimate graduation of multicultural students.

    A. To increase awareness and appreciation of multiculturalism across the academic community.
        1. Survey multicultural students to assess their needs, their concerns, and their recommendations for improving the campus climate.
        2. Offer diversity education workshops to every advisor, faculty and staff member; and ensure that their efforts for diversity are included in performance evaluations.
        3. Encourage student participation in multicultural/diversity training.
        4. Develop and promote events that recognize diverse cultural heritage.
        5. Project a positive multicultural image through publications related to the university.
        6. Hold an annual Multicultural Convocation and Reception.

7. Support and collaborate with a Curricular Diversity Committee in its efforts to increase the number of courses that address multiculturalism and diversity.

8. Include presentations on the university's diversity and its enrollment management recruitment and retention plans for multicultural students during orientation sessions for new faculty, staff and administrators. ,

9. Continue partnerships that will ensure the successful transition for students transferring from other colleges and universities.

10. Continue and develop new working relationships with other minority offices, agencies, and organizations that provide support services for students.

B. To increase incrementally each year the number of faculty and staff of color.

1. Establish yearly meetings with the president with deans and heads of major units to personally reaffirm multicultural hiring goals, with special emphasis on tenure track faculty.

2. Identify staff and financial assistance at the university level to provide incentives for departments and units to hire a more diverse staff.

3. Produce an annual report documenting the number of faculty and staff of color employed by the university.

C. To integrate the campuses and surrounding communities to improve the local racial climate.

1. Expand special living community opportunities to better support multicultural student populations.

2. Host teleconference presentations on campus that address racial issues that would include the university and the surrounding community.

3. Participate in City Council Meetings.

D. To provide opportunities for faculty and staff of color to interact with multicultural students as the students adjust to the campus environment.

1. Implement a biannual reception for faculty, staff and students.

2. Implement activities that celebrate cultural heritage that comprises faculty, staff and students.

E. To provide opportunities for all faculty and staff to interact with multicultural students as the students adjust to the campus environment.

1. Establish a professional mentor program for multicultural students.

F. To provide multicultural students with a permanent space that they can call their own and where they can see an immediate reflection of their cultural heritage.
   1. Allocate spaces for a Multicultural Student Services Office on all campuses.
   2. Provide more artwork across campuses.

II. To provide an academic environment and support structure that is aimed at improving the retention and graduation rates of multicultural students.

A. To coordinate academic retention programs to maximize their effectiveness.
   1. Have each college and branch campus appoint a person to coordinate its retention initiatives, monitor the implementation of these initiatives at the college level, and serve as an active member of a Council on Retention.
   2. Provide this representative with the resources and authority to oversee services to multicultural students in the areas of advising, mentoring, and participation in academic clubs and activities.
B. To systematically assess the effectiveness of retention programs and use the results to improve them.
   1. Provide an accurate database to track all undergraduate students.
   2. Perform annual evaluations of existing retention programs by departments, offices and majors.
   3. Analyze the multicultural student demographic report in regard to retention data to identify trends.
   4. Survey nonreturning multicultural students to identify the reasons why they leave the university.
C. To provide all incoming multicultural students with a pre-college experience.
   1. Continue to provide on and off-campus programs targeting multicultural students in which they are introduced to the history of higher education, how the system works, and the demands and expectations of college life.

D. To develop culturally responsive classrooms that actively engage students in learning.
   1. Assess pedagogical needs of the faculty members.
   2. Encourage faculty members to utilize campus educational centers for the review of curriculum and teaching styles for multicultural inclusiveness.
   3. Facilitate cross-disciplinary collaboration among faculty, administrators, and students in the development of culturally sensitive classrooms.
E. To assist multicultural students with their social, academic, and cultural adjustment to college.
   1. Assess the academic needs of multicultural students and how the university is meeting them.
   2. Monitor multicultural student academic progress.
   3. Establish a Comprehensive University Mentoring Program to assist multicultural students in adjusting to and maximizing on the university experience.
   4. Highlight and recognize multicultural students' academic achievement and scholarship.
F. To provide the ongoing information and guidance necessary to facilitate connecting multicultural students to educational and career programs that meet their needs.
   1. Assist multicultural students to inventory their existing education skills and help focus their interest in selecting a degree program.
   2. Provide multicultural students with sensitive and appropriate academic advising.
   3. Assist multicultural students in accessing academic support services as their need for these services arises.
   4. Promote multicultural student enrollment in the four-year degree agreement.
   5. Provide options and information on post-graduate education and assist with preparation for the application process.
   6. Publicize the academic support structure available to multicultural students.

7. Collaborate with student groups and other units across campus working in existing and future multicultural retention efforts to apply principles of career development and success to educational experiences.
8. Provide a multicultural perspective that enhances career development, employability, and preparation for graduate studies.
9. Provide opportunities for students to link their education with their cultural communities through service learning, observation of service delivery, internships, cooperative education and research.

III. To assist multicultural students in securing adequate financial aid.

A. To assist students and their parents to understand and use the financial aid process and eligibility.
  1. Include financial aid information in all publications and mailings to prospective students.
  2. Include presentations on all types of financial aid as a regular component of recruitment events and new student orientation.
  3. Conduct workshops to assist students in filling out financial aid applications.
  4. Continue to assist students in the aid distribution process.
B. To assist students and parents in identifying suitable scholarships and grants.
  1. Include scholarship and grant information in all publications and mailings to prospective students.
  2. Include scholarship and grant information as a regular component of recruitment events and new student orientation.
  3. Conduct workshops to assist students in filling out scholarship applications.
C. Increase scholarships available to multicultural students.
  1. Create a multicultural scholarship endowment fund.
  2. Increase allocations for multicultural scholarship support from ongoing fund raising efforts.
D. To inform students and parents on loan eligibility and how to apply for guaranteed student loans.
E. To inform students and parents on work-study eligibility and how to qualify and apply for work-study.

F. To obtain resources for an emergency loan program.
   1. Provide interim financial support for students whose aid is delayed.
   2. Provide emergency money for students not eligible for financial aid.

IV. To monitor the implementation of the university's Five-Year Multicultural Student Retention Plan.

A. To provide an accurate database for all students.
B. To maintain periodic meetings to discuss the implementation of the plan and receive and provide feedback to various departments, and redirect efforts as needed.
C. To provide the various departments with a format for the evaluation of their particular efforts regarding the implementation of this plan.
D. To make council members available as consultants to the campus in the development, implementation, and evaluation of specific retention plans.
E. To generate an annual report showing the overall impact of the plan and providing recommendations for improvement as needed.

Mac A. Stewart

MAC A. STEWART is Vice Provost for Minority Affairs at The Ohio State University, where he served as Dean of University College from 1991 to 2001.

As Associate Professor and member of the Graduate Faculty in both the College of Human Ecology and the College of Education, Dr. Stewart has published widely in numerous professional journals. He has been a member of the editorial board of *The Negro Educational Review* since 1983 and editor-in-chief since 1999.

Dr. Stewart is a member of the Board of Trustees of the International Foundation for Education and Self-Help, an organization founded by the late Reverend Leon H. Sullivan. He has worked especially closely with its Teachers for Africa program.

Active in civic and community projects, Dr. Stewart is a member of the Board of Trustees of Mount Carmel School of Nursing and the Columbus Urban League. He has served in similar roles for The Columbus Academy, Buckeye Boys Ranch, and many other organizations. He has received numerous honors and awards, notably the 1992 Frederick Patterson Award of the Greater Columbus United Negro College Fund.

He earned his B.A. degree in Sociology from Morehouse College in 1963, an M.A. in Counseling from Atlanta University in 1965, and a Ph.D. in Higher Education Administration from The Ohio State University in 1973. Following the doctorate he also had educational experiences at Harvard University and the University of Bonn, Germany.

10

EFFECTIVE MINORITY PROGRAMS AT THE OHIO STATE UNIVERSITY

Most minority academics of my generation, who studied as undergraduates in the 1960s, can identify personally with the metaphor of the ship that is being built even while it floats to its next destination. Like a working Website that is continually under construction, the metaphor of a ship floating as it is repaired or refurbished can be used to describe the self as it matures or an academic discipline as it becomes increasingly sophisticated in its knowledge and its methodology. It can equally apply as a framework to analyze in retrospect the ways in which universities, especially predominantly majority institutions, learned to deal with minority groups even while the numbers of minority enrollments were increasing and the programs developed to serve them proliferated, becoming, one hopes, more thoughtful and more effective.

I have worked as a graduate student, a faculty member, and an administrator at Ohio State University since 1970; this is not long enough to have known the school's first African-American graduate who completed his degree in 1892, but long enough to have watched the intense discussion of the early 1970s and to participate in devising many of the programs that emerged from those often confrontational times. I helped put many of those programs in place, to build some of the staterooms on the ship, and I have journeyed, so far, without capsizing for about three decades. To extend the metaphor, I would point out that this particular ship has always needed a captain and a crew, and that during these decades they, like the ship, have been in a continuous process of rebuilding, rethinking, revising, and revitalizing.

The questions we used to ask to move us toward our destination have changed. Early on they were very basic calls for social justice. Our early evaluations were predominantly quantitative: How many new students were enrolled? How often did they take advantage of our services? Measuring with a Likert Scale, how did they feel about what we made available? More recently, as we have gained experience and been able to watch our graduates mature personally and professionally, it seems to me that our questions have become more qualitative. The one most relevant to this collection of essays and to my own experience is this: Can predominantly white institutions prepare black and other minority students for the elite levels of American life to the same degree and in the same way that they prepare white students?[1] It seems to me that this question, formulated in this way, points us in a significant direction, and that struggling to answer it affirmatively requires a high level of academic and administrative work. We were unlikely to ask this question when the journey began in the 1970s, and we would certainly not have understood it in the specific ways we should today. It is, I think, a measure of the distance we have come as educators that we can ask and hope to answer this kind of question for our students.

One last preliminary point: Although our ship, our destination, our program, and most of our crew have changed substantially in the past thirty years, two elements of our enterprise have retained their original character. First, we have learned again and again that flexibility in adapting to altered situations and politics is a crucial skill. Second, we still need to continually recognize that whatever we implement *outside* the classroom must support our students as students inside the classroom, or else the prospects of minority students to attain "the elite level of American life" diminish greatly.

Review of Effective Programs

A decade of social unrest largely fueled by an unpopular war culminated on many campuses in student strikes and other disturbances in the spring of 1970. On our campus, located about ninety miles southwest of Kent State, the seriousness and intensity of the students often were matched by angry voices from faculty. From this context, as the tear gas cleared, there emerged several permanent changes to our campus—notably the Office of Minority Affairs, the Department of Black Studies and the Center for Women's Studies. With little initially as defined programs, the university acted mostly on social commitment and put its faith in a number of new leaders. Among them was Dr. William Jimmerson Holloway, appointed to head the Office of Minority Affairs at its creation in 1970. His values and vision provided the original shape of the office and remain the pillars on which it still depends.[2] Eventually, it became the goal of the Office of Minority Affairs (OMA) to work with units throughout the institution to develop a comprehensive array of services and programs to attract, retain, and promote the academic success of designated minority students. The specific groups targeted as priorities for OMA were identified as African-Americans, Hispanics, Asian-Americans, Pacific-Islanders, Native-Americans, and, acknowledging several counties in Ohio, students from Appalachia. However, given the population of the state and our role as the acknowledged flagship institution, it was clear from the onset that Ohio State's success in dealing effectively with minority populations would be measured predominantly by how we served the African-American student population.

Recruitment Programs

Our earliest contact with students usually occurs through one of our recruitment programs. Through the years, we have learned that students of color come to the university from many different backgrounds, along many different pathways, encouraged and influenced by many different mentors. Within the limits of our resources, we systematically approach prospective students taking these varied paths and mentors into account. For example, although we are located in the Midwest, we annually send teams of our personnel to the areas of the Southwest with a large Hispanic student population in order to attract some of them to enrich the cultural scene of our campus. Of course, the quest is for students who qualify for admission and present a strong likelihood of academic success in the rigorous environment of a research extensive university.

The Young Scholars Program

To ensure that qualified applicants will be available, we begin early with students in the sixth grade. The **Young Scholars Program** (YSP) is a collaborative effort between Ohio State and the urban school districts of Ohio's nine largest cities. Its purpose is to increase the number of college-bound students who enroll at Ohio State and graduate, enhancing diversity in the university community. Young scholars are selected in their home school districts during their sixth-grade year. Nominations are submitted by teachers, counselors, or principals. Once selected, scholars must agree to enroll in a college preparatory curriculum and maintain a minimum cumulative 3.0 GPA through high school. Young Scholars who successfully complete program requirements are guaranteed admission to Ohio State, as well as a financial-aid package based upon their individual verified needs.

The Young Scholars Program was established coincident with the university's decision to implement a policy of selective admission to Ohio State. Many individuals inside and outside the university expressed concern that anticipating higher admission standards, the university should be highly proactive in ensuring the continued and, if possible, increased diversity of entering classes. After considerable discussion with campus groups and state legislators, the Young Scholars Program was put in place in the largest school districts of the state. Since its founding in 1988, YSP has served 2,212 students in Akron, Canton, Cincinnati, Cleveland, Columbus, Dayton, Lorain, Toledo, and Youngstown.

Currently, each year 120 students statewide are designated "pre-Young Scholars" during the sixth grade. They receive a variety of support services, including advising and tutoring, and during their high school freshman year, they are eligible to become "Young Scholars" if they:

- have earned a grade-point average of 3.0 or higher
- are a member of a YSP-designated minority group
- would be first-generation college students
- qualify based on low family income

They must maintain the 3.0 GPA or face probation and eventual dismissal from the program. These students are recommended by their schools and selected by a committee of representatives from the local schools and communities. The academic credentials of those selected are now more competitive than previously. In the early years of the program, some students had only the minimum credentials required for "good standing" in their local schools. The 3.0 GPA requirement has greatly improved both the academic caliber of the students and retention rates in the program.

Students who started as Young Scholars in the sixth grade in 1988 began to graduate from high school in 1994; those YSP students who entered Ohio State in autumn 1994 began to graduate from Ohio State in 1998. We therefore have data for YSP students in OSU entering classes starting in 1994, retention data since 1995, and graduation data since 1998. Graduation data are conventionally (and nationally) available in a six-year time frame, so that our most recent graduation data for national comparison are from 2001 for the cohort entering 1994, the first year YSP students matriculated at Ohio State.

It is encouraging to be able to report that a considerable percentage of YSP participants have attended Ohio State. The following numbers show the contribution of YSP to the African-American enrollments at Ohio State:

Cohorts Entering Ohio State in	1994	1995	1996
African-Americans	492	491	517
Number from YSP	91	144	141
Percentage of entering African-Americans who were in YSP	18.5%	29.3%	27.3%

Other data highlights for the program to date include:

- Sixty-four percent, or 1,417 students out of 2,212 served, completed the pre-college program with a 3.0 GPA or better.

- Eight hundred two YSP students have attended Ohio State.

- From the cohorts entering YSP from 1988 to 1995, 261 have graduated from Ohio State.

- Six-year graduation rates for African-American YSP students entering from 1994 to 1996 compare favorably with the overall average graduation rates for entering black students reported by OSU: for 1994, YSP = 44 percent, compared with 33.7 percent for the total African-American population; for 1995, YSP = 41.7 percent, compared with 35.4 percent for the total African-American population; and for 1996, YSP = 42.6 percent, compared with 35.6 percent for the total African-American population.

These data suggest that without the substantial positive influence of the YSP data factored in, the general totals would show substantially lower enrollments and graduation rates for Ohio State's African-American students.

The focus of the Young Scholars Program is academic; university personnel, however, need to adapt their sense of "academic" to the interests and capacities of high school students each summer when YSP students come to our Columbus campus for a two-week stay. The "Summer Institute," named since 1998 to honor Dr. Samuel DuBois Cook, builds a sense of identity among YSP students, permits them to meet and make friends with students of like ability from many parts of the state, and greatly supports their process of growing accustomed to the college environment. YSP students who eventually attend Ohio State have therefore spent at least eight weeks in residence on campus before they matriculate as college freshmen. They are "old hands" with a sense of comfort and a network of compatriot students, faculty, and staff on the day that their official college lives begin. They have been encouraged to live a disciplined life where studying has a high priority and, because their high school performance has earned them admission with financial aid, they have first-hand experience of the rewards that can follow academic success. In short, YSP has benefited them in many personal ways. This collaboration with nine school boards also benefits the high schools, since YSP students are retained and graduated at levels well above the percentages usual in these large urban school districts. The university also benefits because it has maintained and even increased minority enrollments while greatly raising the standards required for admission. The initial goal of the program—to ensure minority enrollments in the face of rising standards for admission—has been annually achieved.

Scholarship Programs

Integral to the recruitment of undergraduates is effective targeted **scholarship support**. As noted, YSP students receive financial packages that meet their needs according to the common formulas. These YSP awards represent about 10 percent of the undergraduate scholarships that

OMA administers. Serving primarily as the funding resource arm for undergraduate students in OMA's programs, our Minority Scholarship Services (MSS) unit provides financial-aid counseling and facilitates the awarding of need-based grants and merit-based scholarships to students recruited by OMA. MSS personnel report to the Office of Minority Affairs. The university's Office of Student Financial Aid is a separate unit, and MSS works closely with that university-wide office. However, in our experience, it has been advantageous to maintain a separate office with counseling targeted to and tailored for minority students and their concerns.

Our Freshman Foundation Program offers need-based grants up to a current annual maximum of $3,000 to any entering undergraduate Ohio resident in our designated populations. To be eligible also requires demonstrated need, completion of the Free Application for Federal Student Aid (FAFSA) by the priority deadline, and placement in the top half of the student's high school class. Annually, an average of more than 500 entering students receive Freshman Foundation Program assistance.

While need-based financial aid accounts for the majority of assistance provided to students, Ohio State has long believed that academic achievement should be recognized with merit-based scholarships. The university became a sponsor of National Merit and National Achievement Scholars in 1975, and in 2001 it signed on as a sponsor of National Hispanic Scholarships as well. These programs have attracted thousands of students to Ohio State since 1975, and they have provided a means to identify and contact highly qualified prospects for recruitment. However, for minority students, we measure the programs' effectiveness in terms of the quality of some very impressive students rather than in terms of large numbers.

Many more minority students have benefited from Ohio State's own programs of merit-based support. The Minority Scholars Program (MSP) offers competitive scholarships each year to high school seniors with a record of academic and leadership achievements. The largest awards are offered to the most competitive applicants as determined by several criteria: performance in high school and/or ACT or SAT scores, demonstrated cultural awareness (based on essay responses to questions on the application), and committee recommendations. The minimum criteria to be eligible for MSP consideration are a high school rank in the top 20 percent *or* a 3.0 GPA on a 4.0 scale *or* a 23 ACT composite or 1,070 SAT combined score. MSP offers three scholarship award levels, named Distinction, Prestige, and Excellence.

- The Distinction Scholarship Award covers full in-state tuition, room and board, books, and miscellaneous expenses. Annually about ten of these are awarded to new students.

- The Prestige Scholarship Award covers full in-state tuition plus $500. Annually, on average about 200 awards have gone to new students in recent years.

- The Excellence Scholarship Award covers full in-state tuition. About 190 are awarded annually to new students.

About 40 percent of the MSP recipients can also demonstrate financial need and receive Freshman Foundation Program support. Having this array of categories has allowed the institution to compete successfully with America's most elite institutions for able minority students.

Graduate and Professional Student Recruitment

Every autumn quarter, Ohio State hosts a three-day program that brings about 250 prospective graduate and professional students to the Columbus campus. The originator of this effort was Dr. Frank W. Hale, Jr., who joined Ohio State as Associate Dean of the Graduate School in 1971, with duties that included a mandate to increase minority graduate enrollments.[3] When Dr. Hale moved to the position of Vice Provost for Minority Affairs in 1978, the responsibility for the Graduate and Professional Schools Visitation Days (GPSVD) programs accompanied him. Annually, OMA invites honors-level seniors from sixty or more colleges and universities to Columbus where, at university expense, they receive lodging and meals while attending general programs on the campus and city environment for minority students as well as individual/ small group meetings with the academic units in which they have expressed interest. Administrators from their home institutions are also invited—an important program element, which over time has led to long-term professional relationships and a high degree of mutual confidence. Ohio State also pays the expenses for these guests. A travel allowance is included for each visitor. While this is obviously a resource-intensive program, successive generations of senior administrators continue to believe that the results, measured by increased graduate and professional minority enrollments, more than justify the costs.

Ohio State has a long history of providing graduate education to minority students, especially to African-Americans. Through the 1970s, Ohio State ranked as the leading educator of black Ph.D.s in the nation. Even with increasing competition from many elite institutions which have now opened their doors to greater numbers of minority graduate students, we currently rank fourth.

As the program developed an early record of success with graduate enrollments, its net was cast more broadly to include prospective students interested in our professional Colleges of Dentistry, Law, Medicine, Nursing, Optometry, Pharmacy, and Veterinary Medicine. Representatives from all these units, the Graduate School, the Office of Academic Affairs, the Office of Student Affairs, and many department-level faculties all participate in this complex event. This comprehensive commitment of university personnel, the substantial budget of the program, the ongoing relationships between Ohio State and the colleges that provide students as guests—all these contribute to the continued effectiveness of this program. Dr. Hale still participates, and the planning for the program continues on the path he envisioned.

Inevitably, some of these elite students accept bids from other schools; some fail to be accepted by the Ohio State department or college of their choice; and some change their post-graduation plans. Even so, on average in recent years, about 40 percent of those who come to a Visitation Days event enroll at Ohio State within two years. Since the inception of this program, more than 2,000 students who participated have been awarded fellowships by the Ohio State Graduate School.

Minority Continuing Education Opportunities Program

In concluding this section on recruitment, one small but simple and effective program should be mentioned. The Minority Continuing Education Opportunity Program (MCEOP) meets the needs of nontraditional minority students in the Columbus area who work full-time, usually in the day, and who frequently have significant family obligations. Ohio State personnel work with local employers to help their minority employees take advantage of a benefit commonly available, namely, tuition reimbursement. This benefit usually pays the tuition for an employee *after* the employee has earned a designated grade (usually a "C" or better) in a college course. Sometimes employers stipulate that the class must show relevance to the job, but often this is not a requirement.

Unfortunately, many employees find it difficult to come up with tuition before taking the course. MCEOP "fronts" the necessary money; if the employee, now student, completes the class, the funds from the employer are used to repay Ohio State or, in most cases, to cover the next term's tuition. Eventually, the student's final reimbursement covers the university's initial outlay. University investment of time and money is minimal. Most of the administration has been handled by a part-time graduate associate. In 16 years, 200 students have taken advantage of the program, and more than 80 percent have repaid the loans.

Retention Programs

Under the leadership of Dr. William E. Kirwan, Ohio State's President from July 1998 through June 2002, the university developed and began to implement two documents of central significance to the university in general and specifically to the environment for minority students, faculty, and staff. These documents are the *Academic Plan* and the *Diversity Action Plan.*[4] Both of them affirm the importance of diversity to the life of Ohio State. The *Academic Plan* discusses five "core ethical values" of the university, of which one is to celebrate and learn from our diversity. As an institution, we stand for the belief that we value the differences in one another along with the similarities, and we recognize that the human condition is best served through understanding, acceptance, and mutual respect.

The other document, the *Diversity Action Plan*, gives additional reasons for supporting a diverse environment. Among them are the following:

- The quality of education and scholarship is enhanced when it is informed by the perspectives of a diverse community.

- Support for diversity is an affirmation of each individual's intrinsic value.

- A diverse environment tests, shapes, and educates each of us to more fully realize our potential.

- A student entering the 21st century world must be prepared to interact successfully with people from all backgrounds and races.

- In order to succeed, businesses, institutions, and governments must have talented individuals who can excel in diverse settings.

These values are explicitly affirmed in the official policies of Ohio State University. We teach them to new members of our community in orientation programs for students, for staff members, and for faculty. They serve as touchstones for the institution's judgments about behavior in and outside the classroom. And utopian though they may seem to be, I firmly believe that at Ohio State, they are observed far more often than they are broken.

Such an environment is essential for effective retention of minority citizens within a dominantly majority community. Having explicit values to which all university partners (administrators, Trustees, University Senate members representing students, faculty, and staff) subscribe, with diversity as a chief value, makes a difference in our daily lives. If we do not continually strive to realize such an ethical environment, none of our day-to-day programming will be ultimately effective.

Academic Advancement Services

The issue for effective retention programs, therefore, becomes how we make these defining values real in our daily interaction with students. Once students make the decision to attend Ohio State, our next step is to do everything possible to help them succeed. Many studies confirm that the first six weeks on campus are the most critical in determining whether a student will be successful. Our programs in support of student success include a **mentoring program** that pairs staff and faculty mentors with students of similar interests and a **tutorial program** that offers free academic assistance in a wide range of courses. We provide help for custodial single parents who are students themselves, including a comprehensive package to serve their specialized needs.

Students take advantage of these varied programs and services as they themselves perceive their needs or after referral from faculty or staff.

In my view, the most effective retention program that we have for *all* entering students has been the **Minority Advising Program** (MAP). Established in 1971 as a "portal of entry" advising unit where all freshmen were advised, MAP (then known as the Office of Developmental Education) assigned every incoming student to an advisor who taught a required introduction to the university course for his or her advisees; the advisor, therefore, met with them in a classroom setting twice every week and required them to attend individual advising conferences each term.[5]

One guiding tenet of MAP is that academic success is not achieved in a vacuum. Instead, we recognize that personal, social, financial, emotional, developmental, cultural, ethnic, and various other factors may at times affect a student's ability to succeed academically. Therefore, MAP advisers conduct advising from a holistic perspective, using their expertise in working with diverse student populations. Given these expectations, MAP advisers are assigned smaller case loads than advisers in other university offices. This has allowed for more face-to-face interaction as well as more comprehensive advising. MAP advisers, most of whom are themselves persons of color, demonstrate a sensitivity to and an ability to address cultural, ethnic, and social issues that minority students are likely to face within a predominantly white institution. Finally, these staff members have a strong commitment to the retention and success of the individual students assigned to them. They are proactive in following individual students to encourage and monitor good academic habits that lead to academic success.

The Hale Black Cultural Center

Many of our minority students, especially our African-American students, commute from home rather than live on campus. These off-campus students face a problem common to all commuter students without respect to ethnicity—namely, the center of energy in their lives is located away from campus, at home, at a job, or in old friendships formed prior to matriculation. To many commuter students, the university is merely a place to take classes, and consequently their college education lacks some of the transforming power that affects students who live on campus, who work on campus, and whose courses and extracurricular activities form a powerful cathexis with the institution. This binding tie promotes maturation, retention, and ultimately graduation. The lack of it erodes them.

In a word, minority commuter students need a place on campus where they can feel at home. At Ohio State we recognized this need early on and tried to accommodate it in several ways. Eventually, when one of the residence hall commons facilities was slated for renovation, the Black Cultural Center was created and named the Hale Black Cultural Center when Dr. Hale retired from full-time employment at Ohio State in 1988.

The mission of this center is to promote cultural, social, and educational discourse among all students at Ohio State—particularly African-Americans—through its programs, lectures, and cultural activities. Black students, both commuters and residents on campus, are the principal users, but all are welcome and the programs and services of the center attract a diverse audience. The center also reaches beyond the campus, serving as an educational resource for the community on issues of race and diversity. In an average week, the center hosts about 3,000 people for ongoing activities or special events.

A strong program of events and activities has familiarized prospective users with the center's services. Many credit courses are taught there, either regularly or for special class sessions. It has facilities for meetings of student organizations, for lectures by visiting scholars, and for tours by local school children. The center has an extensive collection of art by African-American artists, including traditional African works and paintings and sculpture by avant-garde modernists. The computer lab is open to enrolled students for many hours every day. Of course, the center provides lounge areas that have become popular gathering places. After 10 years, use was high enough that an extensive renovation and enlargement was needed. Outreach to the Columbus area has been successful, partly because there is substantial parking space adjacent to the center but largely because planners have identified some genuine local needs and worked to satisfy them. Two of the most popular offerings are computer training for local senior citizens and a quarterly grant-writing workshop focused on how to find and gain human services grants from local and state funding sources.

To understand the range and quality of programs at the Hale Center, the following additional information may be helpful:

- The Hale Center is a one-level facility with 18,800 square feet of space.

- The center provides a state-of-the-art computer lab with twenty-seven work stations; several classrooms; a research and reading room; a tutorial lab; a community computer center; a large multipurpose room that can be set up in many ways; three art galleries; and a suite of administrative offices.

- The center is the largest employer of African-American students on campus.

- The center is open seven days a week, for a total of eighty-five hours each week.

- About 15 percent of the programs at the center are sponsored and planned by the Office of Minority Affairs. The rest—on average, 85 percent—are programs done by the rest of the university and/or community.

In a recent seven-month period, 643 events were held by student groups; 259 events were sponsored by Ohio State staff members; 112 events were held by Ohio State faculty members; and community groups used the center for 147 events. It is a busy crossroad for many groups and activities and has been frequently used as a model by other colleges and universities.

Thanks to its origins as a residence hall dining facility, the center is located in the heart of the residence hall area where most new students are housed. It is also on the edge of campus near a heavy concentration of low-rent off-campus housing. Therefore, it is well located for convenient access by the students it is meant to serve. All these factors have promoted a successful operation.

Recognition Programs

Educators have always understood the value of recognition as a means to foster good work. In a university setting, recognition programs provide a way to reinforce the academic values of the institution. Therefore,

OMA makes use of several recognition patterns to encourage and reward high academic achievements. One, perhaps neglected in some institutions, is the honorary degree or similar awards of merit. We make a conscious effort to respond when the annual invitations come from those university committees assigned to identify potential recipients of honorary degrees, Distinguished Service Awards, and the like. Recent successful nominees have included Dr. David Satcher, U.S. Surgeon General from 1998 to 2002; Dr. Bill Cosby, performer, author, and educator; Dr. Walter Massey, President of Morehouse College; and the Reverend Leon H. Sullivan, whose work to promote job training in America's inner cities and education throughout Africa is widely known. Making these awards keeps minority models of excellence in the eye of the general public and of university colleagues. Most important, bringing people of this high level of influence and achievement to campus raises a sense of personal possibility in the minority students who see, or hear from, or meet these exemplars. As noted earlier, Dr. Samuel DuBois Cook meets every summer with Young Scholars when they come to campus, with much the same purpose and result.

The Office of Minority Affairs also conscientiously works to recognize the achievements of minority students, faculty, and staff. In a recent year, for example, two African-American faculty members each received major national awards for scholarly achievement in their respective disciplines of English and Political Science. Their work was celebrated at the annual national conventions of these areas, but it seemed appropriate to spotlight their honors locally as well. Such events offer an opportunity for local administrators to honor high levels of achievement and by so doing encourage others in the long process of scholarly authorship.

Undergraduate students are generally recognized for high academic performance by their individual colleges, but truly outstanding performance over several terms should, we believe, receive special attention from a central university office, such as the Office of Minority Affairs in the Office of Academic Affairs. At the recognition event, speakers are selected to give special encouragement for continued study in graduate or professional schools, and information is distributed about such highly prestigious national awards as the Rhodes, Marshall, and Fulbright Scholarships.

Institutional Research

Finally, we value institutional research and make the attempt to review as objectively as we can the programs and services that we offer. Virtually every organized activity (workshops, campus visitation programs, training and orientation programs, etc.) implemented or sponsored by OMA includes an evaluation component. For our most comprehensive efforts, like the Young Scholars Program, we hire unaffiliated consultants to study and reach independent conclusions about our efforts. We read these carefully and take them to heart as we revise for future events. Where there may be broad interest beyond our own uses, we support staff members who attend conferences to report on their works or we publish our studies in national journals and, more recently, online.[6] We also keep track of the work of other schools who are laboring at the same general tasks.

Experience, evaluations, reading, and organized research all contribute to improving our ship, to keeping it on course, and helping our student-passengers on the way to their personal destinations. Can we report with confidence that we have prepared black and other minority students "for the elite levels of American life" in the same way and to the same degree that Ohio State has prepared its white students? I think a fair response might be that for *some* students of color, we have been successful at this task. However, the process continues, just as the ship is still traveling and still being refurbished. As our minority graduates go into the world and some reach the elite levels we hope for them, it is highly encouraging to see that frequently they return to the ship, that they give us their assistance in the rebuilding of it, and that they mentor and nurture our recent graduates when they set sail on their own.

Notes

1. I am indebted to Philip Richards's article "Prestigious Colleges Ignore the Inadequate Intellectual Achievement of Black Students," *Chronicle of Higher Education* (13 September 2002) for some of the language of this question.
2. An especially interesting account of this period can be found in William Jimmerson Holloway's, "My First 100 Days at The Ohio State University," in *The Odyssey of a North American Educator* (Xlibris Corporation, 2001): pp. 290–301.

3. Dr. Hale recounts the history of the development of this program in Chapter 13 of his autobiography, "The Ohio State University: My War Against Under-representation in the Graduate School," *Angels Watching Over Me* (Nashville: James C. Winston, 1996): pp. 255–278.

4. The *Academic Plan* and the *Diversity Action Plan* can be read at the official Website of Ohio State University, www.osu.edu, along with up-to-date information about progress on these two major efforts.

5. The Minority Advising Program is described more fully and in its original context in the essay on Ohio State University in Diane Weltner Strommer, ed., *Portals of Entry: University Colleges and Undergraduate Divisions* (The Freshman Year Monograph Series, No. 12).

6. For example, here are some of the research studies based on just the Young Scholars Program and published since 1993: S.M. Calhoun, *College Graduates' Perceptions of the Toledo Young Scholars Program: A Best-Case Example Evaluation* (Ph.D. diss., University of Toledo, 2002); Denise Forest and Paula Smith, "Projects," *Mathematics Teachers* 93 (2000): p. 357; Leslie S. Jones, "Opening Doors with Informal Science: Exposure and Access for Our Underserved Students," *Science Education* 81 (1997): pp. 633–48; Alfred Joseph, "Partnership Programs: Is There a Relationship Between Self-Esteem and Academic Performance?" *Social Work in Education* 14 (1992): pp. 185–90; Barbara Newman, "The Transition to High School for Academically Promising, Urban, Low-Income African-American Youth," *Adolescence* 35 (2000): pp. 45–66, and "Experiences of Urban Youth Navigating the Transition to Ninth Grade," *Youth and Society* 310 (2000): pp. 387–416; and Philip R. Newman and Barbara Newman, "What Does it Take to Have a Positive Impact on Minority Students' College Retention?," *Adolescence* 34 (1999): pp. 483–492.

JoAnn Moody

JOANN MOODY began her academic career at age 27 as the first and only European-American female faculty member in the English department of thirty-three European-American male faculty. That eye-opening experience has continued to inform her work. Currently, as a diversity consultant, she specializes in the recruitment, mentorship, and retention of graduate students and faculty (U.S. underrepresented minorities and majority women) at predominantly European-American majority campuses and especially science and engineering academic departments. Small liberal-arts campuses such as Middlebury College as well as large research-oriented campuses such as the University of Wisconsin-Madison, Rensselaer Polytechnic Institute, and Michigan Technological University are counted among her clients. She is also director of the Northeast Consortium for Faculty Diversity.

Dr. Moody is a key leader and a co-founder of the National Compact for Faculty Diversity, which awarded her its Outstanding Support Award in 2001. As the founding director of the Excellence Through Diversity Initiative at the New England Board of Higher Education, where she also served as vice president, she developed the minority-advancement Doctoral Scholars Program, the Science Network co-sponsored by MIT, and the Humanities and Social Science Dissertation Scholars-in-Residence Program.

Her publications are practical in orientation and are used extensively by faculty-development offices, graduate deans, and provosts' offices across the country: examples include *Vital Info for Graduate Students of Color and Demystifying the Profession: Helping Junior Faculty Succeed.* Her most recent book is *Faculty Diversity: Problems and Solutions* (2003). Her book-in-progress is the collection *Minority Graduate Students on Majority Campuses: What Works.* Dr. Moody is a member of Phi Beta Kappa and a graduate of the College of William and Mary, University of Minnesota, and Northeastern University Law School.

11

DEPARTMENTAL GOOD PRACTICES FOR RETAINING MINORITY GRADUATE STUDENTS

Introduction

In academic departments where European-Americans predominate, special steps must be taken internally to ensure that non-majority graduate students feel valued and can thrive. While I would be the first to applaud external academic enrichment and financial support programs for underrepresented minorities, I believe that departmental units themselves should bear the major responsibility for ensuring the retention and graduation of their minority students. What should departments do?

The following Good Practices have evolved from my research, my national consulting work with campuses, and my interactions with several science departments participating in the New England Board of Higher Education's Doctoral Scholars Program that I founded in 1994. The Doctoral Scholars Program is affiliated with the national Compact for Faculty Diversity started in 1994 by the Southern, Western, and New England Boards of Higher Education.

The effectiveness of the departmental Good Practices set forth here has been reinforced by two important studies. In 1999–2000, Claremont Graduate University Professor Daryl Smith and her collaborator Sharon Parker, both are diversity experts, were hired by the Ford Foundation to evaluate the national Compact for Faculty Diversity. Site visits were made to several New England departments included in the Doctoral Scholars Program, departments which in 1996 began the process of adopting or adapting the Good Practices outlined in this essay. Smith and Parker found that these practices had already begun to influence institutional and departmental change and that they were benefiting not only minority but also *majority* graduate students in the departments.

Further, the Good Practices described here were reinforced by a 2001 book by Barbara Lovitts, *Leaving the Ivory Tower, The Causes and Consequences of Departure from Doctoral Study,* and by her preview of the book's findings, "Attrition from Ph.D. Programs—The Hidden Crisis in Graduate Education," in the November–December 2000 *Academe* journal. Studying a total of 816 graduate students (mostly majority students) at both a public, rural research university and a private, urban research university, Lovitts discovered that departments in any academic field where graduate students have high completion rates exhibit behavior and follow protocols very similar to those described in the Good Practices. These *high-completion departments* have a variety of intellectual and social mechanisms that create a welcoming and collaborative climate in the department.

The students in Lovitts' study who leave graduate school do so because they have become demoralized—not because, as some faculty invariably infer, the students can't do the intellectual work. The students' academic weakness is not the culprit but rather a department's hostile or *laissez-faire* approach. This approach causes the student to suffer from lack of attentive faculty advising and lack of departmental community; the student develops "a deep conviction that the department is indifferent to one's fate." Nevertheless, students who leave graduate studies often come to blame *themselves* and suffer a loss of self-esteem. In my experience, such blaming of oneself is especially intense for non-majorities—white women and U.S. underrepresented minorities—who during their lives have probably received a steady stream of belittling signals about their abilities. At the conclusion of her study, Lovitts takes a hopeful view which I share: "Departments with high rates of attrition among graduate students need to look to their own practices for answers and solutions . . . high attrition is not inevitable. The good news is that the system can be fixed" (*Academe,* p. 50). The following Good Practices can fix the system and ensure that minority graduate students thrive in majority departments.

Comprehensive Financial Aid

Throughout their graduate school years, students should be guaranteed a *mixed* financial package, including research and/or teaching assistantships, summer research stipends, and ideally a dissertation-year fellowship—all of which will enable students to be part of the teaching and research enterprises in their departments as well as to complete their degrees in a timely fashion.

According to minority-status reports issued annually by the American Council on Education, U.S. minorities on the whole predictably receive less departmental, faculty, and institutional support and assistantships than all other groups of graduate students. Campuses must rectify this long-term pattern and stop making minority students rely on loans and outside jobs for financing their graduate training. But, at the other extreme, fellowships underwriting the cost of all years of graduate work can also be a disservice because fellowship holders who do not become engaged in the teaching life of the department can easily become marginalized from other students and faculty, and consequently drop out. Lovitts found this pattern in her study, and informal evaluations of national fellowship programs likewise suggest high attrition. In short, majority and especially minority graduate students need to be included in the mainstream activities of the department and take pride in their contributions as research, lab, and teaching assistants because, as we all know, teaching a subject deepens our intellectual grasp of it. Nevertheless, graduate students also deserve summer research grants and dissertation-year stipends that enable them to devote uninterrupted time to the completion of important academic tasks.

Orientations

Before graduate work begins, the graduate department should hold one orientation session for all new graduate students. It is amazing that this common courtesy toward newcomers is not uniformly observed. Two additional departmental orientations in September and October, led by advanced graduate students and faculty, should focus concretely on degree timetables, requirements, and especially departmental idiosyncrasies and do's and don'ts. These orientations should also help beginning students understand how graduate work in the department may compare and contrast with their undergraduate studies.

Being at a research university is an exciting and yet predictably bewildering experience for students from liberal arts and other smaller campuses where faculty–student interaction may differ greatly from that found at most research universities. This may be true especially for graduates of small, historically minority colleges who received personal attention and nurturing from faculty and staff during their undergraduate years. Unless these students are clued in to the more impersonal approach in graduate work, they may falter and waste valuable energy trying to decipher what they are doing or not doing to elicit the chillier climate of their new academic setting.

Transitional Mentor from Day One

At the very beginning of the academic year, the department should assign to each new graduate student **a transitional and welcoming faculty advisor** who will meet with the new student at least every two weeks during the first year. This is particularly important for first-year *minority* students who will probably have to expend extra psychological energy as they adjust and make their way in a predominantly majority setting. The advisor's job is to attentively monitor the student's progress and problems. Because drop-outs from graduate school often occur, in my experience, during the first term of the first year, it is essential to be up-to-date on each advisee's psychological and academic adjustment and to intervene when necessary.

Study Groups and Peer Mentors

The department should ensure that students are forming study groups in order to improve their learning outcomes. The department chair and senior faculty, at the early fall orientation sessions, should make clear that all students are expected to aggregate themselves into study groups and that no one should be excluded. Such exclusion based on race has been experienced by several doctoral scholars I have coached. If faculty in the department forcefully express the expectation that study groups and peer-assisted learning will take place, they will.

In addition, each beginning graduate student will benefit from the coaching of an advanced graduate student assigned to him/her. Again, the department should organize this big brother/big sister mechanism because the hope that this arrangement will evolve serendipitously is insufficient. Every entering student, majority and minority, deserves this supportive intervention.

Lab Rotations or Research Seminars for First-year Graduate Students

To visualize the research work expected of them in graduate school, beginning students should spend a month or so working in one and then another departmental lab; doing so allows students to gain an in-depth introduction to various faculty and their research and mentoring styles, the size and composition of their labs, and the intellectual questions they are pursuing. Minority Doctoral Scholars I worked with at the University of Connecticut's Molecular and Cell Biology Department reported that their first-year lab rotations helped them decide which faculty lab most interested them. Their friends at other campuses were envious of how knowledgeable they had become about their department and key faculty researchers in such a short time.

For non-lab disciplines, in areas such as humanities and mathematics, departments can provide several seminars for all beginning students where several faculty and their advanced graduate students talk in depth about their intellectual projects which function as a helpful show and tell. The purpose is to acquaint newcomers with the research enterprise in graduate school and, more specifically, to give them information they can use later in choosing a faculty supervisor, dissertation committee, and dissertation topic. In their studies of first-year graduate students, SUNY-Stony Brook Psychology Professor Robert Boice and his doctoral student Peg Boyle Single (now Associate Research Professor of Education at the University of Vermont) found that exemplary departments not only routinely organized such research seminars but also engaged students in research work with faculty during the summer following the first year of graduate work (Boyle and Boice). Pity the advanced student who has not undertaken, prior to the dissertation year, substantial independent study or gained some research experience. Advanced students who have finished their graduate coursework and passed their comprehensive exams can be bewildered and demoralized because of their lack of preparation for this last stage of independent research and dissertation writing. While lab science departments would not have this problem because their students quickly become part of labs and scholarly enterprises, non-lab departments often do and should move to prevent this problematic shift to independent work for advanced students.

Reasonable Comprehensive Exams

Graduate departments should construct comprehensive exams that fairly test students' mastery of skills and subject matter. There should be no mystery for students regarding how and what to study. Unfortunately, some departments still use archaic, rigid, overwhelming exams which are designed to weed out incompetent students. What actually needs weeding out are exams that prevent students with different learning styles from demonstrating, in a variety of oral and written ways, what they know. In my work with New England's Doctoral Scholars Program, the advisors and I decided to drop one department from our core group because it persisted in requiring students to pass an archaic exam that other departments at other campuses found ridiculously broad. Such an exam seemed deliberately designed to demoralize and thin the ranks of their graduate students. Students typically failed several times; this series of failures occurred after they had devoted several years not only to completing their coursework but also to teaching introductory "service" courses to undergraduates (at very low pay) for the department. Such an approach is unconscionably wasteful of human talent. Given that students from certain minority groups are already severely underrepresented in science, math, and engineering fields, such departments' weeding out process is doubly shameful.

Frequent Tutorial Sessions

Advanced graduate students, hired by the department, can offer regularly scheduled tutorial sessions to benefit all those preparing for their qualifying or comprehensive exams. Departments should avoid playing, or giving the impression that they are playing, the "gotcha" game—a game that involves tripping up unsuspecting students in high-stakes exams. Further, departments should reward advanced graduate students who serve as tutors to beginning students. A departmental bulletin board could announce the specialties of advanced students, their availability, and where they can be reached.

A Cluster of U.S. Minority Graduate Students

A graduate department should work to ensure that it has enrolled a cluster of at least four to six U.S. minority graduate students. Such a cluster will provide the peer support that underrepresented students need in a majority setting where, at times, they are likely to feel psychologically isolated. Being a "solo" and "pioneer" can be a draining experience, as I have frequently observed during my coaching of minority students and faculty in majority settings. Moreover, in my work I have discovered that the adjustment of departmental faculty members to having U.S. minority students is facilitated when there are several, not merely one, in their midst.

A creative way to guarantee such clustering is to "block-enroll" in a graduate department several minority students sent from the same undergraduate department. This strategy has been used successfully by the clinical psychology department at the University of California-Irvine. According to Irvine Emeritus Professor Joseph White, bridges were built to eight graduate departments around the country that were receptive to Irvine students. Each year, a handful of Irvine minority students are enrolled in the same doctoral department, thus providing a community for the new students as well as peer mentoring from more advanced Irvine graduate students already established in the department (Foxhall, p. 62). Similarly, an innovative program for undergraduates called "Posse" enables participating colleges and universities to block-enroll ten students every year, most of whom are minorities, who have completed Posse's training in leadership development and study skills while they were in high school. Posse students enjoy a close-knit community with one another and habitually reach out to include other students on campus in their Posse-sponsored retreats and events (see www.possefoundation.org for more information).

Frequent Get-togethers for All Faculty and Students

Following the suicides of several chemistry graduate students, Harvard is addressing students' psychological overload and alienation. One of the chemistry department's first steps was to sponsor a weekly catered get-together for faculty and students, which has been a resounding success in improving the departmental climate (English, *Boston Globe,* 2001). It is heartening to note that departmental buildings now under construction at Harvard and around the country typically include several large and small areas where faculty and students can congregate, eat, and socialize. Other activities, such as departmental pizza parties, softball games, teas, and informal Friday afternoon research seminars help students feel they belong in the department.

A Central Location or Group Offices for Graduate Students

My own work with departments, together with studies by Boice, Single, and Lovitt, demonstrate the value of "gang offices" where each large office is shared by up to a dozen graduate students. These communal rooms provide places for students to congregate, build intellectual and personal friendships with one another, and share tips about courses and professors. Often those friendships begin, of course, with "griping sessions" about how much work the department or a certain professor expects. Students holding Ford, National Science Foundation, and other pre-doctoral fellowships should be advised that building a community with other graduate students and faculty is essential for their success. Because fellowship recipients will probably not be teaching undergraduates and sharing success and failure stories with others who are Teaching Assistants, they can become isolated very quickly. The department chair should be alert to this danger and move to include fellowship holders in the life of the department. Sharing a group office is one means to this end.

A Faculty Mentor, Coached in Cross-Cultural Mentoring Skills, for Each Graduate Student

Departments must guarantee that by the conclusion of the first year of graduate studies, each student has at least one faculty mentor in the department and that their trusting and candid mentoring relationship is helping the student move closer to becoming an intellectual equal and colleague. Mentoring, for the record, involves the senior colleague in an organization providing to a junior colleague psycho-social support as well as instrumental assistance in career-advancement, such as the mentor's co-authoring articles with the mentee, nominating the mentee for awards, and co-leading a session at a professional society meeting with the mentee. By contrast, an advisor merely gives advice, information, and perhaps monitoring for the short term.

The national Council of Graduate Schools underscores that mentoring is usually the most important factor in graduate students' success. National studies (by Turner and Thompson and a dozen others) have confirmed that effective cross-cultural mentoring is essential for underrepresented minority and women graduate students. Without sponsorship, these non-majority students are being set up for failure. But to guarantee a confident and competent cross-cultural mentor for each non-majority student will require deliberate steps by the department. Why?

First, newcomers most likely to find the only people who receive spontaneous mentoring and inside information are white males already accepted in the old-boy network. Those *least* likely to find such support are minorities and women in departments predominantly European-American and male in composition (Blackwell; Willie, Garibaldi and Reed; Turner and Thompson; Turner and Myers; Single and Boyle). For this reason, the chair and others must intervene to make sure that non-majority students receive mentorship. Secondly, many majority faculty are standoffish and hesitant to interact with U.S. non-majority students; their trepidation is expressed in some version of "I don't have the social skills and fear that I will make matters worse." Overcoming this barrier requires *formal training* so that faculty become comfortable and accomplished in mentoring women and minority students. At the end of this paper, I sketch one fundamental component of the cross-cultural workshops that I organize for departmental faculty and mentors-in-training.

Catching Up for Students—Caveats

If the department or faculty advisor or mentor believes a graduate student should retake an undergraduate course or secure tutoring in order to fill in gaps, then it is important to frame this catching up to the student very carefully. Stanford Professor Claude Steele recommends saying a version of the following: "You may be somewhat behind at this time but you're a talented person. We're going to help you advance at an accelerated rate" or "I (or the department) have high standards. Your work is not yet meeting those but I certainly believe you can meet them" (Steele). This language is especially important for U.S. minorities; the point is to *avoid humiliating* a student who has probably had to deal with belittling racial/ethnic stereotypes on a steady basis if he/she has grown up in the United States.

At Rice University, Professor Richard Tapia in his exemplary applied math program scrupulously avoids such humiliation even though women and minorities working with him often must spend, on average, two years longer than white males in earning their doctorates. Boasting an exceptionally high retention and graduation rate for women and minorities who enter the program with *average* credentials, Tapia's program has garnered numerous awards.

Attendance at Professional Conferences with the Mentor

Beginning early in graduate studies, the student who attends professional meetings can be socialized to the discipline, come to understand the latest intellectual developments and arguments, become acquainted with the movers and shakers in the field, and grow in confidence in the mentor–mentee relationship. While science graduate students typically do accompany their mentors to these conferences and gain practice in presenting poster sessions and talks, this is—sadly—not the case for many humanities and social science students. Departments in these areas must be more scrupulous in the professional development of their doctoral scholars.

Manageable Tutoring and Teaching Assignments

Graduate students need practice in teaching, making presentations of various kinds, assessing undergraduate students' learning outcomes, leading discussions and lab sections, grading papers and assignments, and developing courses. But the national Council of Graduate Schools sensibly urges graduate departments to *calibrate* the responsibilities assumed by their Teaching and Lab Assistants: first, begin with tutoring of undergraduates; followed by a reduced-load TA assignment or lab section; and finally, full responsibility for an undergraduate course or lab section.

Careful Supervision of Teaching Assignments

Teaching assistants, tutors, and lab assistants deserve continuous supervision and coaching by senior faculty and more advanced graduate students. Without this constructive attention, graduate students can feel enormous anxiety at dealing all alone with undergraduates, and their bad teaching habits can calcify.

Faculty Guidance and Departmental Workshops on Job Options and the Job Search

The department chair, faculty mentors, and other senior faculty should frequently review with graduate students the various career paths they are and could be considering and find out what questions and misperceptions they may have about various corporate, academic, and governmental post-doctoral appointments and first jobs. It would be wise to invite outside experts to help the department address these questions and misperceptions.

Occasional departmental workshops can give students the chance to do dress-rehearsal practices of job interviews, to receive tips for sprucing up their resumes, and to gain pointers not only on getting their scholarship funded and published but also on handling rejections from funding agencies and publishers. When initiating the job search, advanced graduate students should be coached on how to use to maximum advantage their mentors' and other colleagues' contacts and allies throughout the nation and world.

Cross-Cultural Workshops for Departmental Faculty and Mentors

The above Good Practices are essential, yet I have learned from my consulting and program work that *fundamental and often unspoken* concerns must also be addressed: While majority faculty may possess the will to be encouraging mentors and colleagues to their non-majority graduate students, they hesitate to do so because they feel cross-culturally incompetent or at least awkward. Such awkwardness and hesitancy, I suggest, are prompted by unexamined cognitive schema and stereotypes that probably all or most of us tend to employ in an attempt to reduce the complexity around us. Practice in recognizing these schema and then developing strategies for rising above them are the purposes of the highly interactive cross-cultural workshops I organize for faculty and administrators (as briefly noted above). Additional nuts-and-bolts sessions are provided to mentors-in-training.

Although space does not permit my delineating the structure and leadership of these cross-cultural workshops beyond noting my use of mini case studies, I do want to highlight three schema that are central in these sessions. Because, for centuries, U.S. society and various media have promoted the use of these *three schema or cognitive shortcuts* for sorting people into superior and inferior groups, they are deeply ingrained in almost all of us, myself included.

Racial/Ethnic Schema. Laura Rendon, Professor of Higher Education at Arizona State University who is Mexican-American in background, eloquently describes the belittling that she and other U.S. under-represented minority students have had to deal with as they pursue their ambitions. Messages are sent "loud and clear (from higher education institutions) that only white men can do science and math, that only the best and the brightest deserve to be educated." European-American students are thought to be "inherently smarter than nonwhites," and, in fact, "allowing people of color to enter a college diminishes its academic quality" ("From the Barrio to the Academy," p. 61). Unfortunately, these negative signals endure.

At the Massachusetts Institute of Technology, African-American students and faculty struggle against the ubiquitous stereotype that they cannot excel in math, science, and engineering. In his publication, *Technology and the Dream: Reflections of the Black Experience at MIT, 1941–1999,* MIT Professor Clarence Williams (a contributor to this book) presents more than seventy-five oral history interviews with former and current majority and minority professors, students, administrators, and staff. In his superb introduction, Williams pinpoints how negative stereotypes about African-Americans hamper their fair evaluation and steady advancement on a daily basis. His sad observation: "Ongoing distrust and suspicion about blacks as potential intellectual leaders in science and engineering fields" are alive and well (p. 45). Cornell University Professor Eloy Rodriguez agrees that women and minority students and faculty still face a formidable struggle due to exclusionary schema and business-as-usual procedures that he has seen in operation at various campuses in the country (quoted in Moody, p. 33).

By contrast, European-American men, making up the majority of faculty and graduate students in U.S. colleges and universities, bask in the presumption that they are intellectually qualified and deserve positions of power. Professor Ron Howard, of European-American ancestry, counts the ways that he and his colleagues benefit: Majority males enjoy "having our voices heard, of not having to explain or defend our legitimate citizenship or identity, of seeing our images projected in a positive light, of remaining insulated from other people's realities, of being represented in positions of power, and of being able to tell our own stories" (Howard, p. 62; also see McIntosh; Hu-DeHart). Such privileges are taken for granted by those who hold them; those who do *not* possess such political, legal, intellectual, and social legitimacy have to continually reestablish their voices, stories, citizenship, and rights to be included and heard. Princeton History Professor Nell Painter observes that whereas women and minorities have to constantly "prove that they're not dumb," white men enjoy the assumption that they are automatically well-qualified. She points out that the expression "well-qualified white man" is simply not in our lexicon (pp. 6–7).

Gender Schema. Even when *majority* women attempt to enter certain educational, workplace, and policy arenas, they are viewed by many as innately less competent than men. In her book, *Why So Slow? The Advancement of Women,* Hunter College Psychology Professor Virginia Valian discusses the conventional gender schema that encourage men—because they are assumed to be innately aggressive, rational, and independent—to become professionals, managers, academic deans, and chief executive officers. By contrast, women are discouraged from such posts because they are assumed to be innately passive, emotional, and dependent.

These gender schema lead academic and corporate power-holders to underrate the intellectual performance and promise of women while overrating that of men. Examples abound. At MIT, tenured women faculty in science have documented how their lab spaces, salaries, and institutional resources have been invariably less than those of their male colleagues; and how only men have ever served as chairs or deans in the sciences despite the women's receipt of distinguished national and international awards and membership in the prestigious American Academy of Science. "The heart of the problem," the women have analyzed in a faculty newsletter, "is that equal talent and accomplishment are viewed as unequal when seen through the eyes of prejudice." They add that while male colleagues carefully avoid overt and ugly expressions of prejudice, some of them nevertheless make decisions and evaluations informed by subtle but pernicious prejudice. MIT's president and several faculty committees are taking campus-wide, long-term steps to eradicate this prejudice (MIT Faculty Newsletter, March 1999). Studies are revealing that external federal agencies and their peer-review committees typically require a greater number of publications from women applicants for research funding than from men applicants (Wenneras and Wold; Glazer-Raymo).

Immigrant versus Non-Immigrant Schema. Repeatedly in my consulting and program work, I notice that some majority faculty assume that immigrant minority students and faculty who have voluntarily chosen to locate in the United States are more intellectually promising than non-immigrant U.S. minorities whose families have lived in this country and its territory for generations—namely Mexican-Americans from the Southwest, Puerto Ricans, Native Hawaiians, American and Alaskan Indians, and African-Americans. Why is this? A number of distinguished anthropologists, psychologists, philosophers, novelists, political scientists, and economists have documented and dramatized this pattern: People whose ancestors have been incorporated into the United States (or any other country) against their will—through slavery, conquest, colonization, or forced labor—are typically viewed as *inferior* by many in the conquering, dominant group.

Generation after generation, the conquered and stigmatized groups are kept at the edges of the mainstream society and predictably encounter the highest obstacles to economic, educational, and political advancement. By contrast, immigrants to this country from China, Europe, Africa, South and Central America, the Caribbean, India, Japan, and Korea, who may face enormous challenges when they arrive in their new homeland, enjoy *higher* status and more opportunities than do domestic minorities whose origins are based on force, not choice (see, for example, Steele, Martinez, Ogbu, Morrison, Lee, Gibson, Shorris, Hochschild). Immigrants come voluntarily, with "extravagant dreams" (in UCA-Berkeley Professor Ron Takaki's phrase), and most believe that they and their children are entitled to and can indeed secure upward social mobility in accordance with the inspiring political rhetoric of the American democracy.

Thus, it is important for departmental faculty to understand and rise above the unspoken, *positive* assumptions they may be making about international (immigrant) graduate students and concomitantly the unspoken, *negative* assumptions they may be making about domestic minority students. Moreover in this country, certain domestic minority groups have to struggle against a stigmatized, caste-like status that holds that they are inferior. Because this often daily struggle by students requires enormous energy and resolve, departmental faculty and mentors should recognize this fact and help shore up their defenses. Applied Mathematics Professor Christopher Jones (formerly at Brown University and now at the University of North Carolina-Chapel Hill) explains: "I see a critical part of my role as mentor being to persistently bolster the confidence of mentees. This is particularly important in mentoring women and minorities as I have been struck by how often and to what extent they underestimate their intellectual abilities" (personal correspondence). There are, of course, understandable reasons for this underestimation.

Conclusion

For majority and especially minority graduate students to thrive, academic departments should adopt and adapt these Good Practices. While some of these practices and protocols may already be operative, those not in practice deserve consideration and implementation. Essential are interventions such as interactive workshops and follow-up coaching for departmental faculty and mentors-in-training. Without interventions, many majority faculty will continue to use ingrained schema and will hesitate to reach out to certain students with backgrounds different from their own. With assistance, majority faculty can grow in confidence and competence as they participate in cross-cultural and cross-gender interactions. As a result, both the faculty and the students in a department will be the richer, particularly the women and U.S. domestic students of African-American, Puerto Rican, Mexican-American, Native Hawaiian, Native Alaskan, and American Indian heritages.

References

Blackwell, J. 1991. "Graduate and professional education for blacks." C. Willie, A. Garibaldi, and W. Reed (Eds.), *The Education of African-Americans* (pp. 103–109). Boston: Trotter Institute, University of Massachusetts-Boston.

Boyle, P., and B. Boice. 1998. "Best practices for enculturation: Collegiality, mentoring, and structure." M. Anderson, ed., *The Experience of Being in Graduate School: An Exploration* (pp. 87–94). No. 101, Spring 1998. San Francisco: Jossey-Bass.

English, B. 2001. "Grad-student suicides spur big changes at Harvard chem labs." *Boston Globe* (1/2/01): pp. 18–20.

Foxhall, K. 2001. "Mentoring giant [UC-Irvine Professor Emeritus Joseph White] almost didn't find his own way." *Monitor on Psychology:* pp. 60–62.

Gibson, M. 1991. "Minorities and schooling: Some implications." J. Ogbu and M. Gibson, eds., *Minority Status and Schooling: A Comparative Study of Immigrant and Involuntary Minorities* (pp. 357–382). New York: Garland.

Glazer-Raymo, J. 1999. *Shattering the Myths: Women in Academe.* Baltimore: Johns Hopkins Press.

Hochschild, J. 1995. *Facing up to the American Dream: Race, Class, and the Soul of the Nation.* Princeton, NJ: Princeton University Press.

Howard, G. 1999. *We Can't Teach What We Don't Know.* New York: Teachers College Press, Columbia University.

Hu-DeHart, E. 2000. "Office politics and departmental culture." M. Garcia, ed., *Succeeding in an Academic Career: A Guide for Faculty of Color* (pp. 27–38). Westport, CN: Greenwood Press.

Lee, Y. 1991. "Koreans in Japan and the United States." J. Ogbu & M. Gibson, eds., *Minority Status and Schooling: A Comparative Study of Immigrant and Involuntary Minorities* (pp. 131–168). New York: Garland.

Lovitts, B. and C. Nelson. 2000. "Attrition from Ph.D. programs: The hidden crisis in graduate education." *Academe* (Nov–Dec. 2002): pp. 44–50.

Lovitts, B. 2001. *Leaving the Ivory Tower: The Causes and Consequences of Departure from Doctoral Study.* Lanham, Md.: Rowman and Littlefield.

Martinez, O. 2001. *Mexican-origin People in the United States.* Tucson: University of Arizona Press.

McIntosh, P. 1989. "White privilege: Unpacking the invisible knapsack." *Peace and Freedom* (July/August 1989): pp. 10–14.

MIT Faculty Newsletter (March 1999) web.mit.edu/fnl/women/women.html.

Moody, J. 2000. "Tenure and diversity: Some different voices." *Academe* (May–June 2000): pp. 30–33.

Morrison, T. 1992. *Playing in the Dark: Whiteness and the Literary Imagination.* New York: Random House.

Nell Painter. "Making it as a woman of color in the academy." *Diversity Digest* (Fall 1997): pp. 6–7. Washington, D.C.: Association of American Colleges & Universities.

Ogbu, J. 1978. *Minority Education and Caste: The American System in Cross-Cultural Perspective.* New York: Academic Press.

Rendon, L. 1992. "From the Barrio to the Academy: Revelations of a Mexican-American 'Scholarship Girl.' " S. Zwerling and H. London, eds., *First-generation students: Confronting the Cultural Issues* (pp. 55–64). No. 80 (Winter 1992). San Francisco: Jossey-Bass.

Shorris, E. 1992. *Latinos, A Biography of the People.* New York: Norton.

Steele, C. "Race and the schooling of black Americans." *Atlantic Monthly*, 269 (April): pp. 68–75.

Steele, C. and J. Aronson. 1995. "Stereotype threat and the intellectual test performance of African-Americans." *Journal of Personality and Social Psychology*, Vol. 69, No. 5: pp. 797–811.

Takaki, R. 1993. *A Different Mirror: A History of Multicultural America*. Boston: Little, Brown.

Takaki, R. 1989. *Strangers from a Different Shore, a History of Asian-Americans*. Boston: Little, Brown.

Turner, C., and J. Thompson. 1993. "Socializing Women Doctoral Students: Minority and Majority Experiences." *The Review of Higher Education* (Spring 1993) Vol. 16, No. 3: pp. 355–70.

Turner, C., and S. Myers, Jr. 2000. *Bittersweet Success: Faculty of Color in Academe*. Needham Heights, Mass.: Allyn & Bacon.

Valian, V. 1998. *Why So Slow? The Advancement of Women*. Cambridge: MIT Press.

Wenneras, C., and A. Wold. 2000. "A chair of one's own: The upper reaches of academe remain stubbornly inaccessible to women." *Nature*, Vol. 408 (December 2000): p. 647.

Williams, C. 2001. *Technology and the Dream: Reflections on the Black Experience at MIT, 1941–1999*. Cambridge: MIT Press.

Willie, C., A. Garibaldi, and W. Reed, eds. 1991. *The Education of African-Americans*. Boston: Trotter Institute, University of Massachusetts–Boston.

Myra Gordon

MYRA GORDON has recently joined the administration of Kansas State University and brings with her a twenty-seven-year track record in successfully addressing issues of diversity and the needs of people of color in mental health, career development, and higher education. In her previous position at Virginia Polytechnic Institute and State University, Dr. Gordon proved to be a powerful agent in promoting diversity and creating institutional change, including designing and implementing a college-wide diversity planning process, and initiating and completing a three-year pilot project on revised faculty search procedures in the College of Arts and Sciences which averaged 66 percent diverse tenure-track hires.

Dr. Gordon's activities in international education have focused on building partnerships in higher education between American and West African universities to facilitate collaborative research, faculty exchange, curricular enhancement, technology transfer, distance learning, student study abroad programs, and the development of African female faculty.

Dr. Gordon is a child of the segregated south and graduated valedictorian of her high school class. She was among the first black students to integrate Cornell University. After graduating, she served as Program Coordinator for the Committee on the Status of Minorities for the Board of Trustees at Cornell University, where she designed and implemented a research methodology to statistically evaluate the status of minorities on campus. Dr. Gordon then went on to complete an M.S. and Ph.D. in psychology at the State University of New York at Buffalo. Following graduate school, Dr. Gordon served as Executive Director of the Niagara Community Action Program, Inc. in Niagara Falls, New York; as supervisor of the Mental Health Component of the Erie County Head Start Program in Buffalo, New York; and, in higher education, as a Coordinator of Clinical Services (1985–93), a Director of University Counseling Services (1993–96), and as Assistant Vice President for Student Affairs (1996–98).

12

DIVERSIFICATION
OF THE FACULTY

FRANK TALK FROM THE FRONT LINE
ABOUT WHAT WORKS

The literature on diversity is replete with references to the need for diverse faculty, and many books and articles provide guidance on the matter (e.g. Aguirre, 2000; Knowles and Harleston, 1987; Opp and Smith, 1994; Phillips, 2002; Stein and Trachtenberg, 1999). However, despite small recent gains, this has been the least successful aspect of campus diversification. Most campuses have elaborate mission statements about valuing diversity, a full complement of multicultural student organizations, an office of minority affairs, legions of multicultural events and speakers, TRIO programs, scholarships, and recruitment initiatives; yet when it comes to faculty demographics, improvements have been painfully slow (Harvey, 2002).

Why is this the case? Most answers center around pipeline issues and bidding wars (Atkinson, 1989; Norrell and Gill, 1991; Shuster, 1992). In the first instance, the belief is that there just aren't any minority Ph.D.s available; and in the second instance, the belief is that for the few minority Ph.D.s that do exist, there is so much competition to hire them that one must be prepared to pay astronomical salaries. As is the case with most beliefs, this thinking contains kernels of truth, but it also contains considerable myths. That is, no one can deny that there are supply and demand dynamics in the labor pools from which we are attempting to recruit diverse candidates. However, the work of Daryl Smith and her colleagues (1996) has shown that the majority of minority doctoral recipients of prestigious scholarships and fellowships are neither highly sought after nor exorbitantly paid. It is easy for people to say we would hire them if we could find them or if we had enough money but I, like others, question whether these are the main problems underlying the failure to diversify faculty (Cross, 1994; Washington and Harvey, 1989).

The real reason for a general failure to diversify lies in the culture and practices typically associated with faculty hiring. For the most part, the faculty search and selection process is one of the most privileged activities that occur on a predominately white university campus and, in this arena, the faculty rule supreme. They have been given, they expect, and they even demand the sole right to select their colleagues. As they do so, their allegiances usually are only to their disciplines and to their professional organizations, with little, if any, attention paid to the additional considerations which increasingly affect the life of the academy. Faculty live in their own world with little understanding of themselves or those of the real world. On surveys, they say of themselves that they are egalitarian and color-blind, but in truth, many of them harbor unconscious stereotypes and prejudices; they so fear that academic excellence will suffer because of diversity that they cannot possibly be fair when left to their own designs. Historically, this combination of privilege and bias, whether conscious or unconscious, has always spelled disadvantage for women and minorities.

Another problem with the typical faculty search process on predominately white campuses is that it appears to be public on the face of things but, in truth, it is very closed and private in its essence. Despite sunshine laws and admonitions to be transparent, usually no one knows what goes on in the search committee. This is not so much a matter of confidentiality but rather a matter of privilege, which makes this "our business." Affirmative action offices attempt to monitor the various phases of searches to ensure equal opportunity, but such offices are seldom close enough to the action to be able to make a real difference. Most of the time, affirmative action offices suffer from too few personnel and too many complaints requiring investigation and resolution. Any one smart enough to get a Ph.D. can figure out in a heartbeat what one must do in most cases to get signatures from the office of affirmative action and still not produce diverse hiring outcomes. So the culture and practices associated with faculty searches continue largely unchanged and, not too surprisingly, they yield hiring outcomes that are largely the same.

For four years I worked directly on faculty diversification in one very large college of an elite research institution in the south. In the departments of this college were some of the most brilliant people in the world and those who aspired to be. Also in these departments were people who were very enlightened about diversity issues, those who were educable, and those who could care less. Like most colleges, we were entering a period of unprecedented hiring due to faculty retirements (Bowen and Shuster, 1986; Bowen and Sosa, 1989; El-Khawas, et al., 1990; Tack and Patitu, 1992). The desire of this college's cultural diversity committee and its dean was to devise an approach to faculty hiring that would capitalize on these hiring opportunities to add more women and minorities to the faculty. Working alongside me on the front-line were two amazing culturally competent associate and assistant deans. Moreover, the work was supported by personnel in the affirmative action office, an associate provost, and the vice president for multicultural affairs. The remainder of this report will discuss the outcomes of this effort and what worked.

The first year of this endeavor was spent laying the foundation for what would become a pilot project on revised faculty-search procedures. During that year, I identified and reviewed every piece of institutional data on diversity issues, such as university climate as viewed from different perspectives, search committee composition, and baseline hiring outcomes. I also observed the way faculty searches were being run; reviewed the existing hiring policies, procedures, and paperwork; reviewed the literature on the recruitment of diverse faculty; identified best practices; compared the best practices with existing practices to identify deviations; rewrote the procedures; revised the paperwork; created the concept of hiring as a partnership rather than a privilege; designed and implemented a retreat for department heads to introduce this concept; wrote a charging script for search committees; and, toward the end, began intervening in some very problematic searches. For the next three years, I led the implementation of the pilot project to see whether the culture and practices of faculty hiring could be changed and, if these practices were changed, whether hiring outcomes also would change. We gave ourselves five years to produce measurable results.

Well, the answer to both questions was a resounding, "yes." To our utter astonishment, measurable results occurred in the very first year of implementation. The practices associated with faculty hiring could most definitely be changed and hiring outcomes did become more diverse . . . not just a little more diverse, but *significantly* more diverse. In the baseline year, the percentage of women and minorities hired was 35 percent. It rose to 48 percent during the year of scrutiny, study, and limited intervention. During the first full year of implementing the pilot, the percentage rose to 62 percent, was 57 percent the second year, and 90 percent in the third year. The writer ended the pilot after the third year and the institution was then left to contemplate what it was going to do about university-wide implementation.

So what worked?

Having Committed, Involved, and Savvy Leadership at the Dean's Level Works

The literature tends to discuss the importance of presidential leadership, but my experience indicates that committed, involved, and savvy leadership at the dean's level is critical. In this case, the dean, a white male, was committed to equal opportunity and was willing to admit that opportunity had not been equal. Just as important, he was willing to make changes and take risks. Upon the recommendation of the college diversity committee, he created an associate deanship to lead efforts related to diversification in the college. After I was hired for the position, he allowed me to work directly on the faculty-search process and he empowered me with signature authority. But he did not leave me on the front-line alone. He helped educate faculty and broaden their views by consistently articulating a vision for and describing the value of diversity for the faculty, the department, the college, the university, the state, and the nation. During the first year of implementing the pilot, this very overworked dean went to and charged every one of twenty-six search committees. He expressed his expectations and answered all search committee questions. Throughout the hiring cycle, he kept abreast of what was going on.

Savvy is an intangible aspect of the dean's role in the hiring process, but it is invaluable when it is there. It is in the way the dean negotiates, explains, rewards, persuades, backs off, sets limits, thinks creatively, compromises, and, if necessary, defers searches until there is greater agreement on the processes and expected outcomes. Savvy is an art, the art of knowing what to do, how to do it, and when to do it. Savvy presumes an understanding of people and is predicated on doing the right, if not always the popular thing. This combination of commitment, involvement, and savvy made this dean an exceptionally effective and visionary leader. To be sure, American higher education is blessed with many, many great academic leaders at the dean's level but unfortunately, most of them lack vision and skills when it comes to leadership for diversity (Ramirez, 1996). So many of them are still faculty members at their cores and thus, cannot think outside of that box on these matters. Yet, without them, I am convinced little progress can be made because, as the reader will see, they play pivotal roles, not only at the beginning of searches but all throughout and at the end.

Introducing Accountability Works

For the most part, there is little to no accountability associated with faculty hiring on the dimension of diversity. What exists is exercised by affirmative action offices whose ability to affect change has either been eliminated completely or eroded into impotence by negative campus climates, fear of litigation, and successful attacks on affirmative action elsewhere. In addition, affirmative action offices are not always headed by people who are willing to use every legal means necessary to bring about diversity, but rather those who are timid, conservative, or incompetent and who, over time, end up engendering feelings of no-confidence or marginalization in the very constituencies their offices were created to serve (Aguirre, 2000).

What worked for us was introducing accountability into every phase of the hiring process. A Faculty Search Activity Record (FSAR) was created by the assistant dean on the team which required review and approval for (1) the composition and leadership of the search committee; (2) the wording of the position announcement and the advertisement; (3) the recruiting and advertising plan; (4) the screening and evaluation of applicants; and (5) the short list of candidates to be invited to campus. Where approval in the past had been proforma, given hastily due to the "urgency" of every search, there was now real accountability. To create this accountability meant labor- and time-intensive work for all involved, but it ensured that all phases of the process were inclusive, well-justified, and completely documented.

In our process, there was a Dean's Office Review Team led by the writer, an African-American female, in her capacity as associate dean for diversity. The two other members of the team were the associate dean for finance, a white male, and the assistant dean for administration, a white female. Each of us reviewed every aspect of every FSAR; we agreed on our evaluations or discussed them until we did; we requested changes as needed; and then, I signed off. Having a diverse review team guarded against bias at the level of the dean's office. Having real accountability at the level of the dean's office made the work of the affirmative action office easy.

Admittedly, this level of accountability slowed down the faculty search process, much to the dismay of some departments. While we attempted to turn around paperwork in one to three days, the departure from the practice of rushing in, interrupt whatever was going on to get the perfunctory signature, and then running out the door was often perceived, especially in the first year, as a delay that would cause the best candidates to get away. In addition, even people who then knew exactly what was required would not comply by submitting their paperwork and then would become upset when the paperwork was returned without a signature and needing changes. Holding the line on accountability eventually taught people to do their work correctly and thoroughly so that paperwork could speed through in the minimum amount of time.

Thoughtfully Structuring Search Committees Works

In general, too little attention is paid to who leads and comprises the search committee. In most cases, search committees are composed largely of senior faculty so junior faculty have more time to invest in teaching and research. While this is a laudable motive, the lack of junior faculty on search committees eliminates voices at the table which may be more sensitive to diversity issues because of the recency of their education. In addition, it is junior faculty who will work the longest with new hires, and thus they have the greatest vested interest in who is hired.

Since rank and race/ethnicity are negatively correlated, the typical search committee composed of senior faculty means the search committee is most likely composed of white males with, perhaps, a female or person of color added for purposes of representation. While tokenism is better than nothing, it is extremely difficult for a lone woman or person of color to advance a different perspective in a group that is overwhelmingly male and white. We know from the communication studies literature that the comments of women and minorities are often devalued unless they are repeated by a white male, in which case they will command attention. So while the token person can have an effect, most often they will not. They will not be heard and, if theirs is a dissenting view, they will be out-voted. Hence, their presence configured this way is often ineffective in terms of search committee deliberations, but useful in passing muster with affirmative action officers who look for female and minority representation on the search committee.

What works is a search committee that is diverse with respect to rank, gender, and race/ethnicity. It is difficult to give a formula, as one size cannot fit all, but a useful rule of thumb is 50 percent men, 50 percent women; 50 percent senior faculty, 50 percent junior faculty; and 50 percent whites, 50 percent non-whites. In departments with little to no diversity, these numbers are impossible to achieve. In that case, one can look for search committee members from (1) related departments on campus; (2) the same departments in neighboring colleges or universities, including historically black colleges and universities, historically Spanish institutions, and tribal colleges, which do not have a similar search in progress; and (3) alumni and graduates of other universities who work in neighboring industry or government positions. Keep in mind also that many people in black faculty and staff associations and Hispanic alliances on campus are often willing to serve on search committees. All of these individuals can bring fresh perspectives and new networks to search committees while departmental members continue to serve as discipline and research experts.

It must be noted that there can be very elitist, exclusionary attitudes voiced and/or exhibited when a search committee is faced with the prospect of involving someone from "the outside." Such people can be viewed as not knowing anything about the discipline, as having nothing to contribute, and as "spies" or "administration watchdogs." Every attempt should be made to work through these attitudes. In the process, the attitudes should either subside or give way to other creative and acceptable alternatives.

The choice of search committee chair is critical in positioning a search committee for the greatest probability of success in producing a diverse hiring outcome. The search committee chair needs to be a person (1) who understands and is committed to the value of diversity on the faculty; (2) who is willing to do the extra work it takes to find qualified candidates who are women and people from historically under-represented groups; (3) who understands, can recognize, and can work through the biases that often affect the evaluation of diverse candidates; (4) who possesses great professional credibility; and (5) who is willing to partner with the dean's office in hiring faculty. This person will be at the very heart of the faculty search process; who this person is will make a major difference in the way things go.

Writing Position Descriptions with Attention to Required and Desired Qualifications Works

When a faculty position becomes vacant, the tendency is for the department chair to pull out the position announcement that was last used to recruit for the position, make a few changes here or there, and then get that old document into the discipline's professional journal as quickly as possible. Very often, the haste with which this task is undertaken precludes input from others, thoughtfulness about how the position can be reconfigured to better serve the needs and future directions of the department and, most importantly, a careful consideration of the required and desired qualifications.

This issue of required and desired qualifications is very important for at least two reasons. The first is that every person hired *must* meet the required qualifications. This is the law, and there is no latitude in this. The same, however, is not true about desired qualifications. Many times, qualifications that are desired are listed as requirements. When they are written this way, they must be met.

Second, there is a rule about which one should be ever-cognizant if one is trying to increase the pool of applicants. That rule is that the longer the list of required qualifications, the smaller the pool. Of course, one does not want to state required qualifications that are so few or so broadly written that sociologists, for example, will be applying for positions in chemistry; this is idiocy. On the other hand, one does not want to write so many required qualifications that potential applicants do not see themselves as having a chance to be considered and thus do not apply. An important balance needs to be struck here which should occur in the context of a full discussion within the search committee.

Truly Searching for Diverse Applicants Works

There are definite supply and demand dynamics in the labor pools from which we are attempting to recruit diverse candidates. Moreover, these supply and demand characteristics vary from discipline to discipline and are further complicated at times by the region of the country where the job is located, competition from other institutions of higher education and from industry, resource issues in higher education generally, and the lack of women and domestic diversity on many of our campuses and in many of our communities. This is true.

But it is also true that the production of Ph.D.s from diverse groups has not stopped; today, women and minorities account for more than half of all new Ph.D.s. Maybe I am alone in this but I believe that if there is even one minority Ph.D. produced in a discipline in a given year, it is the obligation of the search committee to find that person and get the institution to consider that person. Many highly desirable candidates from diverse backgrounds who want to go into the professoriate never get one recruiting telephone call. Is that a supply issue or a search issue?

The traditional mentality of "place the ad and they will come" is usually not enough. It also is not enough to deluge HBCUs, HSIs, and tribal colleges with position announcements. The search committee must live up to its name and *really search*. It must (1) review the Chronicle of Higher Education and relevant Websites to find scholars with prestigious fellowships; (2) see who is presenting at conferences and approach them; (3) identify the top degree producers for minorities in their particular discipline and then go directly after their graduates; (4) attend the regional conferences for the Compact for Faculty Diversity; and (5) contact special professional caucuses or interest groups for referrals. Professional relationships cultivated over time can attract potential applicants or encourage a person who might already be interested to give an institution serious consideration. Really searching is work and it constitutes behavior that is new to most search committees. They feel awkward doing it and sometimes put upon. But searching for something that is in short supply is very serious business. It is necessary to pull out all the stops and you get there first.

Leveling the Field in the Evaluation of Candidates Works

In my experience, it is infinitely more difficult to get diverse candidates out of the applicant pool than it is to get them into the pool (Michelson and Oliver, 1991). Because the number of Ph.D.s who are women and minorities is growing slowly, more and more diverse candidates are showing up in our applicant pools. However, once diverse candidates are in the pool, a whole host of biases and institutionalized racism can come into play and kill a minority person's candidacy (Schwindt et al., 1998; Washington and Harvey, 1989). These biases include inflexible preferences for certain schools over others with the accompanying assumption that no excellence can exist outside of them; distinct preferences for the linear career path when we know that many women and minorities have more circuitous paths; distinct preferences for some types of research while devaluing others.

All of these things work against the candidacies of many women and minorities. Sometimes, the bias is to evaluate an international person more positively than a domestic minority person because the department already has had experience with them and "they work out just great." We must confront head-on the narrow notions of who is the "best qualified," as these definitions favor white males and, now, Asian males. Is it really the white male with thirty-five publications over the female candidate with twenty-one publications when half the students in the department are female, there is only one female faculty person in the department, and when we know women can face special obstacles when it comes to publishing? Well, maybe, maybe not. Is the Asian male with forty-five publications and some teaching experience better qualified than an African-American female with eighteen publications, a teaching excellence award, and an interest in mentoring students and when we know that black faculty often have no one with whom to collaborate in order to pump up the number of publications? Well, maybe, but maybe not. The point is there are many configurations of excellence, not just one. But we must be able to see them and then debate them in the context of a diverse search committee.

There are two other dynamics that can create problems in fairness. One is the tendency of search committees to be "looking for God on a good day." They want a superstar at all costs, ignoring much fabulous talent and unique assets along the way (Brown, 1996). They also ignore the fact that they may not be superstars themselves; distinguished and accomplished, yes . . . superstars, no. And yet, the reality often is that a department that is not all superstars can still produce outstanding scholarship, classroom excellence, and notable outreach efforts. We know this because often our superstar candidates turn us down and we move on to hire someone else, someone who looks much better to us after the superstar is out of the picture. That person did not change; we did in the way we looked at that person.

The second dynamic comes into play because of stereotypes, neurotic fears of lowering academic standards, and discomfort with those who are different (Swoboda, 1993; Talbot and Kocarek, 1997). This dynamic causes people to demand that female or minority candidates satisfy all required *and* desired qualifications in order to be seen as minimally competent. A letter of recommendation written by a superstar for a woman or minority candidate gets dismissed as boilerplate language, while a similar letter for a white male candidate is taken as evidence of his excellence. Sometimes, the smallest thing a woman or minority person does is counted against him or her as a major deficit, while a similar occurrence with a white male is rationalized and minimized. We simply must stop creating these extra hurdles for some people while we erase them for others.

At the same time, it must be said that it does no one a favor to bring forward from the pool a female or minority candidate who cannot be successful in the department. To do so is insulting, demoralizing, and humiliating for the woman or the minority. It is a waste of the department's time and precious resources and an incontrovertible piece of evidence for skeptics and naysayers who believe that excellence and diversity cannot exist at the same time in the same place.

Running a First Class Campus Visit Works

All visitors to campus should be treated like guests in one's home, and nowhere is this more important than when faculty candidates visit. The campus visit is the chance *to sell* candidates on the desirability of working in the environment (Brooks and Hammons, 1993). The schedule should be well-planned and *humane*. The candidate should feel genuine warmth, real enthusiasm, and true acceptance. Search committee members should be knowledgeable about and comfortable talking about basic aspects of campus diversity. Under no circumstances should they take this as an opportunity to air their grievances or disgruntlements.

One important feature of the pilot project was the dean's office involvement in interviewing every faculty candidate. After the hiring plan for the year was approved, the three associate deans were assigned to work with various searches. In addition, all minority and female candidates had a separate meeting with this writer. All candidates for associate and full professor positions met with the dean.

These meetings with the dean's office staff provided first-hand experiences with all finalists and a basis for discussing qualifications that did not rely solely on the vita. The meetings with this writer also gave women and minority candidates an opportunity to discuss any issues deemed by them too sensitive to discuss in the search committee. For me, these meetings were an opportunity to sell candidates on the vision of a truly multicultural learning and research community and to assess the degree to which they would be able to contribute to making this vision a reality. I also took this opportunity to inform candidates that the dean and I played active roles in the dispute-resolution process as appropriate. Thus, my meetings were meant to inform, to assess, to excite, to flatter, to reassure, and to positively influence candidates in every way possible (Rynes and Miller, 1983). Whether we offered the position to them and whether they accepted the position, the goal was to have candidates leave our campus with nothing but good things to say.

Having Search Committees Submit Profiles of Excellence Rather than Select Candidates through Ranking Works

After candidates have visited the campus, the typical scenario is for the search committee to gather feedback, meet with the faculty, and then send to the department chair its ranked choices. This list gets forwarded to the dean and to the affirmative action office for proforma approval. The candidate ranked number one is then called and offered the position. The search committee is acting as a hiring committee.

In the pilot, search committees were asked not to rank the final candidates. Instead, they were first asked to indicate whether any of the candidates was unacceptable and why. Then, for the remaining candidates, they were asked to create *profiles of excellence* based on the unique configurations of talent exhibited by each of them. The detailed profiles of excellence were presented by the search committee chair to the dean and the department chair together. The latter would ask questions and seek other clarifications as needed to be able to fully appreciate the views of the search committee and the faculty. Then, after considering these views and broader factors, the dean and the department chair made the decision about the order in which offers were to be made.

This is where faculty hiring as a partnership differs from faculty hiring as a privilege. When faculty hiring is a privilege, there is no meaningful role in the process for either the department chair or the dean. They merely carry out the wishes of the faculty. In a partnership, everyone has a role. The search committee and faculty ensure that a group of diverse candidates has what it takes to be successful in the department. Then the dean and the department chair weigh those evaluations and discuss the broader issues, set-up costs, dual career development, departmental and interdisciplinary directions, and departmental and college demographics. In the final analysis, the people with hiring authority determine the order in which offers are to be made.

This approach represented a marked departure from institutionalized practice. In the first year of implementation, many search committees and faculty questioned and resisted the loss of total freedom, total privilege and total autonomy. It did not matter that the order of offers was supported by the profiles of excellence the search committee prepared. Their resistance was based solely on the principle that they had not exercised the final decision-making. Some faculty felt they were not being trusted; that the dean was forcing people down their collective throat; and sometimes that, from only their point of view, the best person was not offered the position first.

This is where the commitment, involvement, and leadership of the dean at my institution was the most crucial. Together with the department head and using all search documentation, he exercised hiring authority to bring to the university all kinds of people, *including white men*, who could meet the needs at every level. Although some people were unhappy about this process, they could not say they were unhappy with the new-hires because all of them have gone on to perform in a stellar fashion. For years, the college had been trying to get people to grow their thinking in ways that would bring more faculty diversity. In the pilot project, a fair process brought more diversity to the faculty and people started to grow their thinking.

I would like to leave the reader with three points for reflection. One is that this work is not for the faint-hearted. Trying to change extant culture and practices surrounding faculty hiring is some of the hardest work ever done. This culture is entrenched, it's the status quo, and it rises up to fight back. Second, this work is not for the uniformed. Those involved must know what they are doing; they must know the literature, best practices, their institution, and network of support. Third, this work is not for those without staying power. It will take working year-after-year, hiring cycle after hiring cycle to change the culture, and practices surrounding faculty hiring. The effort cannot just be a flash in the pan or the process will drift right back to where it was before. All of this work takes place at the front-line, and sometimes the front-line is not a pretty place. But the front-line is a place where important causes are advanced and a positive difference can be made.

References

Aguirre, A. 2000. "Academic storytelling: A critical race theory story of affirmative action." *Sociological Perspectives*, 43(2): 319–339.

Aguirre, A., Jr. 2000. *Women and Minority Faculty in the Academic Workplace: Recruitment, Retention, and Academic Culture.* Washington, D.C.: ERIC Clearinghouse on Higher Education.

Atkinson, R. C. 1989. *Supply and Demand for Science and Engineering Ph.D.s: A National Crisis in the Making.* Remarks to the Regents of the University of California (February 16).

Bowen, W. G., and J. A. Sosa. 1989. *Prospects for Faculty in the Arts and Sciences: A Study of Factors Affecting Demand and Supply, 1987 to 2012.* Princeton, N.J.: Princeton University Press.

Bowen, H. R., and J. H. Shuster. 1986. *American Professors: A National Resource Imperiled.* New York: Oxford University Press.

Brooks, L. R., and J. O. Hammons. 1993. "Has higher education been using the wrong marketing approach?" *Journal of Marketing for Higher Education*, 4(1–2): 27–48.

Brown, S. V. 1996. "Responding to the new demographics in higher educa-tion." *Educating a New Majority: Transforming America's Educational System for Diversity*, edited by L. I. Rendon, R. O. Hope, and Associates. San Francisco, Calif.: Josey-Bass Publishers.

Cross, T. 1994. "Black faculty at Harvard: Does the pipeline defense hold water?" *The Journal of Blacks in Higher Education*, 4: 42–46.

El-Khawas, E., C. Cartwright, T. W. Fryer, R. Corrigan, and T. Marchese. 1990. "Faculty Shortages: Will Our Responses Be Adequate?" [Excerpt from ses-sion at 1990 American Association for Higher Education National Confer-ence]. *American Association for Higher Education Bulletin* 42(10): 3–7.

Harvey, W. B. 2002. *Minorities in Higher Education: Nineteenth Annual Sta-tus report*. Washington, D.C.: American Council of Education.

Knowles, M. F., and B. W. Harleston. 1997. *Achieving Diversity in the Pro-fessoriate: Challenges and Opportunities*. Washington, D.C.: American Council on Education.

Michelson, R. A., and M. L. Oliver. 1991. "Making the short list: Black can-didates and the faculty recruitment process." *The Racial Crisis in Ameri-can Higher Education*, edited by P. G. Altbach and K. Lomotey. Albany, N.Y.: State University of New York Press.

Norrell, S. A., and J. I. Gill. 1991. *Bringing into Focus the Factors Affecting Faculty Supply and Demand: A Primer for Higher Education and State Policy-makers*. Boulder, CO: Western Interstate Commission for Higher Education.

Opp, R. E., and A. Smith. 1994. "Effective strategies for enhancing minority faculty recruitment." *Community College Journal of Research and Prac-tice*, 10: 147.

Phillips, R. 2002. "Recruiting and retaining a diverse faculty." *Planning for Higher Education*, 30(4): 32–9.

Ramirez, B. C. 1996. "Creating a new kind of leadership for campus diver-sity." *Educating a New Majority: Transforming America's Educational System for Diversity*, edited by L. I. Rendon, R. O. Hope, and Associates. San Francisco, Calif.: Josey-Bass Publishers.

Rynes, S. L., and H. E. Miller. 1983. "Recruiter and job influences on candi-dates for employment." *Journal of Applied Psychology*. 68: 147–54.

Schwindt, L., K. Hall, and R. Davis. 1998. "Affirmative action in action: A case study of faculty recruitment at one major land-grant university." *NWSA—Journal*, 10(3): 73–100.

Shuster, J. H. 1992. "Academic labor markets." *The Encyclopedia of Higher Education*, Vol. 3, edited by B. R. Clark and G. R. Neave. Oxford, Tar-reytown, N.Y.: Pergamon Press.

Smith, D. G., L. E. Wolf, and B. E. Busenberg. 1996. *Achieving Faculty Diver-sity: Debunking the Myths*. Washington, D.C.: Association of American Col-leges and Universities.

Stein, R. H., and S. J. Trachtenberg, eds. 1993. *The Art of Hiring in America's Colleges and Universities*. Buffalo, N.Y.: Prometheus Books.

Swoboda, M. J. 1993. "Hiring women and minorities." *The Art of Hiring in America's Colleges and Universities*, edited by R. H. Stein and S. J. Trachtenberg. Buffalo, N.Y.: Prometheus Books.

Tack, M. W., and C. L. Patitu. 1992. *Faculty Job Satisfaction: Women and Minorities in Peril*. Washington, D.C.: ERIC Clearinghouse on Higher Education.

Talbot, D. M., and C. Kocarek. 1997. "Student affairs graduate faculty members' knowledge, comfort, and behaviors regarding issues of diversity. *Journal of College Student Development*, 38(3): 278–87.

Washington, V., and W. Harvey. 1989. *Affirmative Rhetoric, Negative Action: African American and Hispanic faculty at Predominately White Institutions*. Washington, D.C.: School of Education and Human Development, George Washington University.

Freeman A. Hrabowski, III

FREEMAN A. HRABOWSKI, III, has served as President of The University of Maryland, Baltimore County since May 1992. He joined the university in 1987, serving first as Vice Provost then as Executive Vice President.

Born in 1950 in Birmingham, Alabama, Dr. Hrabowski graduated at 19 from Hampton Institute with highest honors in mathematics. At the University of Illinois at Champaign-Urbana, he received his M.A. in mathematics one year later and his Ph.D. in higher education administration/statistics at age twenty-four.

Dr. Hrabowski serves as a consultant to the National Science Foundation, the National Institutes of Health, the National Academy of Sciences, the U.S. Department of Education, and universities and school systems nationally. He is a member of numerous boards, including the American Association of Colleges and Universities, the Baltimore Community Foundation, the Baltimore Equitable Society, the Baltimore Museum of Art, the Carnegie Institution of Washington, Marguerite Casey Foundation, Center Stage, Constellation Energy Group, Corvis Corporation, McCormick & Company, Inc., the Mercantile Safe Deposit & Trust Company, the Merrick & France Foundations, and the University of Maryland Medical System.

Examples of recent awards include election to the American Philosophical Society and the American Academy of Arts and Sciences, the McGraw Prize in Education, named *Marylander of the Year* by the editors of the *Baltimore Sun*, the Council on Chemical Research's first Diversity Award, Educator Achievement Award (NSF), Outstanding Science Educator Award (Eli Lilly & Company), and U.S. Presidential Award for Excellence in Science, Mathematics, and Engineering Mentoring (awarded to Dr. Hrabowski's university). He also holds honorary degrees from Franklin and Marchall College, the Medical University of South Carolina, Binghamton University, Brooklyn College (City University of New York), and Mercy College.

His research and publications focus on science and math education, with a special emphasis on issues involving minority participation. He is co-author of two books: *Beating the Odds* (1998), focusing on parenting and high-achieving African American males in science; and *Overcoming the Odds* (2002), on successful African-American young women in science.

13

OVERCOMING THE ODDS
PRODUCING HIGH-ACHIEVING MINORITY
STUDENTS IN SCIENCE AND ENGINEERING

Major demographic and workforce trends, coupled with the persistent achievement gap between minority and white students, pose serious challenges for America's colleges and universities in the recruitment and education of minority students for the national workforce, particularly in science and engineering. The racial and ethnic composition of the population continues to shift dramatically and, during the first decade of the new century, the proportion of white Americans is expected to decline from about three-quarters to two-thirds of the population.[1] College and university enrollments also will become increasingly diverse, extending the trend of the past decade. During the 1990s (1990–99), the number of African-American, Hispanic, Asian-American, and American-Indian undergraduate students increased by approximately 45 percent (from almost 2.5 million to 3.6 million) and made up 28 percent of all undergraduate students in 1999 compared with only 21 percent in 1990. In 2000, they also accounted for 22 percent of all bachelor's degrees awarded and 28 percent of all associate degrees awarded, compared with 14 and 17 percent, respectively, in 1991.[2]

Demographic shifts in the national workforce also are significant. We expect that during the next decade, the total labor force will expand by approximately 17 million people (12.3 percent), from about 138 million to 155 million,[3] and that minorities and women will constitute a growing portion of the workforce. Also during this period through 2008, the number of new scientific and engineering jobs in America is projected to grow by nearly 2 million (51 percent), from 3.8 million to 5.7 million positions.[4] The nation will need to produce far more minority and female scientists and engineers to meet the substantial increase in demand for S&E workers during the next decade and to respond to the serious and persistent underrepresentation of these groups in science and engineering. Currently, minorities and women make up only about one-third of all American scientists and engineers.[5]

We need to focus considerable attention on African-Americans and Hispanics, in addition to American-Indians and selected Asian groups, because they represent the nation's two largest minority groups, and they trail substantially behind whites in academic achievement.[6] In 2000, Hispanic students who completed high school lagged behind white students by almost 22 percentage points (60 vs. 82), while African-Americans trailed whites by 5 points (77 vs. 82). Among 18 to 24-year-olds, 39 percent of African-Americans and slightly more than one-third of Hispanics were enrolled in college compared with 43 percent of their white counterparts. There also are large differences in college graduation rates. In 2000, the six-year graduation rates for African-Americans and Hispanics were 38 and 46 percent, respectively, compared with 59 percent for whites. We also find that about one-quarter of all bachelor's degrees earned by African-American students in 2000 were awarded by historically black institutions (HBIs), even though only about 14 percent of all African-American undergraduates were enrolled in HBIs in 1999. Similarly, Hispanic-serving institutions (HSIs) awarded 48 percent of all bachelor's degrees earned by Hispanic students in 2000, substantially exceeding the percentage of Hispanic students enrolled in HSIs in 1999.

These data show that whether these students are enrolled in historically black, Hispanic-serving, or predominantly white institutions, a great many of them simply are not succeeding. Their failure to achieve academic success in large numbers stems chiefly from lack of preparation and the achievement gap throughout their K–12 education. The retention and graduation rates for these groups are significantly lower than those of whites. Moreover, as the College Board points out in *Reaching the Top*,[7] its 1999 report on minority high achievement, the achievement gap is most pronounced in mathematics and science.

Expanding the Pool of Successful Minority Students

Colleges and universities seeking to recruit minority students certainly want to project their institutions' attractive qualities and focus on minority student "success stories" and their institutions' commitment to minority groups. Unfortunately, though, recruiters frequently find far too small a pool of students with competitive grades and standardized test scores. A key reason for minority students' chronic underachievement is that many of them simply have not had the course work or special preparatory work needed to succeed. Furthermore, some in minority communities simply lack confidence in standardized tests or do not accept their importance.

For example, some families in urban America have heard for years that standardized tests are culturally biased and that therefore they should not be concerned about them. I recall talking at an inner-city Baltimore high school a number of years ago, when one of the students interrupted me to say that while she knew she could read well, she had never done well on standardized tests because, as one of her teacher's had stated, the test had not been developed with her in mind. When I asked her to explain, it was clear that the student had been led to believe that the test was developed by and for whites only. Although I was not surprised by this sentiment, I was disconcerted to hear the misperception so clearly and strongly stated.

Fortunately, growing numbers of people in Baltimore and elsewhere in the nation are working to correct this message and to help all families understand that standardized tests are indeed a useful and important part of life in our society. They are discussing the important role that standardized tests play not only in assessing students' academic skills but also, unfortunately, as an obstacle to further academic progress, particularly for minority students. Such perceptions about these tests are held not only by minority students but also by teachers and families; sometimes these perceptions prevent the students from focusing on the tests' inevitable importance in higher education (e.g., at many universities, testing in such courses as organic chemistry or genetics is often standardized) and in the professions (e.g., MCATs, LSATs, and various board exams). To succeed in science and engineering at the undergraduate and graduate levels, students need many of the same skills that are important for success on standardized tests, including especially strong reading, math, and thinking skills. While colleges and universities should continue relying on a variety of factors in addition to the SAT to make admissions decisions, we should also consider how we can help students—especially minority students—to perform well on standardized tests generally.

At my university, we emphasize standardized tests for all students in addition to weighing applicants' grades, the rigor of their high school programs, and, for our special scholarship programs, students' attitudes and motivation. Although colleges can identify students who have performed better than their low test scores would have predicted, the fact remains that in certain disciplines—especially science and engineering—standardized test scores, together with information about grades and course background, provide a fairly accurate picture of which students are most likely to succeed. As I frequently tell students, parents, and educators, the issue of standardized test performance is not about race. After all, who wants a doctor, regardless of race, who cannot pass the test? We need to hold all students to a very high standard, at the same time giving them the support they need to reach that standard.

A major problem related to standardized testing is that many people assume that because certain groups have not done well on the test, they will always do poorly. My campus colleagues have rejected this assumption and have been working to support local schools in students' test preparation, building students' reading and math skills, and helping to set high expectations for the students, teachers, families, and ourselves. It would be inappropriate for those of us in colleges and universities to look simply for well-prepared students or to accept students who need special support and place them in developmental programs. As educators, our responsibility is more comprehensive, and we should examine our relationship with K–12 feeder schools. We should look for ways to develop partnerships involving tutoring, having college students serve as role models and guides, working with teachers in challenging schools, and strengthening our teacher-education programs by designing them to be more responsive to the needs of minority and low-income students. We should also work with communities to focus their attention on issues involving minority student achievement, redoubling our efforts to work with families and help them understand their responsibilities for supporting their children.

Colleges and universities—especially admissions staff, advisors, and university faculty and students who deal with minority students before and after their admission—have a responsibility to give the students a realistic assessment of what they must do to succeed in college, while also not discouraging them. It takes special sensitivity to help students develop high aspirations and self-confidence while making them aware of the skills, preparation, and work required. Students interested in the sciences must be made especially aware of the demands of college-level course work and what college faculty expect. If they do not, they are more likely to flounder, fail courses, and sometimes leave the institution.

To avoid such missteps, institutions have a responsibility to work with families and schools, and with middle-and high-school staff and students, helping to prepare students for their college experience rather than waiting until they are freshmen and ill-prepared to perform well.

This is particularly crucial for minority students from poorly funded high schools, where expectations are often lower than at wealthier schools. Without high expectations, many minority students have no idea how hard they will have to work to succeed, and students unaccustomed to studying several hours nightly during high school are unlikely to arrive at college and automatically change their study habits. For this reason, programs like Upward Bound, which offer supplementary academic work to high school students in the summer and during the academic year, are so important. Upward Bound, a federally funded program, has proved to be a highly effective college–high school partnership in which first-generation college students, including large numbers of minority students, benefit from supplemental education in reading, math, and writing during summers in high school. In some cases, such programs, often located on college campuses, help low-income high school students with their academic work; high school students get help preparing for standardized tests, touring campuses, and developing their college financial-aid materials. This program and others like it are often successful because their approach is holistic, taking into account not only the students' academic needs but also the obstacles they will face gaining admission to and succeeding in college. One especially effective component of Upward Bound is a summer bridge program for students after high school graduation. It is designed to help students prepare for college-level courses and the expectations of faculty, and to offer them opportunities for interacting with peers and college faculty and staff. A number of institutions have implemented similar pre-freshman programs to support students' transition to the college.

The Significance of the First-Year Experience

The significance of the first-year experience, particularly for underrepresented minority students, cannot be overstated. It is a crucial determinant of whether these students succeed academically or not. Three indicators of institutional effectiveness in this area include (1) how well schools provide academic support for students—from orientation, advising, and tutoring to support in regular courses (especially after students complete developmental courses); (2) how successful they are in helping students become connected to the institution so they develop a sense of belonging and become enthusiastic about learning; and (3) the level of faculty commitment to the students' success.

The first question college and university administrators must ask themselves is how high an institutional priority is freshman academic performance? The answer is relatively easy. Something is clearly a priority when sufficient resources are applied to it. For freshman academic performance, institutions need to look at the quality of the faculty who teach first-year courses, the extent to which faculty regularly examine instructional practices and develop and revise teaching materials, and the extent to which the institution understands the factors most critical to first-year students' (particularly minority students') success. Such factors include the rigor of students' high school preparation, the students' attitudes about college work, their willingness to take advice and engage in supplemental support work, their level of motivation to succeed, and the extent to which the school encourages students and highlights high academic achievement.

Other questions relate to data analysis. Has the institution evaluated relevant data about students' grades and course loads to determine who succeeds in the first year, who does not, and the differences between the two groups? To what extent does the institution use data on first-year students' performance and attitudes to shape and reshape policies and practices related to admissions, orientation, advising, tutoring, and curriculum? Also, does the institutional research office work with faculty and administrators to assess levels of effectiveness of different initiatives and strategies to help all freshmen? The last question is especially important because institutions where first-year minority students succeed typically focus on the first-year experience in general. Many of the strategies helpful to students in general will also help minority students. Furthermore, it is not sufficient simply to gather and analyze the data about academic performance; discussing the data in focus groups involving students, faculty, and staff also is vital.

For minority freshmen, the orientation process is an especially valuable opportunity to help them adjust to their new environment. The process can help them focus academically and become socially and emotionally comfortable. It is important for faculty, staff, and upperclass students to spend time with freshmen discussing expectations about behavior and how institutions celebrate differences among students. General programming as well as residence hall orientation activities should focus on multicultural issues and race relations, giving students the chance to talk about their backgrounds, personal experiences, and what they bring to the campus community because of their cultural heritage. Whether the minority students live on campus or commute, they are more inclined to stay on campus and interact with student peers, faculty, and staff if they become involved in activities outside the classroom. These co-curricular activities help students develop a sense of belonging and to view themselves as valuable members of the campus community.

Most important, perhaps, is the extent to which freshmen are engaged with full-time tenured and tenure-track faculty. Are these faculty (in addition to part-time faculty, instructors, or graduate students) sensitive to the important roles they play in determining whether students succeed their first year? If graduate students are used extensively, to what extent do they receive special training and support during the process? To what extent are these professors involved in professional development aimed at improving their instructional effectiveness in general and *vis-à-vis* minority students in particular?

Some of the most successful strategies and practices involve faculty and administrators engaging in discussions about student performance (e.g., grades and retention in first-year courses) and having departmental and interdepartmental discussions designed not to point fingers at students or faculty, but rather to understand the level of student performance by course, and even by section and faculty member. Understandably, the faculty need to be assured that the purpose of such conversations is to improve performance and not to embarrass anyone.

In one institution's chemistry department, for example, where nearly half the students were performing below a C in the first-semester course, the initial reaction of some faculty during these conversations was simply that students were either poorly prepared, working too many hours on the outside, or not serious enough about studying. After more discussion with students, though, faculty discovered that students needed more feedback earlier in the semester (e.g., graded homework and quizzes); that students did not always see the connection between lectures and graded exams; that most of the students had little or no experience studying in groups, but rather were relying only on themselves individually to study for tests; that few students took advantage of the department's tutorial center because they mistakenly saw it as a place for poor students only; and that no one had talked with them about the crucial relationship between the number of hours of outside part-time employment and amount of time devoted to studying in the course to ensure success in it. As a result, many students in general—not just minority students—were not succeeding.

Since that time, that department has changed its first-semester chemistry course, making it more interesting to students by using a team-teaching approach and by arranging for some of the department's most productive faculty to talk about their research in relationship to concepts introduced in the course so that students can see connections to real-life science. This is especially worthwhile because students also sense the faculty members' enthusiasm for their work. In addition, the department encourages students to work in groups. In fact, some assignments require group work as a way to encourage collaborative work and to teach students how to collaborate. Also, the chemistry tutorial center is now a place where students go when they want to earn As, not simply passing grades. Considerable time also is devoted at the beginning of the semester, both through orientation and in classes, to discussing the connection between outside commitments and study hours required for success in first-year and subsequent courses.

What we have learned is that when students do poorly, the reasons frequently are more complicated than simply assuming that one group—faculty or students—is not doing what it should be doing. Instead, key themes have become very clear. When student performance has improved, faculty have taken ownership of the problem by looking at the data on student performance in great specificity. Also, discussions with faculty, students, and support staff (possibly through focus groups) to discover the attitudes and perceptions of each group are important because they become the bases for proposing and implementing initiatives designed to strengthen teaching and learning.

We also have found that providing feedback to first-year students through additional homework assignments and quizzes is particularly effective. New freshmen often receive much less feedback, much later in the semester, than they were accustomed to receiving in high school. In one case, when the college department chair suggested giving much more feedback to students, the response she received from one of her faculty was, "We don't want to spoon-feed the students," to which the chair responded, "If spoon-feeding leads to more students having a strong foundation in their first-year courses, then let's spoon-feed them."

In another instance involving a first-year biology course, one faculty member worked with a science-education faculty member who observed and evaluated the biology instructor's teaching and helped devise strategies for him to have more interaction with his students, to use technology more effectively to enhance learning, and to give more students added time and opportunities to absorb materials and ask questions.

Discussions involving faculty and administrators also can root out inaccurate assumptions that both faculty and students sometimes make about the students' performance in the classroom. In one case, faculty and students began the semester with the assumptions that if a minority student earned a C in organic chemistry, the student was doing well. In this case and others, frank discussions about previous performance of minority students in particular courses and the expectations of faculty and students can lead to surprising and useful outcomes. Minority students also tend to do best when departments identify those faculty who have been most effective in motivating and working with minority students, including, for example, when faculty have selected minority students to work with them on research projects.

Ensuring Success Beyond the First Year

The past few years, Richard Light's book, *Making the Most of College*,[8] has been the focus of discussions among faculty and administrators across the country. It emphasizes ways in which colleges and universities—and students themselves—can strengthen students' education and their connections to the campus and, in turn, improve their chances of success. Administrators and faculty are beginning to see, for example, that encouraging students to use departmental and university tutoring resources helps them to improve course performance (raising Bs to As, and not simply achieving passing grades). Also, faculty and staff encouragement to participate in study groups not only produces better academic performance but also teaches students how to collaborate in teams, how to formulate specific questions, and how to explain concepts to their classmates. Study groups give students an opportunity to examine problems from different perspectives. Many institutions now give great importance to the contributions of faculty and staff mentors. Faculty, regardless of their discipline or race, have much to offer in stimulating minority students' interest in research. Equally important, staff members can support students on a personal level by showing their interest in the students' academic progress, co-curricular and career interests, and personal well-being.

Campuses with high minority student retention rates tend to recognize the importance of providing a family-like social and academic support system for these students throughout their academic careers. Such a system includes opportunities for older students to support younger ones and cultivating implicit expectations that student peers will support each other both academically and personally; that it is smart to seek support from various sources; that it is useful to establish clear and achievable academic goals; and that it is important to explore possible careers related to one's major.

Successful campuses also emphasize the value of service by encouraging students to work with needy people of all ages. Tutoring and guidance, or focusing on special projects such as Habitat for Humanity, can put students' studies and their potential for contributing to the larger world in healthy perspective.

A Model Program

Many of the observations, suggestions, and practices discussed here reflect the success of the Meyerhoff Scholars Program for high-achieving minority students in science and engineering at my campus, the University of Maryland, Baltimore County (UMBC). It is a public, predominantly white research campus where minority student retention rates are higher than those of whites, and where the combined mean SAT scores (approaching 1,220) and high school grade point averages (3.5) of all freshmen are virtually the same.

Since the Meyerhoff Program was created in 1988, it has become one of the nation's leading producers of minority graduates, particularly African-Americans, who go on to postgraduate study and research careers in science and engineering. In 1999, UMBC ranked first nationally in the number of undergraduate biochemistry degrees awarded to African-Americans and produced nearly one-third of all undergraduate biochemistry degrees awarded to blacks. It also ranked second in the number of undergraduate biochemistry degrees awarded to minority students, in general, and fourth (tied with Yale) in the number of undergraduate biochemistry degrees awarded.[9] Approximately 500 competitively selected undergraduates have enrolled in the program from its inception, and since the first group of graduates in 1993, nearly 300 Meyerhoff students have earned degrees in science and engineering, with 85 percent matriculating into graduate and professional programs nationally. Most important, these graduates are part of a pipeline that has begun to produce a stream of minority Ph.D.s, M.D.s, and M.D./Ph.D.s. By 2004, the program will have sent more than 400 minority students to science and engineering postgraduate programs.

One of the Meyerhoff Program's distinguishing features is its operating assumption that every student selected has the ability to succeed in science and engineering, given appropriate opportunities and resources. Collectively, the program's components create an environment that continually challenges and supports students from their pre-freshman summer through graduation and beyond. The components include (1) recruiting top minority students in math and science; (2) providing a summer bridge program including math, science, and humanities coursework, training in analytic problem solving, group study, and social and cultural events; (3) offering comprehensive merit scholarship support; (4) actively involving faculty in recruiting, teaching, and mentoring the students; (5) emphasizing strong programmatic values, including outstanding academic achievement, study groups, collegiality, and preparation for graduate school; (6) involving the Meyerhoff students in sustained, substantive summer research experiences; (7) encouraging all students to take advantage of departmental and university tutoring resources to optimize course performance; (8) ensuring the university administration's active involvement and support; (9) providing academic advising and personal counseling; (10) linking the Meyerhoff Scholars with mentors from professional and academic fields in science, engineering, and health; (11) encouraging a strong sense of community among the students; (12) encouraging the students to engage in service in the larger community; and (13) involving the students' parents and other relatives who can be supportive by keeping them informed of students' progress, and inviting them to special counseling sessions if problems arise.

Notwithstanding the success of the Meyerhoff Program and other programs for minority students, e.g., the University of California-Berkeley's Biology Scholars Program and Yale's Science, Technology, and Research Scholars (STARS) Program,[10] our studies have confirmed that without special support these minority students would not succeed for various reasons, ranging from academic and cultural isolation to low expectations for performance.[11] During the past three decades, I have studied minority student achievement from various perspectives and in different institutions ranging from urban and rural historically black institutions to a large Midwestern land-grant university and, for the past fifteen years, a predominantly white research university in Greater Baltimore. The past several years, I also have worked with a number of school systems, community colleges, and four-year colleges and universities around the nation, addressing minority academic achievement and[12] that my colleagues and I have written two books on parenting and educating academically successful African-American college students in science and engineering. In my career, I have observed certain characteristics common to minority students who succeed in college: (1) most notably, the ability to read well, take notes, and study; (2) the willingness to attend class regularly; (3) the ability to adjust to campus life; (4) willingness to seek and take advice; (5) "fire in the belly"—a passion for learning and excelling; and (6) the resilience to recover and learn from making mistakes and experiencing setbacks.

Finally, from an institutional perspective, I have concluded that minority student success depends on administrators, faculty, and staff clearly and explicitly communicating high expectations; creating an academic climate that is both challenging and supportive; striving always to bring out the best in these students academically and personally, encouraging them to become involved in co-curricular activities on campus and service activities in the community; and engaging a variety of people on the campus, from faculty and staff to upperclass students, to take ownership of the challenge of elevating minority student performance.

Notes

1. U.S. Census Bureau, *Statistical Abstract of the United States: 2000*. While whites accounted for 75 percent of the nation's total population in 2000 (211.5 million of 281.4 million), they are projected to represent just over 67 percent of the population in 2010 (202.0 million of 299.9 million).
2. American Council on Education, *Minorities in Higher Education 2001–2002: Nineteenth Annual Status Report*. Washington, D.C., 2002.
3. U.S. Bureau of Labor Statistics, Employment & Earnings, Monthly Labor Review (November 1999), U.S. Census Bureau's *Statistical Abstract of the United States: 2000*.
4. National Science Foundation, *Science & Engineering Indicators 2000*, Volume 1, Text Table 3–20.
5. National Science Foundation, *Women, Minorities, and Persons with Disabilities in Science and Engineering: 2000* (September, 2000) Table 5–4.
6. ACE, *ibid*. Note that the data in this paragraph on high school completion, college participation, and college graduation rates, and type of institution attended are all derived from the ACE report.
7. The College Board, *Reaching the Top: A Report of the National Task Force on Minority High Achievement*, 1999.
8. R. J. Light, *Making the Most of College: Students Speak Their Minds*. Harvard University Press, 2001. Also see "A Harvard Professor Becomes a Guru on Helping Students in Colleges Nationwide Turn to His Book and His Ideas" *The Chronicle of Higher Education* (August 17, 2001).
9. American Society of Biochemistry & Molecular Biology, Graduation Survey, *ASBMS News* (January–February, 2000). In 1999, UMBC awarded twenty-one of the sixty-seven undergraduate biochemistry degrees earned by African-Americans in the nation. It also awarded forty-five undergraduate biochemistry degrees to minority students, the second highest number national, and seventy-two undergraduate biochemistry degrees overall, the fourth highest number (tied with Yale).
10. *Science* (31 August 2001), Volume 293: pp. 1611–1612, identifies the programs at Berkeley and Yale, along with UMBC's Meyerhoff program, as exemplary.
11. K. I. Maton, F. A. Hrabowski, and C. L. Schmitt, 2000. "African-American College Students Excelling the Sciences: College & Post-College Outcomes in the Meyerhoff Scholars Program." *Journal of Research in Science Teaching*: 37(7), pp. 629–54.
12. F. Hrabowski, K. Maton, J. Greif, *Beating the Odds: Raising Academically Successful African American Males* (Oxford University Press, 1998). Hrabowski, F., Maton, K., Greif, J., Greene, M., *Overcoming the Odds: Raising Academically Successful African American Young Women* (Oxford University Press, 2001).

Donald Brown

DONALD BROWN has served as the Director of the Office of AHANA Student Programs at Boston College for twenty-two years. An acronym for African-American, Hispanic, Asian, and Native Americans, the goal of the Office of AHANA Student Programs is to provide an array of support services aimed at assisting in the optimal academic performance, retention, and eventual graduation of AHANA students from Boston College.

Prior to his arrival at Boston College, Dr. Brown served as a Regional Director for the Boston Region of the Massachusetts Department of Youth Services where he was responsible for the care and placement of 800 youth adjudicated delinquent. Prior to DYS, Dr. Brown served as Director of the Upward Bound Program at the University of Massachusetts-Amherst.

Over the years, Dr. Brown has written about and made presentations on retention issues and has received citations for his work of structuring model retention programs. In addition to his full-time job, Dr. Brown derives a great deal of satisfaction from his work as President of Christian Soldiers, Inc., where he holds the rank of major. The aim of this initiative is to shape character and to assist in the academic, social, and most importantly, spiritual growth and development of youth between the ages of seven and fifteen. In addition to Christian Soldiers, Inc., Dr. Brown serves as Co-Director of Bridging Bridges, an initiative aimed at bringing together eighteen to twenty organizations serving black males throughout the Greater Boston area.

Dr. Brown received his B.A. in Community Leadership and Development from Springfield College, a M.Ed. From Springfield in Rehabilitation Counseling, and a Doctorate in Educational Policy, Planning, Research, and Administration from the University of Massachusetts-Amherst.

14

THE COMBINATION OF OPPORTUNITY AND SUPPORT EQUALS SUCCESS

THE OPTIONS THROUGH EDUCATION PROGRAM AT BOSTON COLLEGE

During the summer of 2002, I had the good fortune to participate in a wonderful retreat that required participants to pause and reflect on three major questions: What are you passionate about? What are you good at? What do you see as the world's greatest needs? I did not have to think very long about these questions, which conjured up thoughts about my work with students at Boston College over the past twenty-four years where I have served as Director of the Office of AHANA (African-American, Hispanic, Asian, and Native-American) Student Programs. More specifically, I thought about my work with more than one thousand students who, during my tenure, have come to the university through my office's six-week summer Options Through Education Transitional Summer Program (OTE). Because these students were afforded an opportunity to participate in OTE and were supported both during the summer and throughout the academic year, virtually all of them have become highly productive and contributing members of society. Indeed they have become doctors, lawyers, nurses, ministers, educators, bankers, and entrepreneurs.

When I reflect on what it is I am good at, I am proud of my achievement at developing and implementing an academic support program that has contributed to altering a retention rate of 17 percent twenty-five years ago to a current retention rate of 95 percent.

On the question of the world's greatest needs, from my vantage point there is profound need to ensure that AHANA students, who in a few short years will become this nation's majority, are prepared to assume positions of leadership as our nation moves further into the next century.

In this essay I will describe the Options Through Education Transitional Summer program. I will share the program's mission, goals, and objectives. Additionally I will share strategies that have contributed to the program's success. I will provide advice to those who wish to launch a similar program. Moreover, I will discuss the kinds of support services that are critically important to the survival of under-prepared students during the course of the academic year. Finally, I will share what some of the graduates of the OTE program are doing today.

Launched in the summer of 1979, the continuing objective of the six-week summer Options Through Education Program is to ensure that the forty to sixty participants are provided with the academic support and assistance that will give them a head start as they begin, in earnest, their four-year journey at Boston College in the fall. Specifically the summer program seeks to: build skills, especially in the areas of math and English; introduce participants to various campus resources; strengthen students' self esteem; and give students a sense of what college is like.

The target group for the OTE Program is students who have high levels of motivation and potential; they are the first in their family to attend college; and they are leaders in their high school and community. Given their performance on the SAT exam, which is 300 points below the typical Boston College student, candidates are told that they are admissible to Boston College if they participate in the mandatory six-week OTE Program. In addition to looking at SAT scores, Boston College ranks students on a scale of 1 to 10. One is the best-prepared student and 10 is the least-prepared. Candidates for OTE are ranked between 7 and 10.

All students complete the same application process for Boston College. These students' applications are flagged because it is felt that if they are required to attend the mandatory six-week summer Options Through Education Program, there is a far better likelihood that they will graduate from Boston College.

Boston College's Admissions Office and the Office of AHANA Student Programs supports the view enunciated in numerous studies that such factors as high school curriculum, test scores, and class rank are excellent predictors of success especially among African-American students (i.e., Perna, 2000; Adelman, 1999). But we also champion the belief expresses by Sedlacek and Webster (1978) in the late 1970s that non-cognitive variables are also important predictors of academic success especially among black and Latino students. These variables include positive self concept, realistic self appraisal, understanding and ability to deal with racism, preference for long-term goals, availability of a strong support person, leadership experience, demonstrated community service, and knowledge acquired in a field.

Evidence of these variables is sought when reviewing the applications of OTE students. Particularly important among these non-cognitive variables, for the program's purposes, are preference for long-term goals. This is important because throughout the program we attempt to instill in our students that the pursuit of a college education may not be accomplished in the traditional four years. Indeed, in some cases a student might have to "stop out or drop-out" for a period of time. This is acceptable as long as he or she eventually completes their undergraduate studies.

Once the admissions office and the Office of AHANA Student Programs make a determination, OTE students are notified that their acceptance is conditional upon participation in the six-week summer orientation program, which commences around the fourth week of June. The program begins with a two-hour orientation for participants and their parents. Information about classes, rules, regulations, and expectations are enunciated for students. Further, students are asked to stand and repeat, along with the program's director, a contractual agreement. The agreement says that the Office of AHANA Student Programs commits to assisting participants throughout the summer and throughout their four-year stay at the university if the student agrees to utilize the resources available to him or to her.

In a separate room parents are given an explanation of the program, introduced to the contract, and advised about ways they can assist the program in meeting their sons' and daughters' needs both during the summer and throughout the academic year. A key component of the orientation is that OTE students meet for the first time their preceptor (peer counselor), who is crucially important to guiding the student through the program. Preceptors live with an assigned group of students on the dormitory floor; they introduce them to the campus; they assist in the resolution of difficulties that the student might encounter; and they provide tutorial assistance in the evening. The literature corroborates the critically important role that students play in helping other students. Payne (1987) put it very succinctly: "A truly holistic approach to providing social support to high risk students must also involve other students."

Following this Sunday orientation, several things transpire before students begin attending classes. Paramount among them is that the students participate in a two-day orientation with other first-year students at Boston College. In addition to receiving a vast amount of information about Boston College, OTE students meet and participate in groups with white students. These interactions have proved invaluable in the past in promoting an appreciation of the various cultures represented at Boston College.

Along similar lines, prior to starting classes, OTE leaders spend an entire day focusing on the various cultures represented in the program. Through an exercise titled "drawing one's culture," role-playing, and skits, students gain an understanding of the various cultures represented in the program.

OTE Academic Course Offerings

Three to four days after they have arrived on campus and continuing for the next four weeks, OTE students participate in an academic regimen that has been likened to a boot camp experience.

Class Schedule

Mathematics	Monday through Friday 8:30 to 9:30 a.m. 11:30 to 12:30 p.m.
English	Monday through Friday 9:30 to 11:30 a.m.
Contemporary Social Issues	Monday through Thursday 1:30 to 3:30 p.m.
Freshman Year Experience	Monday through Thursday 1:30 to 3:30 p.m.

Course Offerings

Introduction to Literary Studies, 3 (elective credits)

After completing an English placement examination, students are grouped and placed in an English class that approaches writing as a necessity for success in college and focuses on practical rather than theoretical issues, such as how to construct a thesis, an argument, and a paper. Accuracy, economy, and clarity are emphasized in the course.

Format is lectures and small groups.

Pre-Calculus, 3 (elective credits)

Depending on the outcome of a diagnostic test, students are placed in either a basic course covering algebra and geometry, which is not offered for credit, or a pre-calculus course, which is offered for credit. The pre-calculus course covers a number of topics that are preliminary to calculus. Among such topics are sets, functions, inequalities, some college algebra, trigonometric, exponential and logarithmic functions, and the analytic geometry of the straight line and conic sections.

Format is lectures, small groups, and individual instruction.

Contemporary Social Problems/Oral Communications (non-credited)

Through the study of topics such as intimacy, prejudice, AIDS, and substance abuse, students will explore personal feelings and learn how to effectively communicate with others. Each student brings his or her own preferences, attitudes, customs, and values about various issues. When understood, these enrich the larger community; when misinterpreted, they may lead to misunderstanding and stereotypes. The second component of the class focuses on oral communication. Communication is self-expression. Speech is a major tool of effective communication. Through an awareness of how students express themselves orally (e.g. their ideas, opinions and feelings), they can improve the way they communicate to others.

Format is readings, discussions, hands-on activities, and films.

Freshman Year Experience Seminar (non-credited)

The Freshman Year Experience Seminar teaches students critically important survival and coping strategies necessary to adapt to and excel in college. The major issues highlighted are study techniques, time management, communications, and interpersonal dynamics involving instructors, roommates, and peers. This course also teaches students who do not already know how to use a computer.

Format is role-play, discussion, and interaction with upperclassmen who participate as teaching assistants.

Weeknight Study Hall

Each weeknight between 6:30 and 9:30 p.m. tutorial assistance is provided to students in mathematics and English. This assistance is provided by program instructors who are assigned a weeknight in the program and by preceptors who live with students in the dormitory and who have been hired in large part to provide academic assistance to students. Following study hall, students are allowed to unwind until the midnight curfew.

Town Meetings

Each Wednesday night from 5:30 to 7:00 p.m. OTE students attend a Town Meeting. The purpose of the Town Meeting is that of affording students an opportunity to communicate to program administrators and preceptors their thoughts, feelings, and aspirations for the program. These meetings are essential because they represent student ownership of the program and afford an opportunity to make changes where needed.

Weekend Excursions

Each weekend, for four weeks, students are expected to participate in excursions that expose them to the beauty of the Commonwealth of Massachusetts. For many of them it will be the first, and perhaps only, time that they will visit Martha's Vineyard on the south shore of the Commonwealth and Six Flags in the western part of the state. In addition, students attend plays, go roller-skating, and participate in barbecues and a host of other activities. All of these activities are geared to mitigate anxiety and fear of being away from home, in many cases, for the first time.

Closing Ceremony

The culminating event for the Options Through Education Program is a closing ceremony. At this event students, faculty, and staff eat a hearty meal, laugh, cry, and share reflections on the six-week program. A student speaker represents the class in capturing the six-week experience and offers a word of gratitude to the program coordinator, instructors, preceptors, and senior staff. In addition to wishing students well during brief visits home before starting the school year, students are reminded of the contractual agreement they signed which says that they will meet with an assigned advisor, entrusted with responsibility of monitoring their performance, at least three times each semester. Further, if they are experiencing difficulty in any of their courses, they must agree to use tutorial and other resources provided by the Office of AHANA Student Programs.

Lastly, OTE graduates are encouraged to bring roommates, friends, and other AHANA students who did not have the benefit of participating in the OTE Program to a barbeque/orientation on the first day of classes. At that orientation, the staff of the Office of AHANA Student Programs makes clear to all entering AHANA Students that while its focus was on OTE students during the summer, the resources of the office are available to all AHANA students during the course of the academic year.

Advice to Those Who Wish to Start Similar Programs

For the most part, the Options Through Education Program has not changed its structure over the past twenty-four years. When sound recommendations have come from students, faculty, and others involved in the program, we have made adjustments. As a result the program has grown stronger. In the light of twenty-four years of experience, I suggest that institutions wishing to start a program similar to OTE consider Brown's (1996) advice about the essential components of summer programs for AHANA students who lack preparation. Brown opines that these programs should, at the very least, do the following:

- Convey very honestly to the student that, given weaknesses in math, English, or other subjects, acceptance to the university will be conditional upon successful completion of a summer academic enrichment program.

- Resolve that if the courses are offered for credit, the program should be no less than six weeks in length.

- Enter into a contractual agreement with students, clearly enunciating what the program expects from the student and, conversely, what the student can expect from the program. Expectations should be spelled out not only for the summer but for the academic year as well.

The specific objectives of comprehensive summer programs akin to OTE are crucial. Such a program should do the following:

- Diagnose students' academic ability levels and develop programs that respond to their needs.

- Offer programs of instruction in English and math.

- If a student can show that he or she is able to handle a rigorous program in mathematics, science, or English he or she should be encouraged to do so.

- Provide students with instruction in the use of computers and other technology that might aid in their learning.

- Introduce students to the broad array of campus resources, e.g. libraries, laboratories, Financial Aid, Deans office, etc.

- Offer classes, workshops, lectures, and seminars regarding the realities of college life.

- Develop workshops aimed at assisting students with time-management, note taking, study skills, budgeting money, etc.

- Collaborate with the institution's Career Center to ensure that students receive information regarding internships, jobs, and graduate school.

- Provide recreational outlets so that students can relax and bond with each other.

- Focus on students' spiritual development. Provide opportunities for those who wish to attend church to do so.

An orientation such as the one described here is essential to the success of students who have been educationally disenfranchised. Equally important, however, is what an institution does over the course of the year to accommodate the needs of students. Boston College recognizes this and through its Office of AHANA Student programs provides a continuum of support services during the academic year that helps OTE students, and indeed all AHANA undergraduates at Boston College, to successfully negotiate the institution. Included among the continuum of services are the following:

Tutorial Assistance The Office of AHANA Student Programs makes sure its students know that students at Ivy League Colleges are willing to pay for tutors. They are willing because they recognize that they are competing for graduate school and job opportunities against the best and brightest students in the world. To ensure that they stand a chance, Boston College students are told that they should use the Office of AHANA Student Program's Jaime Escalante Tutorial Program. If they think they are getting an A in a subject, they should get a tutor and strive to get an A+.

Academic Advisement At most colleges and universities, faculties do a very poor job of advising students and deans are overtaxed. It therefore becomes necessary for other offices to assist in the advisement process. Such is the case at Boston College, where the Office of AHANA Student programs provides a holistic approach to advisement, focusing on the academic, social, cultural, and spiritual needs of AHANA students.

Peer Mentors The Office of AHANA Student Programs believes that students play a vital role in assisting fellow students to adjust to the college campus. Further, upperclass-men and-women know which instructors to take and which ones to avoid. Further, they have a good sense of the courses required for a major or a minor. Recognizing this, the Office of AHANA Student Programs annually hires a cadre of peer mentors whose job it is to serve as ambassadors. As ambassadors, they are expected to assist, where possible, AHANA Students with difficulties they may be experiencing. Central to their responsibilities is encouraging students to meet with a full-time staff member in the Office of AHANA Student Programs.

Academic Performance Monitoring This is an early warning system that asks faculty to provide feedback on students. By knowing early on the problems that a student is encountering, the program is in a better position to help the student pass a course that he or she might otherwise fail.

Career Counseling It is imperative that students see what is in store for them at the end of the proverbial rainbow. With this in mind, the Office of AHANA Student Programs has established a close-working relationship with the university's Career Center. AHANA Students are provided information about internships, jobs and graduate school opportunities; they are assisted in writing cover letters, and their resumes are critiqued. Further, discussions, workshops, and seminars are sponsored by alumni who share some of their experiences while attending the university and what they are currently doing.

Financial Aid Advising One of the frightening realities of attending the nation's colleges and universities are the prohibitive costs. As it stands now, Boston College costs $37,000 for tuition, room, and board. For most students in OTE this is in the vicinity of their parents' annual income. It becomes the student's responsibility and a function of the Office of AHANA Student Programs to work collaboratively with the university's Financial Aid Office to ensure that a student has the money needed to begin or remain at the university. Fisher (1987) correctly states that providing financial aid throughout a student's four-year stay at college is crucial to retention. In our experience at Boston College, when students have agonized over how the tuition bill is going to be paid, this has had serious implications for their academic performance and, in some instances, it has led to them dropping out of school.

AHANA Hotline Newsletter This is the Office of AHANA Student Programs' newsletter. It is a vital link in our array of services. It keeps squarely before students the broad array of resources provided by the Office of AHANA Student Programs; it informs them of activities that may be of interest both on and off campus, and it lets them know about jobs, internships, and graduate school opportunities. Providing students with information is the first step to getting them involved. It has been our experience at Boston College that when students become involved in campus activities, they are more likely to persist to graduation.

The Bowman AHANA Scholars Program and Reception Most offices on college and university campuses serving AHANA students spend considerable time assisting students at resolving adjustment issues, poor grades, or difficulties they may be experiencing with faculty, staff, roommates. Not nearly enough time is spent acknowledging, celebrating, or supporting those students who excel academically. The Office of AHANA Student Programs' response to this is to have an annual ceremony to recognize those AHANA students who have achieved a grade point average of 3.0 or better in a semester. Last year was a banner year for the office as we acknowledged more than 1,200 students. We were especially pleased that a number of the honorees were students who participated in our office's Options Through Education Summer Program.

The Gospel Caravan Marvalene Styles Hughes (1987) was in the vanguard in stating that spirituality plays a critically important role, especially in the lives of black students attending both historically black and predominantly white colleges and universities. On surveying students at both types of institutions, she asked an open-ended question aimed at what contributed to their success in college. At both types of institutions students stated that their faith in God was key to their success.

Recognizing the importance that spirituality and religion plays in the lives of AHANA students, several years ago the Office of AHANA Student Programs launched a van service called "The Gospel Caravan." The aim of The Gospel Caravan is to transport students who wish to attend a Sunday morning worship service to the church of their choosing. All that is required of the student is that he or she is ready to be picked up at a designated location at an agreed upon time.

Community Involvement The isolation that many AHANA students experience on predominantly white campuses can be partially overcome if opportunities are found for students to become involved in off-campus activities. At Boston College, we have identified a number of ways in which our students can make a difference in the community. One of the ways directly involves students in the Options Through Education Program. During the summer of 2002, the entire OTE program twice visited a housing development not very far from the Boston College campus. While there, they spent quality time playing basketball, volleyball, dancing, engaging in arts and crafts, and generally having a good time with the youth. In addition, the youth visited the college campus during the summer. Along with enjoying a wonderful barbecue, the youth were encouraged to begin thinking about one day attending college. Members of the OTE Program entered into pen pal relationships with the little ones and have agreed to work with them over the course of their four-year stay at the university.

AHANA Summer Tuition Remission The Office of AHANA Student Programs is aware that some students, for a plethora of reasons, will either drop out or fail a course during the academic year. When this occurs, if the student has fulfilled his or her obligation to use the resources of the Office of AHANA Student Programs during the academic year, he or she will, in all likelihood, be awarded two or more courses plus housing and dining. As one might imagine, this contributes enormously to student retention.

There is nothing serendipitous about the success that Boston College has experienced at retaining and graduating AHANA students from Boston College. It has come as a result of strong commitment at the highest levels of the university administration and it comes from the efforts of a dedicated and committed summer and academic year staff who continually develop and implement strategies that respond to the academic, social, cultural, and spiritual needs of students. In "Improving Minority Student Retention: A Search for Effective Institutional Practices," Clewell and Ficklen (1986) suggest that successful retention programs possess the following characteristics: presence of a stated policy; high levels of institutional commitment; a substantial degree of institutionalization; comprehensive services; dedicated staff; and non-stigmatization of students. Crosson (1997) corroborates the foregoing in a study of several colleges and universities that centered on factors that contributed to retention and graduation of AHANA students. She reported that they had six characteristics in common:

- They had strong programs to help students with problems in academic preparation.
- They emphasized pre-college programs and had developed relationships with elementary schools.
- They emphasized multicultural environments.
- They successfully resolved the organizational dilemma of separatist versus support programs for AHANA students.
- They developed proactive approaches to financial aid.
- They provided opportunities for on-campus housing.

Over the years the Office of AHANA Student Programs has received numbers of awards, citations, and accolades for its efforts at retaining AHANA Students at Boston College. However, nothing has been more rewarding than hearing directly from or about students who got their start in OTE, graduated from Boston College, and are now making their marks in the world. In this final section of the essay I would like to share several of their stories because their successes are really what this chapter is all about.

Toya M., who was ranked a 9 on Boston College's admission's grid (1 being the best student and 10 being the least-prepared). She was accepted into Boston College's School of Nursing. Although her skills in science and math were not strong, Toya was able to complete successfully two summer courses in math and English during the OTE program. During the academic year Toya experienced difficulty in the rigorous nursing program, earning no more than a 2.0 GPA each semester. Every summer, because she had either withdrawn or failed a course, Toya applied for and was given courses through the Office of AHANA Student Programs' Summer Tuition Remission Program. Each time she passed the courses awarded to her. Throughout her stay at Boston College she was encouraged to transfer out of the School of Nursing. This was unacceptable to Toya; she persisted in her dream of becoming a nurse. At the close of four years, Toya marched across the stage and received her nursing pin and degree. Her story does not end there because Toya, on her very first attempt, passed Massachusetts's very difficult board examination in nursing and is now doing quite well as a registered nurse at one of the world's finest hospitals.

Donna V. was ranked a 9 on Boston College's admissions grid. In light of her performance on the SATs, it was thought that she would benefit from the Options Through Education Program. She did well in the program. If there was a concern it was that while very amiable, she was not as verbal as we would have liked. In the fall Donna began her major in communications and soared. She began to open up. At the close of four years Donna moved to Florida, where she accepted a job as a news reporter. Today, she is an anchor on a local television station in the Miami area.

Mya B., at 15, was the youngest student ever accepted into the OTE Program. Her family had moved from Ethiopia a few years prior to her applying to college. Because she was prepared well in Ethiopia, Mya skipped two grades in the Boston Public Schools. If there was a weakness in Mya's preparation, it was her mastery of English. When she took the SATs, she did not do well on the English portion of the exam. Given her strong high school record, Mya applied and was accepted to Boston College through the OTE Program. She was rated a 7. Mya did well in OTE and throughout her four years at Boston College. She used the resources of the Office of AHANA Student Programs and graduated in four years. After graduating, she went on to get an MBA. Following that, she worked for Inroads for a number of years. Recently, Mya called the Office of AHANA Student Programs to thank us for assisting her in her journey through Boston College and to inform us that she had been accepted into a Ph.D. program at Stanford University. Not only that, she was awarded a 3D Fellowship; this, we are told, is an acronym representing Diversity, Distinction and Degree.

Jorge Miranda, ranked an 8 on the admissions grid, also entered Boston College through the Options Through Education Program. Jorge had graduated from the Hartford Public Schools, which, at the time, had been taken over by the state of Connecticut because of poor performance. Shortly after beginning OTE, Jorge began hanging around with several students who did not take the program seriously. He began mimicking some of their negative behaviors, including putting forth as little effort as possible. Then something wonderful happened. Jorge was asked to write an essay on something that he was passionate about. The result was a brilliant piece of work. His instructor told him that his writing ability was akin to that of a graduate student in writing. After that word of encouragement, Jorge began to apply himself in both English and mathematics. He removed himself from the negative influences of other students. Near the end of the program he applied for a mentor through our office's Benjamin Elijah Mays Mentor Program. His mentor was the director of residential life with whom Jorge met throughout his stay at the university. Jorge graduated with a GPA of 3.7 and was inducted into Phi Beta Kappa. Jorge had the difficult decision of deciding whether to attend Harvard Law School or Columbia University Law School. He chose Columbia, and while there, Jorge wrote for the Columbia Law Review. He graduated in May 2002 and accepted a job at a prestigious New York City law firm.

Conclusion

The aim of this chapter has been to point out that if AHANA students who are identified as being underprepared academically at the time of admissions are supported both during the summer and during the academic year, they will not only succeed but thrive on our nation's college and university campuses. Our nation needs to do more by way of ensuring that our youth are provided with every possible means of support. Indeed, if for no other reason than enlightened self-interest, we must make sure that such is the case. We would do well as a nation to look at the major demographic changes that have and will continue to occur in our nation. Here is something for our nation to ponder: In 1950, whites accounted for 86 percent of school-age youth. By 2000, their share had declined to 65 percent. In 2040, whites for the first time will comprise less than 50 percent of the school-age population, with Latinos comprising a full 28 percent, African Americans 14 percent, Asian Americans 8 percent, and Native Americans 1 percent (Source: U.S. Census Bureau, Population Projections, *Education Week*, 27 September 2000).

The message should be crystal clear to all. If this nation is concerned about its future well being, it must do whatever it takes to ensure that its young people graduate from high school and then enroll in one of our nation's colleges or universities. If the Options Through Education Program at Boston College and its attendant academic year support program have proven anything, it is that if students are afforded an opportunity and provided with academic support, they can and will succeed at our nation's colleges and universities.

References

Adelman, C. 1999. "Answers in the toolbox: Academic intensity, attendance patterns, and bachelor's degree attainment." Jessup, Md.: Education Publications Center, U.S. Department of Education.

Brown, D. 1996. "Increasing Retention Rates Among Students of Color: The Office of AHANA Student Programs at Boston College." C. Ford, ed. *Student Retention Success Models in Higher Education*, pp. 14–15. Tallahassee, Fla: CNJ Associates.

Clewell, B., and M. Ficklen. 1986. *Improving Minority Retention In Higher Education: A Search for Effective Institutional Practices*. Princeton, N.J.: Educational Testing Services.

Crosson, Patricia H. 1987. "Environmental Influences on Minority Degree Attainment." Paper presented at an annual meeting of the Association for the Study of Higher Education. (21–24 November 1987). Baltimore, Md.: Ed 292415. 34 pp. MF-01: PC–02.

Fisher, Frederick J. 1987. "Graduation-Contingent Student Aid." *Change* 19(6): pp. 40–47.

Hughes, M. S. 1987. "Black Students' Participation in Higher Education." *Journal of College Student Personnel.* Vol. 28: 532–537.

Payne, Jarize. 1987. "My Experience with the peer Mentoring Program." *Children Today,* 16(4): 20.

Perna, L. W. 2000. "Differences in the Decision to Attend College among African American, Hispanics and whites." *The Journal of Higher Education, 71:* 117–141.

Sedlacek, W. E., and D. W. Webster. 1978. "Admissions and Retention of Minority Students in Large Universities." *Journal of College Student Personnel* 19:242–248.

U.S. Census Bureau, "Population Projections," *Education Week* (27 September 2000).

Linda S. Greene and
Margaret N. Harrigan

LINDA S. GREENE, a University of California Berkeley Law School graduate, is the Evjue-Bascom Professor of Law at the University of Wisconsin Law School. She teaches Constitutional Law, Civil Procedure, Race Conscious Governmental Action, and the Life and Legacy of Thurgood Marshall. She has been a civil rights attorney at the NAACP Legal Defense and Education Fund, a tenured associate professor at the University of Oregon, a visiting professor at Harvard and Georgetown law schools, and Counsel to the United States Senate Judiciary Committee. She is Associate Vice Chancellor for Faculty and Staff Programs at the University of Wisconsin Madison. Her responsibilities include faculty strategic hiring initiatives, the Interdisciplinary Cluster Hiring Initiative, dean and department chair professional development, new faculty programs, faculty pay equity, women faculty mentoring, and human resources policy and strategic planning.

MARGARET N. HARRIGAN is a policy and planning analyst in the Office of Academic Planning and Analysis at the University of Wisconsin–Madison. She analyzes educational and academic policy issues important to the work of the Provost, the Vice Chancellor for Administration, the University Academic Planning Council, and other task groups. For more than ten years, she has focused on gender equity in pay and promotions for faculty and other professional staff. She has authored many papers on important faculty and student issues for external and internal audiences and speaks frequently to numerous campus administrative and governance groups. She holds degrees from George Washington University and the University of Wisconsin.

15

STRATEGIC PRIORITIES AND STRATEGIC FUNDING

MINORITY FACULTY HIRING AT THE UNIVERSITY OF WISCONSIN-MADISON 1988-2003

Introduction

In this essay, we discuss the experience of the University of Wisconsin-Madison that has provided central funding for minority faculty hiring at various times since 1987. Part II discusses the period from 1982–83 to 2002–03, which includes two significant periods of central funding availability, the Madison Plan (1988–93) and the Strategic Hiring Initiative (1997–2002). We review the terms and conditions of that funding, the financial commitment associated with that funding, and the amount of minority faculty hiring associated with the presence and absence of central funding. In Part III, we analyze minority faculty hiring statistics associated with the availability and absence of central funding and conclude that the provision of central funding had a significant positive effect on minority faculty hiring. Other factors, such as the number of faculty hired each year, may also have contributed to the increase in minority hiring during the periods of central fund availability. However, we conclude that the existence of the fund and the manner in which it was administered kept the importance of minority faculty hiring in the foreground of faculty hiring discussions. Moreover, the augmentation of departmental budgets provided a tangible financial benefit, which rewarded successful efforts to recruit minority hires and further reinforced the significance of increased faculty diversity. At the University of Wisconsin-Madison, minority faculty hiring increased when central funding was available and decreased when central funding was not available. While the optimal outcome would be greater minority faculty hiring without central administration intervention, on the basis of this experience, the University of Wisconsin-Madison has reinstated a central fund as one tool to raise the number of minority faculty at our institution.

Strategic Funding and Minority Faculty Hires at UW-Madison 1982–83 through 2002–03

Background

In the past twenty years, the University of Wisconsin-Madison has had two periods of central funding to encourage hiring a more diverse faculty: the Madison Plan, introduced in 1988; and the Strategic Hiring Initiative, which began in 1997. Both programs lasted for approximately five years. To measure the effect of central funding to increase faculty diversity, this chapter divides the years between 1982–83 and 2002–03 into five periods: pre-Madison Plan (1982–83 through 1987–88); Madison Plan (1988–89 through 1992–93); post-Madison Plan (1993–94 through 1996–97); Strategic Hiring Initiative (1997–98 through 2001–02); and post-Strategic Hiring Initiative (2002–03).

At the University of Wisconsin-Madison, faculty hiring decisions are made at the school or college level. The dean of the school or college authorizes a department to conduct a search, setting aside dollars and full time equivalent data (FTE) for the new position. Generally, the dean must have funds and FTE resulting from retirements or resignations in order to approve a search. Historically, the university's central administration did not normally play a role in the faculty recruitment process. During the Madison Plan and the Strategic Hiring Initiative, university central administration was proactive by providing additional funds to departments that successfully recruited minority faculty.

Pre-Madison Plan Period: No Strategic Funding between 1982–83 and 1986–87

During the period from 1982–83 through 1986–87 there were no central funds set aside for hiring minority faculty. Throughout this pre-Madison Plan period, the percentage of minority faculty hired varied between 7 percent and 11 percent (See Figure 1 and Table 1). In 1987,

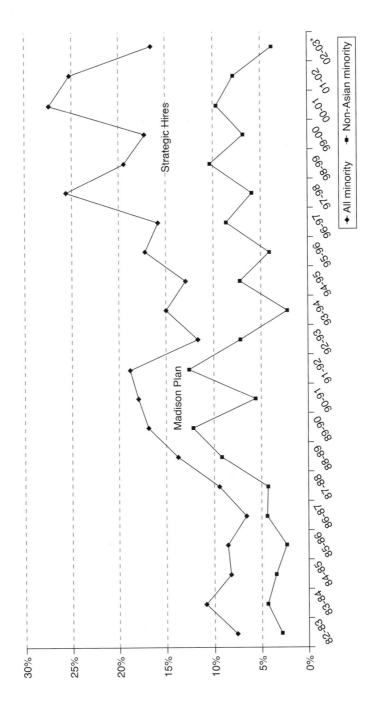

Figure 1 Minority Faculty Hires as Percent of All Faculty Hires

Table 1 Minority Faculty Hires at UW Madison 1982–83 through 2002–03

Year of Hire	Total Faculty Hired	Minority Faculty Hired						Percent Minority	Percent Non-Asian Minority
		Total	Black	Asian	Native American	Hispanic			
Pre-Madison Plan									
1982–83	106	8	0	5	0	3		8%	3%
1983–84	138	15	2	9	0	4		11%	4%
1984–85	146	12	2	7	2	1		8%	3%
1985–86	129	11	0	8	0	3		9%	2%
1986–87	92	6	2	2	0	2		7%	4%
1987–88	117	11	0	6	1	4		9%	4%
Madison Plan									
1988–89	197	27	4	9	2	12		14%	9%
1989–90	148	25	7	7	2	9		17%	12%
1990–91	145	26	5	18	0	3		18%	6%
1991–92	128	24	7	8	1	8		19%	13%
1992–93	112	13	3	5	2	3		12%	7%

Mann-Whitney U one-tailed test (p-value)
comparing Madison Plan and pre-Madison Plan period   (0.002)   (0.004)

Post-Madison Plan

1993–94	94	14	0	12	0	2	15%	2%
1994–95	70	9	2	4	0	3	13%	7%
1995–96	76	13	2	10	1	0	17%	4%
1996–97	70	11	2	5	0	4	16%	9%

Mann-Whitney U one-tailed test (p-value)
comparing Madison Plan and post-Madison Plan period (0.365) (0.095)
comparing Madison Plan and pre- and post-Madison Plan periods (0.025) (0.010)

Strategic Hiring Initiative

1997–98	86	22	3	17	0	2	26%	6%
1998–99	98	19	6	9	0	4	19%	10%
1999–00	134	23	3	14	2	4	17%	7%
2000–01	157	43	9	28	0	6	27%	10%
2001–02	155	39	7	27	2	3	25%	8%

Mann-Whitney U one-tailed test (p-value)
comparing Stratergic Hiring Initiative and post-Madison Plan period (0.008) (0.143)

Post-Strategic Hiring Initiative

2002–03	134	22	2	17	0	3	16%	4%

NOTES: 2002–2003 hiring data are preliminary and are based on deans' reports of offers accepted during 2001–02. These numbers will differ from hires during 2002–03 since some offers are accepted with a start date more than one year in the future.

SOURCE: University of Wisconsin–Madison Equal Employment Opportunity and appointment databases, Office of Academic Planning and Analysis

UW-Madison had 2,360 faculty. Of these, twenty-five were Black (1.1%), eighty-six Asian (3.6%), three Native American (0.1%), and twenty-five Hispanic (1.1%) (See Table 2). In 1987, after black students began to express concerns about the racial climate on campus and racial tensions were further exacerbated by a fraternity's offensive caricature of a Fijian, the central administration began a fledgling effort to use central funds to encourage the recruitment of women and minority faculty in underrepresented areas. When Donna Shalala became Chancellor on January 1, 1988, she incorporated that program into a more expansive effort to increase diversity on the campus. That effort is now known as The Madison Plan.

The Madison Plan Provides Strategic Funding from 1988–1993

On February 8, 1988, just one month after she became Chancellor, Donna Shalala announced the beginning of The Madison Plan "conceived to address the University's need for diversity"[1] She stated, "today we do more than denounce racism, sexism, and discrimination of all kinds. Today we commit our skills and our resources to the task."[2] Shalala linked the goal of diversity to excellence. "Diversity and pluralism are absolutely essential on this campus; they are necessary parts of a superb education for all our students."[3] The Madison Plan addressed student recruitment, student retention, outreach to minority middle school and high school students, academic staff recruitment and retention, curriculum, establishment of a multicultural center, and the goal of achieving a non-discriminatory environment. The Madison Plan also announced the goal of attracting and retaining an increased number of minority faculty.

The Madison Plan was a response to the Final Report of the Steering Committee on Minority Affairs, the report of a campus committee that during 1986–87 examined the causes of racial tensions on the Madison campus. The Steering Committee, also known as the Holley Committee after student chair Charles Holley, reported its findings and recommendations in December of 1987. Chancellor designate Shalala had visited the campus several times before her official start date of January 1988. During these visits, she discussed the Holley Committee and pending Holley report with Interim Vice Chancellor Phil Certain

Table 2 Headcount of Faculty by Gender and Race/Ethnicity at University of Wisconsin–Madison

		Percent Minority	Black	Asian	Native American	Hispanic	White/ Other	Total
October 1987: Prior to Madison Plan	Women	6%	7	9	0	5	337	358
	Men	6%	18	77	3	20	1,884	2,002
	Total	6%	25	86	3	25	2,221	2,360
October 1996: Prior to Strategic Hiring Initiative	Women	11%	17	19	2	13	415	466
	Men	9%	24	95	5	38	1581	1,743
	Initiative Total	10%	41	114	7	51	1,996	2,209
October 2001: Current Faculty	Women	16%	28	39	2	18	459	546
	Men	12%	32	123	6	42	1,464	1,667
	Total	13%	60	162	8	60	1,923	2,213

Note: The category White/Other includes those who choose not to report race/ethnicity.

Source: University of Wisconsin - Madison Office of Academic Planning and Analysis

and others. In the course of these discussions, Chancellor Shalala decided to make a response to the Holley Report the highlight of her first six weeks on the University of Wisconsin-Madison campus. The Madison Plan emerged from those discussions.

In the faculty-related portion of the Madison Plan, the university set a goal of hiring seventy minority female and male faculty by the end of 1991. More specifically, the Madison Plan aimed to hire twenty-five tenured faculty and forty-five tenure track faculty over a period of three years as well as visiting professors during a transition period.[4]

The Madison Plan

The portion of the Madison Plan designed to recruit a more diverse faculty began with three components. Departments hiring a tenured minority faculty member received a permanent budget allocation of $67,500. Recruitment of a minority or female assistant professor in an under-represented area garnered a $10,000 budget increase for the department. This increase was renewable annually for as long as the assistant professor remained on campus. With the granting of tenure, the supplement became a permanent part of the department's budget. Finally, departments that hired visiting minority faculty received a one-year supplement of $10,000 for the appointment of an assistant professor and a one-year $25,000 supplement for an appointment at the associate or full professor level.[5]

Over time, the financial incentives in the Madison Plan were modified.[6] After 1988–89, the central administration discontinued the subsidization of women faculty hires. Allocations for senior minority faculty hires remained with the department only for as long as the faculty remained with the university and were recaptured by central administration when/if the minority faculty departed. In 1990–91, the supplement for visiting faculty was discontinued and the supplement for probationary faculty was modified. Instead of providing a renewable allocation, the central administration provided temporary supplements for probationary minority hires equal to the lesser of $25,000 or half of the individual's salary for up to two years upon approval by the Provost. Beginning in 1993–94, the campus provided for the renewal of previously awarded amounts for tenured and untenured faculty but did not provide new positions or allocations for newly hired faculty.[7]

In the 1988–89 academic year, the university committed $1.6 million to fund the first cohort of Madison Plan hires.[8] At its peak, the university spent nearly $2 million annually in permanent and transitional dollars to fund the Madison Plan. Currently, approximately $1 million in permanent base budget allocations per year is attributable to the Madison Plan minority hires.

The Effect of the Madison Plan on Minority Faculty Hiring

During the five years of the Madison Plan, the central administration made contributions to salaries of 110 tenured and tenure-track faculty: sixteen minority senior faculty, forty-three minority assistant professors, and fifty-one women assistant professors in underrepresented areas. During the first year of the Madison Plan, total minority faculty hired increased to twenty-seven, 14 percent of the total faculty hired that year. In the four subsequent years that Madison Plan funding was available, minority hiring as a percentage of total number of faculty hired varied between 12 percent and 19 percent (See Table 1). Our analysis will show that the increase in minority hires during the Madison Plan years is statistically significant.

A review of the number of faculty hires per year shows that the number of minority hires seems to rise and fall with the number of overall faculty hires (See Figure 2). Table 3 shows the average number of faculty hires per year in each of the five time periods. In the six years before the Madison Plan was implemented, an average of 121 faculty members were hired each year. On average, ten to eleven new hires per year were members of a minority group, with Asians making up about 60 percent of the minority hires. Minorities comprised nine percent of total hires.

The Madison Plan was adopted at a time when the university received additional funding and more than 100 new faculty positions from the State of Wisconsin to improve undergraduate education. Thus, the average number of faculty hires per year grew to 146 during the five-year period. During the Madison Plan, minority hires climbed to twenty-three per year, or 16 percent of all faculty hires—an increase of about 78 percent over the previous time period. The increase in hires occurred for all minority groups. Black faculty hires increased four-fold, from an average of one per year to more than five per year—about 4 percent of all faculty hires in the period. Both Native American and

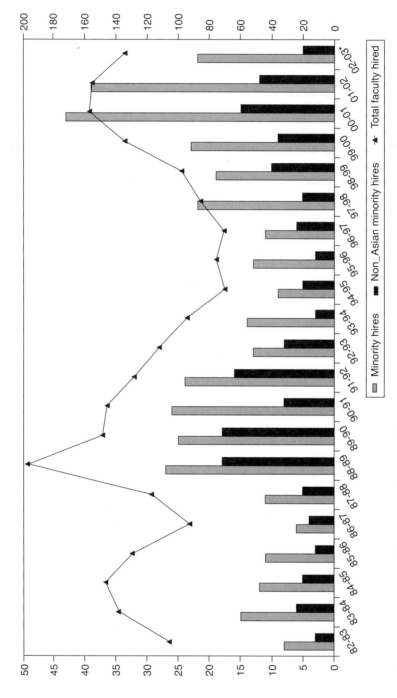

Figure 2 UW Madison Faculty Hired in 1982–83 through 2002–03

Table 3 Faculty Hires at UW Madison from 1982–83 through 2001–02 by Minority Status

Time Period	Total Hired	*Average Number of Faculty Hired Per Year*						Minority Hires as % of Total	Non-Asian Minority Hires as % of Total
		All Faculty	All Minority Faculty	Black	Asian	Native American	Hispanic		
Pre-Madison Plan (1982–83–1987–88)	728	121.3	10.5	1.0	6.2	0.5	2.8	9%	4%
Madison Plan (1988–89–1992–93)	730	146.0	23.0	5.2	9.4	1.4	7.0	16%	9%
Post-Madison Plan (1993–94–1996–97)	310	77.5	11.8	1.5	7.8	0.3	2.3	15%	5%
Strategic Hiring Initiative (1997–98–2001–02)	630	126.0	29.2	5.6	19.0	0.8	3.8	23%	8%
Post-Strategic Hiring Initiative (2002–03)	134	134	22	2	17	0	3	16%	4%

NOTES: 2002–2003 hiring data are preliminary and are based on deans' reports of offers accepted during 2001–02. These numbers will differ from actual hires during 2002–03 since some offers are accepted with a start date more than one year in the future.

SOURCE: UW–Madison appointment data, Office of Academic Planning and Analysis.

Hispanic hires increased by more than 150 percent. Native American hires averaged one to two per year during the Madison Plan. Hispanic faculty hires rose to an average of seven per year. Asians, the largest minority group on campus, also showed gains. Asian faculty hires rose from an average of about six per year between 1982 and 1987 to about nine per year during the Madison Plan. Non-Asian minority hires were 56 percent of all minority hires during the Madison Plan years.

A simple statistical test can be used to compare minority hires during the Madison Plan with years when no central funding was available. We used the Mann-Whitney U test (95% confidence level, one-tailed test) to compare the percent of minorities hired during the Madison Plan years with the pre-Madison Plan period, the Post-Madison period, and both periods combined (see Table 1). Minorities made up a significantly greater proportion of faculty hires during the Madison Plan years than in the years immediately preceding the Madison Plan. The difference between the Madison Plan period and the combined periods with no central funding is also statistically significant. Compared to the post-Madison Plan period alone, however, there is no significant difference in the percent of minority faculty hired. The Madison Plan period also shows a statistically significant increase in non-Asian minority hires compared to the pre-Madison plan period and the combined years when no central funding was available.

Post-Madison Plan Period: No Central Funding between 1993–94 and 1996–97

From 1993 to 1996, the campus did not provide any additional central funds to reward the hire of minority faculty.[9] However, the vice chancellor informed deans and department chairs that the university hoped to continue to make progress on recruiting underrepresented minority faculty. Departmental requests for assistance for senior minority faculty hires would be considered on a case-by-case basis. The vice chancellor also offered temporary assistance for recruiting new minority assistant professors, and continued the Anna Julia Cooper post-doctoral fellowships, a six-year-old program designed to give the campus a competitive edge in the recruitment of junior minority faculty.[10]

The state budgetary situation was bleak as well. The state adopted major budget cuts to the university of about $13 million in 1995–97. Limited state funds meant fewer faculty hires in the mid-90s. On average, only seventy-eight faculty were hired each year of the post-Madison Plan period—a drop of almost 50 percent. The number of minority hires decreased, but new minority faculty as a percentage of new hires did not fall to the pre-Madison Plan level. Fifteen percent of all new faculty during the period were minority hires, compared with 16 percent during the Madison Plan years.

However, in the absence of significant central funding for diversity, Asians once again comprised more than 60 percent of all minority faculty hired. Non-Asian minority faculty were 9 percent of hires during the Madison Plan years and 5 percent of total hires from 1993–94 through 1996–97. Black faculty hires fell to about 2 percent and Hispanic hires to about 3 percent of total hires in the later period (See Table 3). Central administration's concern about the diversification of the faculty led the administration to seek funding to be used to encourage minority faculty hiring.

The Faculty Strategic Hiring Initiative (SHI) 1997–2002

Description of the Strategic Hiring Initiative

On October 9, 1996, Provost John Wiley announced the beginning of a strategic hiring initiative to increase the number of hires in three major areas: minority faculty, women faculty in the sciences and engineering, and the spouses or partners of dual career couples. This initiative was funded with a large portion of one-time only funds provided through the Wisconsin Alumni Research Foundation (WARF), called the Faculty Enhancement Fund. The Strategic Hiring Initiative provided negotiable, varying percentages of short-term funding (hereinafter *bridge funding*) to departments that hired women faculty in the sciences and engineering, minority faculty, and spouses or partners of faculty.[11] Department chairs and deans frequently consulted the associate vice chancellor (hereinafter *AVC*) for advice on search strategies or for clarification of existing campus policy on strategic funding availability. The AVC also provided advice on interview strategies as well as referrals to other campus offices (such as the Equity and Diversity Resource Center or Office of Human Resources) that might provide assistance or advice. The AVC was also available to meet with or talk by telephone with minority candidates to answer questions about the campus commitment to faculty diversity or to network candidates with minorities on campus and in the surrounding Madison community. The AVC also provided referrals for the discussion of issues such as start-up packages and space needs, and explained campus resources and programs for new professors.

After departments identified hires and deans approved those hires, deans or designated associate deans sent requests for central funding directly to the Provost. The funding arrangements varied depending on the needs of the department requesting funds. This was negotiated with the AVC responsible for the oversight of the faculty strategic hiring fund.[12] Finally, the AVC wrote memoranda (for Provost signature) documenting agreements to provide assistance.

The Graduate School managed the overall Faculty Enhancement Fund and also provided valuable services in connection with the Strategic Hiring Initiative. The Graduate School provided fund accounting services, advised on the structuring of bridge funding arrangements, and arranged for the transfer of funds to the appropriate departments.

With respect to the Strategic Hiring Initiative, during the period between 1997 and 2002, the campus committed about $3.5 million to bridge funding arrangements for tenure-track minority faculty hires. A portion of this funding, about $900,000, funded Anna Julia Cooper Post Doctoral fellowships for minority faculty who had also been offered and had accepted tenure-track positions upon the completion of the Anna Julia Cooper Fellowship.

Although the Strategic Hiring Initiative was maintained as a single fund without specific amounts set aside for the strategic categories, the expenditures in the various categories was fairly equal. During the five-year period strategic expenditures to recruit or retain dual career couple faculty and staff were $4.2 million. Minority faculty related expenditures—Anna Julia Cooper Post Doctoral Fellowships, salary, and other expenditures for recruitment and retention—were $3.6 million. Women in Science faculty related expenditures for recruitment or retention were $3.7 million.

The Effect of the Strategic Hiring Initiative

Both the total number of faculty recruited and the number of minority faculty hires increased during the Strategic Hiring Initiative. As noted above, between 1993–94 and 1996–97, when the campus provided no central funding, minority faculty hiring varied between 13 percent and 17 percent. In contrast, during the Strategic Hiring Initiative, 1997–98 through 2001–02, the percentage of minority faculty hired ranged from 17 percent to 27 percent of the total hired (See Table 1).

In 1998, when the university commenced the Madison Initiative, "a four-year investment plan to strengthen UW-Madison as it provides students an outstanding education and help Wisconsin expand its competitiveness in the global economy."[13] This program, although not targeted to increase campus diversity directly, did include plans to recruit 100 faculty "in new and emerging academic disciplines that cross traditional departmental and college lines."[14] Thus, overall hiring increased in the past three years under SHI, reaching more than 150 new hires in both 2000–01 and 2001–02.

Minority hires reached a new high at the university during the Strategic Hiring Initiative—more than 23 percent of faculty successfully recruited during the period were members of a minority group. Asians made up 15 percent of the total new faculty hired. (In comparison, minority hires of all races in the previous four years amounted to 15 percent.) As a percent of all new faculty, non-Asian minority hires averaged 8 percent over the SHI years, a 60 percent increase over the post-Madison Plan period (See Table 3). Black hires returned to the Madison Plan levels of 4 percent of total hires. Hispanic faculty hires remained at 3 percent of the total, as they had been in the mid-90s when there were no diversity funding incentives in place.

The SHI provided temporary funding to departments for a total of ninety-three faculty hired between 1997–98 and 2001–02[15] (See Table 4). Forty-two were members of minority groups. Of the forty-two minority faculty hired with SHI funds, twenty-one (50%) were black, twelve (29%) were Asian, seven (17%) were Hispanic, and two (5%) were Native American. The Asian faculty hires included three as diversity hires and nine hired under the women in science or dual career couple programs.

Table 4 Faculty Hired with Strategic Hiring Initiative Funds by Race/Ethnicity

	Headcount Of Faculty Hired with SHI Funds						Total Faculty Hired					
Year of Hire	Black	Asian	Native American	Hispanic	White/Other	Total	Black	Asian	Native American	Hispanic	White/Other	Total
1997–98	3	4	0	1	15	23	3	17	0	2	64	86
1998–99	6	1	0	3	14	24	6	9	0	4	79	98
1999–00	2	1	2	2	10	17	3	14	2	4	111	134
2000–01	6	5	0	1	9	21	9	28	0	6	114	157
2001–02	4	1	0	0	3	8	7	27	2	3	116	155
Total	21	12	2	7	51	93	28	95	4	19	484	630

NOTES: Strategic Hiring Initiative (SHI) Funds supported the following hiring programs: Dual Career Couple, Women in Science, Anna Julia Cooper Post-doctoral Fellowships, Diversity, and Vision hires. A limited amount of funds were available to be realloca

SOURCE: UW–Madison Office of Academic Planning and Analysis

The forty-two minority faculty members funded in part through SHI comprised less than one-third of all minority hires during the period. Departments hiring black faculty were most likely to benefit from the SHI—three-fourths of all black hires were covered by the program. Half of Native American, 37 percent of Hispanic, and 13 percent of Asian faculty hired between 1997–98 and 2001–02 were funded through SHI.

A Mann-Whitney U test shows that minorities made up a significantly greater proportion of new faculty during the Strategic Hiring Initiative than in the preceding four years. Although the Strategic Hiring Initiative also showed substantially more non-Asian minority hires—a 60 percent increase over the post-Madison Plan period—this difference is not statistically significant (see Table 1).

Post-Strategic Hiring Initiative 2002–2003

After the exhaustion of the Faculty Enhancement Fund, the Provost considered options for the continuation of the Strategic Hiring Initiatives. The modified program was announced in late November 2001. The program provided that schools and colleges with relatively large numbers of faculty and corresponding financial flexibility would assume responsibility for funding strategic hires including minority strategic hires. Under the new program, small schools and colleges with fewer numbers of faculty would continue to seek strategic funding from the Office of the Provost.[16]

Data is not currently available on the number of minority faculty whose appointment began during 2002–03. However, based on deans' reports of offers accepted during the prior year, an estimated 16 percent of new faculty hires in 2002–03 were members of a minority group. Further, the deans anticipate about 4 percent of these new faculty hires will be non-Asian minority faculty. In comparison, minority faculty hiring was 25 percent during the previous academic year; non-Asian minority faculty comprised 8 percent of the total. The 2002–03 data represents only one year and is only an estimate of actual hires. Nonetheless, it is consistent with our past experience that minority hires at the University of Wisconsin-Madison increase in years when central funds are made available to encourage diversity hiring.

Effects of Central Funding on Minority Hiring

In this section, we discuss the impact of central funds on faculty hiring. As noted earlier, from 1988–1993 when the Madison Plan was underway, the university showed a statistically significant increase in the proportion of new faculty who were members of a minority group. The years corresponding to the Strategic Hiring Initiative, 1997–98 through 2001–02, also showed a significantly greater proportion of minority hires than the post-Madison Plan period.

However, the centrally funded initiatives were designed to encourage underrepresented minority hires. Departments hiring Asian faculty members were only eligible for incentive funding in areas where Asians were underrepresented, generally Arts and Humanities, or if the hire also met other criteria, such as women in science. The Madison Plan period showed a statistically significant increase in non-Asian minority hires as well as total minority hires. Although the percent of non-Asian minority hires under the Strategic Hiring Initiative increased compared with the post-Madison Plan period, this difference is not statistically significant.

Outside pressures on the university's budget influenced the total number of hires in these time periods. The availability of additional funds and positions for faculty recruitment also corresponded to years when central diversity funds were made available. Only in the first two years of the SHI were there limited numbers of new faculty hired at the same time as a centrally funded diversity initiative. In those two years, minority hires comprised 26 and 19 percent of total hires—higher than in the preceding four years. However, non-Asian minority hires—the primary focus of the Strategic Hiring Initiative diversity hires—were 6 and 10 percent of total hires, similar to the post-Madison Plan period (See Table 1). Thus, it is difficult to discern whether central funds were the most significant factor contributing to increased minority hires or whether expansive overall budgets were necessary as well. Perhaps one factor associated with our increase in minority faculty hiring is the total number of faculty hires, and another factor—at least at Wisconsin—was the availability of central funding assistance.

The context in which central funding was made available is relevant to the question of whether central funding was a necessary ingredient in UW-Madison's successful effort to increase minority faculty hiring. As the description of the Madison Plan and the SHI indicate, the amount of the funding and the terms of the funding varied from full faculty lines to a percentage of the initial funds necessary to make the hire. But despite this variation, the availability of the funding was associated with an increase in minority faculty hires.

These results suggest that the very existence of some central funding signals and reinforces the strategic importance of minority faculty hiring to departments and colleges. Nonetheless, departmental initiatives remained crucial to minority hiring. Funding was only available to a department if the department conducted a search that culminated in the choice of a minority candidate for the opening. The availability of funding to a department depended upon the department's ability to persuade the college to seek central funding *and* the college's successful negotiation of a financial agreement with the office of the Provost.

These factors suggest that departmental and college level readiness and motivation were also important ingredients in the use of central funding. In fact, the evidence shows that while a fair number of departments across a range of departments and colleges did seek assistance, some schools and departments did not. Nearly every academic department at Wisconsin (about 120) successfully recruited one or more new faculty members between 1997–98 and 2001–02. About 60 percent of the departments hired a minority faculty member (including Asian faculty) during that period. However, only twenty-four departments used strategic hiring funds for minority faculty recruitment during the five-year period.

Did the existence of central funding create a more favorable climate for minority faculty hiring? The existence of central funding did create opportunities for communication about minority hiring among departments, colleges, and the office of the Provost. Faculty and administrators frequently contacted the Associate Vice Chancellor for advice on the search and assistance in the recruitment of minority candidates. A plausible inference may be that existence of the strategic hiring fund stimulated discussion between departments and colleges and the central administration on the subject of minority faculty hiring. The fact that success in the recruitment of minority candidates might be rewarded with increased budgetary flexibility may have also created a positive climate for faculty diversification efforts. In addition, the availability of funding and the resulting discussion provided an opportunity to encourage, coach, and reward departmental leaders for their efforts. The increase in faculty hiring may also have been stimulated by Provost-sponsored workshops for department chairs and deans on recruiting and hiring. During these workshops, which covered a variety of subjects relevant to faculty hiring, the subject of minority hiring was included and the availability of strategic hiring assistance discussed.

What would the number of minority hires have looked like in the absence of SHI and the Madison Plan? The number of minority faculty hired varied quite a bit from year to year, although a general upward trend in minority hires is evident during the past 20 years. It seems likely that this increase may also be associated with increases in availability of minority Ph.D.s. The number of Ph.D.s granted to minority candidates rose from 2,728 in 1980–81 (9.5% of all doctoral degrees to U.S. citizens) to 6,050 in 1999–2000 (18%).[17] In addition, implementation of recruitment strategies to increase diversity may have also had an impact on minority hires, particularly during those years in which more dollars were available for faculty hires, generally.

Notwithstanding these reservations, the number of minority faculty at the University of Wisconsin-Madison has increased for the period since 1987. In the fall of 2001, the University of Wisconsin-Madison had 290 minority faculty, including sixty Black, sixty Hispanic, 162 Asians, and eight Native Americans. Both the number and percent of minority faculty has more than doubled, from 139 (6%) in 1987, the year before the Madison Plan was initiated, to 290 (13%) in 2001 (Table 2). On the basis of this experience, the University of Wisconsin-Madison has reinstated central funding as one tool to increase the number of minority faculty.

Conclusion

The University of Wisconsin-Madison experience provides twenty years of data from which to assess the effect of central funding on minority hiring. On the basis of this limited set of data, we found a statistically significant increase in minority faculty hires during both periods when central funding was available. Furthermore, the Madison Plan period was associated with a significant increase in non-Asian minority hires. Hiring of non-Asian minority faculty also grew during the Strategic Hiring Initiative years, although the increase was not statistically significant. We also acknowledged other factors that may have also influenced the degree of minority hiring including the level of overall faculty hiring, minority Ph.D.s supply, as well as the manner in which the fund was administered.

The University of Wisconsin-Madison experience was not a controlled experiment. Thus, it is difficult to sort out the effects of strategic funds from other possible factors that may contribute to the level of minority hiring. In particular, the years of expansive budgets and associated increased faculty hiring closely paralleled the years when central finding was made available. Only during the first two years of the Strategic Hiring Initiative were there limited numbers of faculty hires at the same time that the campus had a centrally funded diversity initiative. Thus, it is difficult to discern whether central funds were more important to successful recruitment of minority faculty or whether expansive budgets were necessary as well.

However, on the basis of our overall experience we can conclude that the existence of central funding for minority hires has been associated with an overall increase in the level of minority faculty hiring. On the basis of this experience, the University of Wisconsin-Madison has reinstated central funding as one tool to increase the number of minority faculty.[18]

Notes

1. *UW-Madison Announces Minority Initiatives* (9 February 1988), University of Wisconsin-Madison News Service.
2. The Madison Plan Executive Summary, The University of Wisconsin-Madison, (9 February 1988).
3. 1987–1988 UW-Madison Budget Instructions (9 April 1987).
4. 1988–1989 UW-Madison Budget Instructions (1 April 1988), 1989–1990 UW-Madison Budget Instructions (20 April 1989), 1990–1991 UW-Madison Budget Instructions (13 March 1990), 1991–1992 UW Madison Budget Instructions (18 April 1991), and 1992–1993 UW-Madison Budget Instructions (1 April 1992).
5. 1993–1994 UW-Madison Budget Instruction (30 March 1993), 1994–1995 UW-Madison Budget Instructions (17 February 1994), 1995–1996 UW-Madison Budget Instructions (30 March 1995) and 1996–1997 UW-Madison Budget Instructions.
6. Although central funding for diversity hires was announced during 1987–88, faculty hired during this year are included in the category of pre-Madison Plan hires (with no central funding). This was done because

it generally takes a year or more from the time a recruitment effort begins until a new faculty member arrives on campus. The tables included in this study contain information on when an individual's faculty appointment began, rather than when the recruitment effort took place. Departments received central funds for three minority faculty whose appointments started in 1987–88.

7. A limited amount of funds were available to be reallocated when faculty members hired under the Madison Plan left the university. These funds were held in reserve until new minority faculty hires were made. Between 1994 and 1996, two faculty members were hired with these reallocated funds.

8. Memorandum to Deans, Chairs, and Directors from Interim Vice Chancellor Richard Barrows, September 15, 1993.

9. Memorandum to Deans, Department Chairs, Program Chairs/Directors, and Center Directors from Provost John D. Wiley, January 2000. The initiative also included funding for Anna Julia Cooper post-doctoral fellowships that were available to women minority assistant professor appointments.

10. In 1997–99 the AVC was Paul Barrows; in 1999–2001 it was Linda Greene.

11. "Program Description." *UW-Madison Office of the Provost Cluster Hiring Initiative.* http://wiscinfo.doit.wisc.edu/cluster/progrmdesc.html

12. "Program Description." *UW-Madison Office of the Provost Cluster Hiring Initiative.* http://wiscinfo.doit.wisc.edu/cluster/progrmdesc.html

13. A limited amount of funds were available to be reallocated when faculty members hired under the Madison Plan left the university. These funds were held in reserve until new minority faculty hires were made. Between 1997–98 and 2000–01, two minority faculty members were hired with these reallocated funds.

14. Memorandum to Deans, Department Chairs, Program Chairs/Directors, and Center Directors from Provost Peter D. Spear, dated 28 November 2001, and revised version, 25 January 2002.

15. *Digest of Education Statistics, 2001.* National Center for Education Statistics (April 2002).

16. Memorandum to Deans, Department Chairs, Program Chairs/Directors, and Center Directors, Cluster Hire Search Committees from Provost Peter D. Spear, dated 31 October 2002.

William E. Sedlacek

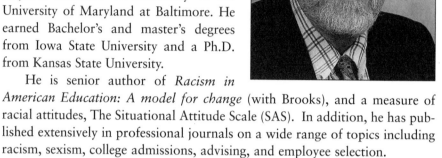

WILLIAM E. SEDLACEK is a Professor of
Education and Assistant Director of the
Counseling Center at the University of
Maryland, College Park. He is also an
Adjunct Professor of Pharmacy at the
University of Maryland at Baltimore. He
earned Bachelor's and master's degrees
from Iowa State University and a Ph.D.
from Kansas State University.

He is senior author of *Racism in
American Education: A model for change* (with Brooks), and a measure of
racial attitudes, The Situational Attitude Scale (SAS). In addition, he has published extensively in professional journals on a wide range of topics including
racism, sexism, college admissions, advising, and employee selection.

He has served as editor of Measurement and Evaluation in Counseling
and Development. Also, he has consulted with more than 250 different organizations, colleges, and universities on interracial and intercultural issues, and
has served as an expert witness in race and sex discrimination cases. In 1993,
he received the Ralph F. Berdie Memorial Research Award "for research
affecting directional changes in the field of counseling and college student personnel work" which was presented by the American Counseling Association.
In 1997, he received the research award from the American Counseling
Association for his article titled "An Empirical Method of Determining
Nontraditional Group Status" published in *Measurement and Evaluation in
Counseling and Development*. In 1998, he was named a Senior Scholar by the
American College Personnel Association. In 2002, he was recognized by the
American College Personnel Association as a Diamond Honoree for his service
and research in student affairs.

16

A MULTICULTURAL
RESEARCH PROGRAM

When we think of programs to support students of color, we usually think of advising, counseling, tutoring, admissions, and financial-aid programs that may directly affect students. If we think of research at all, it is an afterthought or something not directly relevant to the well being of students of color. In this chapter, I will develop the logic of the necessity of basing any effective program on sound research. Without such research, I believe it is much more likely that racism will flourish. It will flourish through the insensitivity of those making decisions about students of color, be the decision-makers hostile, skeptical, or well-intended.

I will describe a research program that students, colleagues, and I have engaged in for more than thirty-five years. I will discuss studies, cite references, and indicate evidence of the effects of each study. The studies presented will represent only a sample of those conducted and will cover a variety of types and topics. I will conclude with a discussion of the reasons why I believe the research program has been effective. I will leave it to you to decide how well I have made my case.

I will discuss the research as being in one of three areas (Sedlacek, 1998). The first research area is *information*. Anything factual such as demographic information, frequency counts of events, or correct answers to test items would fit here. We often need information to identify the issues or to know which way to go. Previously, learned people thought that earth, wind, fire, and water were the four elements in nature. Without research we would have no reason to think otherwise.

Sometimes information is compelling and results in immediate change. This is seldom true, however. The people and systems we are trying to reach can often ignore or rationalize facts: African-Americans prefer to live in certain neighborhoods, women cannot handle management responsibilities, welfare recipients are lazy, etc. Sound familiar?

Researchers have often assumed that the facts speak for themselves. Galileo assumed that once he presented his observations about the earth not being the center of the universe, the church would accept them. It did, but it was some 350 years later. Most of us would prefer a quicker response.

The second area for research questions is *attitudes*. Here the focus of the research is any affective data concerning feelings, opinions, or perspectives. The link between attitudes and information is complex. Presenting information generally does not change feelings but, as part of a larger strategy, the two may be linked. For example, we found that information about cultural and racial differences and racism that is followed by attitude measurement can lead to the desired reductions in racist behaviors (Sedlacek and Brooks, 1976). But if you are interested in changes in feelings, do not confuse that with information or behavior. When one is trying to change attitudes among groups, several conditions are required. First, all groups should view the negotiating conditions as favorable; second, there should be equal power among the groups to affect the outcome; and third, conditions for continued positive feelings should be developed (Dovidio and Gaertner, 1986). Doing assessments of feelings to determine the status of each of these conditions would be important in any attitude change process. As part of our research program, my colleagues and I developed a method of measuring prejudice (Situational Attitude Scale or SAS) that can be applied to a variety of situations, using experimental and control forms of a questionnaire (Sedlacek, 1996).

The third area of focus for research is *behavior*. Here is an area where we often wish to concentrate, but where it is difficult to get change and where information and feelings commonly do not lead to behavior change. I believe it is best to concentrate on reinforcing people to engage in the desired behavior without necessarily getting them to understand the information behind it or to feel good about it. If you get legislators to sponsor legislation which will help your cause, let the legislators do it for their reasons and not yours. If a university can increase its population of students of color by using different admissions procedures, do not worry about school officials not understanding the issues. Concentrate on research which will achieve the desired behavioral outcomes. Thus, in developing research questions one should generally pick one of the three areas (information, attitudes, or behavior), focus the questions to be answered, and not look for change in other areas. It is very difficult to answer questions in more than one area in one study.

Information

How Many Students Are We Talking About?

In the 1960s and 1970s, many universities were reluctant to get involved in recruiting and admitting students of color. Very little information was available on numbers of students of color attending various schools. We did a series of yearly studies, partially funded by the American College Personnel Association, documenting the enrollments of students of color at large universities in the United States (Sedlacek and Brooks, 1970; Sedlacek, Brooks and Horowitz, 1972; Sedlacek, Brooks and Mindus, 1973; Sedlacek and Pelham, 1976; Sedlacek and Webster, 1978). Using these data, a number of schools began to see patterns of enrollment, or lack thereof. At the time, the University of Maryland was not engaging in any racial census of students. The methodology for the first several studies we did was to spread out on campus and, through a series of contacts, try to identify, one-by-one, all the black students we could find (Brooks and Sedlacek, 1972). Black undergraduate enrollment was about 1 percent of 32,000 students. These studies remain the only record that Maryland has of its black enrollment during those years. In the mid 1990s, the president of the University, William Kirwan, contacted me for copies of those studies for a speech he was making on the progress the university had made in enrolling students of color. As of 2002, undergraduate enrollment of students of color at Maryland was about 36 percent, including 14 percent African-American.

By providing national norms, schools were able with see how they compared with like institutions. At the University of Maryland these studies were an important part of establishing the first "minority recruiting" office on campus. At the time of the studies, Maryland was considerably behind other schools in the numbers of enrolled blacks, particularly compared with the population of blacks in the state. While many other activities were taking place nationally and in Maryland, officials from a number of schools, including Maryland, indicated to me that they used the data in confronting the issue of low "minority" enrollments. Eventually, the U.S. government and other organizations were collecting such data, so we moved on to other research.

It's "Pop Sociology"

The idea for a course on racism was developed in the late 1960s during a period of political and social turmoil in the United States. At that time, the University of Maryland offered a few very specialized courses touching on racism, taken mainly by graduate students. The content was also largely academic and theoretical rather than practical and focused on what people could do about racism. There were no courses on racism offered by the College of Education. Given what was happening in the country and in the education system, a graduate student and I decided to develop a course that could be taken by undergraduate and graduate students (Sedlacek and Brooks, 1973).

The course was to be rigorous and would incorporate research, theory, and practical ideas. Course goals included the acquisition of information about racism, confronting attitudes about racism (one's own and others), and engaging in behavior to eliminate racism in education (Roper and Sedlacek, 1988). We also wrote a book to be used in the class, since we felt there were none available which adequately covered the material we thought important (Sedlacek and Brooks, 1976). However, the Dean of the College of Education was opposed to what he viewed as "pop sociology" (Sedlacek and Brooks, 1973). Using information we had on examples of racism on campus, we were able to convince enough people to force the Dean's hand and get the course approved in 1975 (Roper and Sedlacek, 1988).

As more students of color entered the university and expectations for diversity programs grew, the course was allowed to meet a diversity requirement for undergraduate students added in 1988. Currently, the course is consistently over-subscribed and is typically offered every semester. New faculty were hired, including some of color, in part to teach the course. Thus, the course had moved from a special topics oddity of apparent little interest on a nearly all-white campus to a visible part of many multicultural offerings on a highly diverse campus (Sedlacek, in press).

What's the Difference?

Here I will discuss several of many studies in which we have documented differences among various groups of students and provided a basis for meeting their needs.

Your Cult Is My Religion

We found that the University of Maryland was considering some religions to be cults and trying to force the groups off the campus (Majors and Sedlacek, 2001). However, some of those so-called cults were considered religions by some Asian-American students. An analysis of university policies toward religious practices, including absence from class to celebrate religious holidays and providing facilities, strongly favored Christian students (Schlosser and Sedlacek, in press). The university is currently reviewing its policies toward religious groups and is using the research studies to inform their decisions.

No Hablo Español

Not all Latino students speak Spanish. We found that this is one of the major forms of racism Latino students must face (Sedlacek, in press). How Latino should they be? Should they join the Latino student group? Should they change their name and "pass"? Including this information in faculty workshops has been seen by faculty as useful, particularly to those who may speak some Spanish and who may use it to approach Latino students. The diversity within any racial group is great, and language variations can be a useful way to make this point.

Attitudes

Studies of prejudicial attitudes have been an important part of the research program discussed here. These have served as the basis for much of the anti-racism work that I and others have done over the years. In a six-stage model to eliminate racism that colleagues and I have developed, confronting racial attitudes is a necessary step (Sedlacek and Brooks, 1976; Sedlacek, Troy and Chapman, 1976; Sedlacek, 1995, in press). I will discuss several examples of programs that have been developed using the SAS. Many different versions of the SAS have been developed to assess attitudes toward such groups as African-Americans, Arabs, women, gays, American-Indians, Latinos, and Jews, among many others (Sedlacek, 1996).

The Model Minority

Liang and Sedlacek (in press) demonstrated that student affairs professionals have more positive attitudes toward Asian-Americans when race is not considered in a situation. At first glance, attitudes in the positive direction may be construed as good or harmless. However, attitudes based on stereotypes that depict Americans of Asian descent as well adjusted, only interested in technical subjects, and without academic or mental health needs, have hurt many Asian-Americans.

As an illustration of possible problems this could cause, I once had to refer an Asian-American student for counseling because his peers insisted on seeking computer-related help from him, to the point where he had virtually no interpersonal relations on any other basis. His self-concept suffered, and he had begun to get depressed. The student was not particularly interested in computers, but his peers expected him to be, and they thought they were enhancing his self-concept. Forcing an expectation on people from other races is a form of racism, even if that expectation appears to be positive (Sedlacek and Brooks, 1976).

Findings from this study are included in a diversity training program for student affairs staff. Improved programs for Asian-American students on handling prejudice have also been developed from study results.

Is This the Place?

A technique called perceptual mapping can help in identifying physical locations and communities that may be of relevance to students (Mitchell, Sergent and Sedlacek, 1997; Sergent and Sedlacek, 1989). The perceptual mapping approach allows respondents to indicate locations of interest to them and their perceptions of those areas. The unique aspect of perceptual mapping is that respondents use actual maps of interior or exterior spaces and then project their feelings and perceptions on the maps. Research has shown that African-American and white students choose different areas of a campus as positive or negative, depending on their experiences with those areas (Mitchell, Sergent, and Sedlacek, 1997).

For example, the plans to renovate part of a campus student union were changed because African-American students tended to congregate in an area that would have been affected. Since a sense of community has been identified with success in school for African-Americans (Sedlacek, in press), this change in the physical environment was considered to directly affect their retention.

Perceptual mapping was also used to identify problems in the location of a staff ombuds office. This office was designed to assist university employees who were not able to redress their grievances through other channels. However, employees of color, many of whom were in lower paying jobs with less power than other employees, were not taking advantage of the service. Perceptual mapping showed that the location of the office, which was in an administration building, was not a comfortable place for the employees to come to complain. The mapping also identified places on campus which would be better locations. The office was moved, and employee participation increased.

Behavior

The Three Musketeers Problem

While it may be reasonable to hope that a single standardized test could fairly equate applicants, it does not seem reasonable to expect it. I have called this the "Three Musketeers" problem in assessment (Sedlacek, 1994). The rallying cry of "all for one and one for all" is one that we use often in developing fair and equitable measures. If different groups have different experiences and different ways of presenting their attributes and abilities, however, it is unlikely that we could develop a single measure or even a test item that would be equally valid for all.

We have been studying alternatives to standardized tests and prior grades as predictors of success for many years. We have identified, through research, a system of noncognitive variables that measures a wider range of attributes than more traditional methods and is more equitable for students of color (Sedlacek, in press). The noncognitive variables are self-concept, realistic self-appraisal, handling racism, long-range goals, support person, leadership, community, and nontraditional knowledge. We developed the Noncognitive Questionnaire (NCQ) to measure those variables. I will discuss several examples of the application of the NCQ dimensions.

Clarifying the Gray Area

A large state university had about 6,000 applications for 3,000 places in the first-year class. The primary goal in its admission process was to select fairly but, at the same time, to maximize the number of nontraditional students, particularly African-Americans. If it chose strictly by ACTs, the school would accept only about 150 African-American applicants and might get only half of those to actually enroll.

The institution decided to consider both traditional measures (ACT and high school grades) and noncognitive measures. It required the NCQ (Sedlacek, in press) to be completed by all general applicants. Then the university developed two multiple regression equations based on some pilot studies and the NCQ norms. One regression equation was for traditional applicants and the other was for nontraditional applicants. Nontraditional applicants included those of color as well as other groups who had received discrimination (Sedlacek, in press). The approximate weights given were about two-thirds to traditional measures and one-third to noncognitive variables for traditional applicants. For nontraditional applicants, the NCQ was weighted about 60 percent compared to 40 percent for the ACT and grades.

Admission office personnel were trained to make a determination of the traditionality of experience of each applicant to determine which equation to use. Any difficult decisions were assigned to a committee consisting of admission staff, faculty, students, and campus administrators. The assumption was that if the institution wanted nontraditional students, it would have to consider this in the admission process and ensure that the assessments of nontraditional applicants were as fair as possible.

The institution did not change any other aspects of its admission, retention, or recruiting programs or any of its special programs or curricular offerings. By employing the new procedures it admitted 64 percent of the African-American applicants and 208 actually enrolled. The usual graduation rate after six years was about 60 percent for traditional students and about 30 percent for African-American students. After employing the new admission procedures, the six-year graduation rate for traditional students was 65 percent, while it was 56 percent for African-Americans. While the school did not employ a control group for comparison, officials at the institution were pleased with the new system and have begun to think of ways to provide recruiters and advisors with more admission information to perform those functions better.

We Were Never Traditional

Prairie View A&M University, an historically black school in Texas, was under pressure from the state legislature to defend its admissions policies and the very existence of the institution. Officials at the university needed a way to assess the talents and abilities of applicants that were not shown in prior grades and test scores. They knew that traditional measures were never useful in measuring the potential of their applicants. They decided to employ the NCQ in admissions to its program to provide educational assistance and opportunity to students considered "at risk" to persist to graduation. We had done research on the usefulness of the NCQ for this population (White and Sedlacek, 1986).

An institutional study showed that students in the pre-first-year summer program selected with the NCQ got higher grades and completed more credit hours in the year after completing the program than a control cohort. Ninety percent of the students completed the summer program. Applicants to the program also submitted three letters of recommendation and participated in a telephone interview. Uses of prior grades and standardized test scores as criteria for admission were minimized because of their lack of validity for their students. About 75 students entered the program each year.

Gates Millennium Scholars

The Gates Millennium Scholars (GMS) Program set out an ambitious and socially important series of goals for itself. Scholarships are provided to financially needy African-Americans, Native-Americans, Hispanic-Americans or Asian-Americans who are or will be studying mathematics, science, engineering, education, or library science.

Applicants are required to be eligible for Pell Grants as a way of determining that they are in financial need, and awards cover all educational expenses at whatever institution the student is attending.

The noncognitive variables noted above are used to select the scholars as are assessments of the academic rigor of their high school curriculum and their ability to write a good essay explaining their interests in becoming a Gates Millennium Scholar. The goals of the selection process are to judge the academic potential of students of color who show their potential in ways other than the more traditional standardized tests and prior grades.

In the first two years of the program, more than 5,000 students of color were attending more than 900 different institutions in the United States and receiving full scholarships for as long as they matriculated successfully in an institution of higher education. As of this writing, Gates Scholars had college GPAs of 3.86 on a 4.0 scale, so their early successes in school had been established, and the method of selecting them appears to be working well.

The GMS Program is a $1 billion program of the Bill and Melinda Gates Foundation and is planned to last over a 20-year period. At present, a longitudinal study is underway tracking scholars, as well as those not selected, to determine the correlates of the noncognitive variables with a wide range of academic and nonacademic dimensions. This study should yield data which are unprecedented in their potential to provide insights into how to better educate people of color who have shown great potential in ways that we typically do not consider, let alone assess.

Why Does the Research Program Work?

Below are some principles that make for a successful multicultural research program. Some of these are discussed further in Sedlacek (1998).

Understand Your Audience

Whom do I wish to influence with my study? This should be the first question posed by the researcher interested in change. Is it faculty of color? White students? State legislators? For each of these audiences, we would likely perform different kinds of studies yielding different results and present them differently to each of these audiences. The studies discussed above provide examples of the focus on audience.

Define Research Broadly

Research can be defined as any systematic inquiry into a topic. The methods can be quantitative or qualitative, statistical or impressionistic, involving paper and pencil techniques, computer technology, interviews, artistic perspectives, or naturalistic observations. I would recommend using what works best, given your audience and available resources. If you have access to certain resources, e.g., a college research office, computers, or financial resources, by all means use them. If not, use what you have. We once did some behavioral observations of students in a campus union with no budget, five student volunteers, and me as resources. The data were used by some campus clubs in recruiting.

Control the Turf

One valuable function that research can serve in achieving change is to control the area(s) where you wish to hold the argument or debate. Too often, those interested in improving educational situations for people of color react defensively to conditions set up by others. We are told by those in power that the situation is a certain way, and we feel that we have to counter what those in control of the system have set forth. By doing research, we can gain some power and put those in charge on the defensive by causing them to respond to our results.

This principle was made clear to me at a recent education conference. One of the main speakers recommended that those interested in evaluation research should check with their supervisors to find out what they were interested in studying. I suggested during the question and answer period that most of what we know about race and gender issues came from researchers who ask good questions that did not come from those in authority. I believe that research results should be couched in ways that those we wish to affect might be moved to change, either by seeing the issue differently or being made to change by possible implications of the data.

Become the Source

By providing research results over a period of time, one can become a reliable source of data. Part of being a reliable source is to provide data that are fair and honest and not always slanted in a certain direction. As you watch the evening news, whose results are you more apt to trust—a study done by a neutral party or one representing a political party? You should share results regardless of the outcome. By asking the right questions and putting them in a context relevant to the change you wish to bring about, you can give the data the best chance to be used as you wish. However, research that is preconceived as to outcomes often means suppressing undesirable outcomes, thus compromising your role as the source of reliable data.

Group Effort

Most of my research is done in collaboration with others; e.g. students, colleagues, and people in the larger community off-campus. I also look to work with others with different skills, cultural backgrounds, areas of training, perspectives, and interests. I believe that in the ideal project, everyone gains. Students may get training, financial assistance, and dissertation data. Faculty may get publications, grants, and promotions. Administrators may get some answers to questions or guidance in decision-making. Community members may develop a working relationship with university staff. The list goes on. People do things because they are reinforced for them. The researcher needs to understand what motivates the different members of your team and see that they all get what they need.

Up the Conceptual Ladder

Research can help move conceptions of a problem to a higher level. One example of this occurred with one University of Maryland administrator I dealt with over many years. He would tend to see issues concerning students of color as isolated questions with no particular pattern. He wanted simple percentages and frequencies of responses to questionnaire items, rather than anything more complex. However, in a situation where the university was sued by a non-African-American student over his ineligibility for a program intended to "desegregate" the university, this administrator saw the issue in a new light (Sedlacek, 1995).

The university defended the case, in part, by using research on racial climate and issues affecting African-American students that our research team had conducted. The university eventually lost the case after two rounds in the circuit and appellate courts. As the administrator put it after the university had won a round in court, "I was glad we won, but I wish we didn't have to admit we were racist to do it." In that statement, he acknowledged the concept of racism and his role and that of the university in perpetuating it. I had achieved a goal that I had been working toward for many years.

Patience and Persistence

Any educational change activity requires time and persistence. If one thing does not work, try another. The research component in educational change also requires time and many attempts. As noted in some of the examples above, change took place slowly with help from many studies. Do not be discouraged by this. See each study as standing on its own and supporting key points you wish to make. However, also view that research as fitting into a mosaic, as one piece of a larger puzzle. Bigger gains can sometimes come from interconnected studies; however, smaller gains lead to bigger ones. Do not "go for it all" too soon; be content with a smaller gain that moves your issue forward. Those who follow you can benefit from your work. Small victories attract allies and deter opponents (Weick, 1984).

Conclusion

I have attempted to discuss how research can play a vital role in change on educational issues affecting people of color. Research alone cannot bring about change, but dedicated professionals armed with good goals, good data, and guiding principles can make a difference. I hope I have provided some evidence to support my conclusion. Please contact me to let me know what you think or to share some of your experiences with research as a vehicle for change.

References

Brooks, G. C., Jr., and W. E. Sedlacek. 1972. "The racial census of college students." *College and University,* 47: pp. 125–27.

Dovidio, J. F., and S. L. Gaertner. 1986. *Prejudice, Discrimination and Racism.* Orlando, Fla.: Academic Press.

Helm, E. G., W. E., Sedlacek, and D. O. Prieto. 1998. "The relationship between attitudes toward diversity and overall satisfaction of university students by race." *Journal of College Counseling,* 1: pp. 111–120.

Liang, C. T. H. and W. E. Sedlacek. In press. "Attitudes of white student service practitioners: Research and recommendations." *National Association of Student Personnel Administrators Journal.*

Majors, M. S., and W. E. Sedlacek. 2001. "Using factor analysis to organize student services." *Journal of College Student Development,* 42(3): pp. 272–278.

Roper, L. D., and W. E. Sedlacek. 1988. "Student affairs professionals in academic roles: A course on racism." *National Association of Student Personnel Administrators Journal,* 26(1): pp. 27–32.

Schlosser, L. Z., and W. E. Sedlacek. In press. "Religious holidays on campus: Policies, problems and recommendations." *About Campus.*

Sedlacek, W. E. 1994. "Issues in advancing diversity through assessment." *Journal of Counseling and Development,* 72: pp. 549–53.

Sedlacek, W. E. 1995. "Using research to reduce racism at a university." *Journal of Humanistic Education and Development,* 33: pp. 131–40.

Sedlacek, W. E. 1998. "Strategies for social change research." Lee, C. C., & Walz, G. R., eds. *Social action: A mandate for counselors* (pp. 227–39). Alexandria, VA: American Counseling Association.

Sedlacek, W. E. In press. *Beyond the Big Test: Noncognitive Assessment in Higher Education.* San Francisco: Jossey-Bass.

Sedlacek, W. E. In press. "Alternative admissions and scholarship selection measures in higher education." *Measurement and Evaluation in Counseling and Development.*

Sedlacek, W. E., and G. C. Brooks, Jr. 1970. "Black freshmen in large colleges: A survey." *Personnel and Guidance Journal,* 49: pp. 307–12.

Sedlacek, W. E., and G. C. Brooks, Jr. 1972. "Racial attitudes, authoritarianism and dogmatism among university students." *College Student Journal,* 6: pp. 43–44.

Sedlacek, W. E., and G. C. Brooks, Jr. 1973. "Racism and research: Using data to initiate change." *Personnel and Guidance Journal,* 52: pp. 184–88.

Sedlacek, W. E., and G. C. Brooks, Jr. 1976. *Racism in American Education: A Model for Change.* Chicago: Nelson-Hall.

Sedlacek, W. E., G. C. Brooks, Jr., and J. L. Horowitz. 1972. "Black admissions to large universities: Are things changing?" *Journal of College Student Personnel,* 13: pp. 305–10.

Sedlacek, W. E., G. C. Brooks, Jr., and L. A. Mindus. 1973. "Black and other minority admissions to large universities: Three-year national trends." *Journal of College Student Personnel,* 14: pp. 16–21.

Sedlacek, W. E., & Pelham, J. C. (1976). "Minority admissions to large universities: A national survey." *Journal of Non-White Concerns in Personnel and Guidance,* 4: pp. 53–63.

Sedlacek, W. E., W. G. Troy, and T. H. Chapman, 1976. "An evaluation of three methods of racism-sexism training." *Personnel and Guidance Journal,* 55: pp. 196–98.

Sedlacek, W. E., and D. W. Webster. 1978. "Admission and retention of minority students in large universities." *Journal of College Student Personnel,* 19: pp. 242–48.

Weick, K. E. 1984. "Small wins: Redefining the scale of social problems." *American Psychologist,* 39: pp. 40–49.

White, T. J., and W. E. Sedlacek. 1986. "Noncognitive predictors of grades and retention for specially admitted students." *Journal of College Admissions,* 3: pp. 20–23.

Leslie N. Pollard

LESLIE N. POLLARD serves as Vice President for Diversity at Loma Linda University Health Sciences Centers in Loma Linda, California. In this capacity he and his staff lead and manage the six-sided diversity service program for the 500 faculty and 3,000 health-science students of Loma Linda University as well as the 12,000 employees of Loma Linda University Medical Center.

Dr. Pollard is a hands-on leader. He believes that the best diversity programming is real-time programming as opposed to abstract strategizing. Pollard says, "I enjoy that day-to-day administration of real-time programs that make a positive impact on the quality of life at Loma Linda University and in the San Bernardino community."

Dr. Pollard's leadership career began in 1978 in the multi-racial climate of Southern California. After graduating from Oakwood College, he was assigned to work in Santa Monica, California. One of his first tasks was to take over the coaching of a basketball team of ex-gang members who represented his church, since the size of the church could sustain a basketball team.

Dr. Pollard's latest publication is *Embracing Diversity: How to Understand and Reach People of All Cultures,* which has been translated to French, German, and Spanish.

Examples of some of the programming running through the LLU Office of Diversity are:

- **Minority Recruitment and Retention Program**—Invites underrepresented minorities to study at Loma Linda University.
- **Research Apprenticeship Mentoring Program for Minorities**—Invites minority high school seniors to spend a summer participating in scientific research at LLU.
- **Diversity Outreach Teams**—Teams of Latino, Asian, Anglo, and African-American health professional students visit community public schools to promote, and answer student questions concerning, careers in health service.
- **Diversity Awareness Celebrations**
- **Race, Gender, and Disability Training Programs**

17

FOUNDATIONS FOR MAKING
RACIAL DIVERSITY WORK

It is my genuine pleasure to assist Dr. Frank Hale in his latest effort to advance diversity in institutions of higher education. As an esteemed and distinguished educator, speaker, activist, author, colleague, and mentor, Dr. Hale has spent an entire lifetime fighting for and providing equal access to educational opportunity to students of color. This present volume represents one more link in the chain in his string of sterling contributions to diversity. Dr. Hale's clear vision for diversity is borne from his lifetime of leadership in this arena. His unflagging commitment is to be saluted. Congratulations to Dr. Hale on the publication of this volume.

A word about the approach of this article: After reviewing the critical educational research literature for the past twenty years in this area, I concluded that a real-time snapshot of an institution attempting to make diversity work would be a meaningful contribution to this publication. This approach is not intended to set aside or dismiss critical engagement with the research findings discussed in higher education literature. I will leave that important contribution to my esteemed colleagues who are represented in this volume. Rather than submit a review of and distillation from the research literature (which frankly, is the first direction I contemplated after having been approached by Dr. Hale), I will present a university-based initiative now operating in real time at an institution of higher education. Further, I have avoided the inclusion of multiple in-text references in an attempt to smooth out the reading. References will appear as footnotes. I hope that this attempt at a reader-friendly style will not undermine the scholarly substance of this piece.

Since the 1964 Civil Rights Acts and the 1965 Higher Education Act, American institutions of higher education have grappled with the challenge of attracting underrepresented minorities as faculty and students within their institutions. Historically, the method of accomplishing these objectives was through affirmative action. Recently, however, such institutional commitments have met the disapproval of the courts. Reverse discrimination law-suits, such as *Hopwood v. State of Texas,* along with numerous state ballot initiatives (e.g., California's Proposition 209), have limited or eliminated race-based considerations in admissions and promotions. In fact, as this chapter is under pen, the Supreme Court announced on December 2, 2002, that the Court has decided to hear arguments on admissions committees' use of race as a consideration for admission to public universities; the specific affirmative action cases involve the University of Michigan. In *Gratz and Hammacher v. Bollinger* of the University of Michigan, Jennifer Gratz and Patrick Hamacher along with the companion case *Barbara Grutter v. Lee Bollinger,* Caucasians students alleged reverse discrimination in the denial of their applications for admission to the University of Michigan. Such consideration by the Court will test the previous legal ruling of the 1978 *Bakke* decision by the Court to allow race as an admissions consideration. The present legal climate challenging affirmative action has forced institutions to consider alternative strategies for increasing minority presence[1] on campuses of higher education. This article will present a selective sample of one higher educational institution's selected programs intended to facilitate racial, ethnic, and cultural diversity within its residential environment.[2] Examples are selected and edited for purposes of this publication.

About Loma Linda University

Loma Linda University (LLU) is a faith-based academic health-sciences center sponsored by the 12 million-member Seventh-Day Adventist Church. Loma Linda University is a multi-racial, multi-ethnic health science institution accredited by the Western Association of Schools and Colleges. Founded in 1904, Loma Linda University Adventist Health Sciences Center has committed itself to the practice of diversity as an expression of LLU's mission to the global human family. The Loma Linda University Medical Center serves local San Bernardino, Riverside, and surrounding communities. LLU also serves international centers as far away as China and Saudi Arabia. The university consists of seven fully accredited schools: Medicine, Dentistry, Public Health, Allied Health, Nursing, Graduate Studies, and Pharmacology. Registered at the beginning of 2002 were approximately 3,200 students, representing eighty countries, five world religions, and fifty-seven Christian denominations. For the academic year 2002–03, 57 percent of the total student body self-identified as members of the Seventh-Day Adventist Church. The racial composition of LLU consisted of 57 percent Caucasian, 27 percent Asian, 9 percent Hispanic, 6 percent African American, and less than 1 percent Native American. The diversity program at Loma Linda reflects the strong spiritual focus consistent with the historic wholeness mission of Loma Linda. In fact, LLU was founded in 1904 for the purpose of training healthcare professionals in wholistic healthcare delivery.

The LLU Office of Diversity was founded in 1992, although the Office of Minority Affairs has existed since the 1970s. The LLU Office of Diversity at LLU administers the institution's diversity initiatives. In 1993, the LLU Board of Trustees voted to create an inclusive and accessible academic and social environment of healthcare training and delivery. The LLU Office of Diversity coordinates a campus-wide program of education, recruitment, and retention within and beyond the university, the LLU Medical Center, and each local LLU affiliate.

The office has been tasked with the responsibility of creating an inclusive racial, ethnic, and cultural climate by promoting and coordinating diversity education within the schools and academic programs sponsored by LLU. Specifically, the Office of Diversity assists employees and students to understand and serve competently persons in our community who come from a variety of racial, cultural, and ethnic backgrounds. A diversity infrastructure has been created at each of the seven schools. The diversity committee in each school is chaired by a faculty member who convenes the committee on a monthly-to-quarterly basis in order to plan for school-specific diversity initiatives. On a quarterly basis, the university-wide Diversity Steering Committee meets to debrief and plan for the advancement of diversity on the LLU campus. This committee-based infrastructure assists in the institutionalization of the Board's diversity commitment.

This article presents a description of selected programs and activities designed to respond to the educational challenges already copiously documented in the higher education literature. Such challenges include recruitment of racially diverse faculty[3] and students,[4] retention of racially diverse faculty and students, construction of curricular materials within school and discipline-specific programs, international outreach, etc. The practices that follow have been found to be the foundations necessary for making racial diversity work in the institution's campus environment.

Toward Making Racial Diversity Work on Campus

The idea that racial diversity will work in institutions of higher education assumes that educational institutions are interested in recruiting and retaining underrepresented minorities in higher education; furthermore, not only is minority presence on campus desired, but high-level academic performance from them is desired as well.[5] For such efforts to enjoy a measure of success, observation and campus interaction have convinced me that at least five foundations must be embedded in the institution's culture.

Foundation 1: Institutional Commitment

Institutional commitment to diversity on campus begins with the President's announced intention to make diversity a critical part of the institution's organizational life.[6] This public position/announcement must be codified in the institution's charter and operating documents. At LLU, this means that we have had to revisit the strategic plan for the future of the institution. Wholeness, mission, and diversity constitute the three major value-differentiated themes of the university. These three ideas represent the core values of the institution. The LLU Strategic Plan for diversity is built around one of the three key themes of the university. While the themes of wholeness and mission are native to the historic self-understanding of the institution, the theme of diversity accompanies the creation of the 1992 Office of Diversity. Theme V of the plan expresses the role that diversity is intended to play in LLU. The diversity commitment by the institution is codified in this critical document of the university. While the entire theme is not relevant to this chapter, the following institutional commitment is illustrative:

"Loma Linda University is committed to racial ethnic and cultural diversity and gender inclusiveness among students, faculty, staff, and administration as an essential component of a quality educational program. Such diversity will prepare students for successful engagement in a diverse society."[7]

Institutions where diversity is prominent seem, without exception, to have codified their commitment to diversity in their core documents. Such codification serves as an institutional reference point that precedes offices, departments, directors, programs, and activities designed to advance diversity in the residential campus environment.

Foundation 2: Institutional Initiative

Another element that contributes to the advancement of racial diversity in campus environments is the creation of initiatives that drive the efforts of the institution. The following are samples of the some of the intitiatives of LLU's Office of Diversity:

1. "LLU facilitates national and international diversity among the student body, faculty, and staff.[8]

Through targeted recruitment and student referral, underrepresented minority students are encouraged to consider LLU as their institution of preference for acquiring their healthcare training.

2. "Early Exposure Programs designed to expose underrepresented students to research and the health science university environment will be promoted.

High School outreach programs such as MITHS and RAMP (see program display following) introduce young people to healthcare career possibilities through early exposure. These are summer "shadow" programs funded internally or by corporate sponsors.

3. "An academic and residential environment will be nurtured that:
   - recognizes and appreciates the value of diversity.
   - supports the well-being and success of all participants in a multicultural community.
   - encourages a bias-free and non-threatening work and learning environment.
   - creates greater awareness of discriminatory practices, issues of diversity, and the relationships between spirituality and diversity.

LLU Office of Diversity: Annual Programs and/or Events

Program/Event	Date	Audience	Contact persons	Process MAP	Funding
HALL Scholarship Banquet	October or November as close to Hispanic Heritage Month as possible	Hispanic alumni, Hispanic students, Hispanic Community, Administration, Faculty	Office of Diversity assists in contacting corporate and community sponsors for the event	OD works closely with HALL Executive Committee in planning and with Office of Gift Records for processing all donations. Works closely with the deans and schools in choosing the scholarship recipients	The Office of Diversity has provided substantial financial assistance
Diversity New Student Orientation	First or second Monday in October, toward the beginning of the academic year	LLU Minority Students (Black, Hispanic, American Indian)	Office of Diversity invites administration, deans, minority faculty, student services, service departments, student clubs, and faculty forums to speak and give a short welcome	OD plans and coordinates pizza supper. Purchases door prizes. Provides material to assist students in achieving academic success and information about the LLU community	OD Spends approximately $600 providing the supper and door prizes, and copying materials

Event	Timing	Audience	Office of Diversity Role	Planning Partners	Cost
Hispanic Heritage Month Chapel	On or about the third Wednesday in October, assigned by Student Affairs Office	Student body	Office of Diversity coordinates the program details	OD works closely with ALAS in the planning of this chapel service	OD pays the speaker's airfare, hotel, food, car rental, and honorarium. Average cost is about $1,000
Hispanic Student Retreat	Second week of April	Hispanic students from LLU and LSU	Office of Diversity contacts speaker and other participants, such as musicians, etc.	Office of Diversity works closely with ALAS in planning the retreat, and ALAS works with LSU. Approximately 125 attend	Cost: $4,000 to $5,000. LLU, LaSierra University and Alumni cover costs
Black Student Retreat	Second week of November	Black students from LLU and LSU, faculty, and BALL	Office of Diversity contacts speaker and other participants, such as musicians, etc	Office of Diversity works closely with BHPSA in planning the retreat, and BHPSA works with BALL and LSU. Approximately 200 attend.	Cost: $5,000 to $7,000

Table Continued

Program/Event	Date	Audience	Contact persons	Process MAP	Funding
BALL Banquet	Last week of February	Black alumni and friends of LLU and LSU	BALL Executive Committee plans the entire event. Director of Diversity is a member of the Executive Committee	Office of Diversity works closely with BALL Executive Committee	Office of Diversity contributes to the financial support of the event
LLU Diversity Graduate Consecration Service	Middle of May	Minority graduates and parents from LLU and LSU	Invites all minority students and faculty. Administration and faculty from LLU and LSU are requested to march in full academic regalia	Office of Diversity works closely with a planning committee composed of representatives from both institutions and coordinates all arrangements for the keynote speaker and	Cost: $5,000 to $6,000

Activity	Timing	Target	Responsibility	Notes	Budget
				luncheon. Office of Diversity purchases Kinte and ethnic sashes for graduates	
Diversity Leadership Awards	Presented to community leaders in Diversity in February and October	Community leaders	Office of Diversity plans with Steering Committee	The effectiveness of this award lies in its public relations potential. Underscores diversity	Included in Office of Diversity budget
Focus Groups, Partnership Visits to/from minority partner institutions	Fall and spring	Institutions with large numbers of underrepresented students/selected LLU Deans	Office of Diversity	Office of Diversity coordinates	Office of Diversity budget/deans

Table Continued

Program/Event	Date	Audience	Contact persons	Process MAP	Funding
RAMP to Science (Research Apprenticeship for Minorities Program)	July and August (eight-week program) first work day after 4th of July	Underrepresented high school students (preferably seniors) from surrounding high schools and academies	Office of Diversity contacts all the participating lab supervisors, sends out newspaper releases, mails applications to students, sends acceptance and rejection letters, coordinates the physicals, and provides HRM with all necessary paperwork (i.e., work permits, etc.)	OD coordinates the entire program. Office of Advancement applies for funding. Date sequence very important for all the stages of the program. Historically we've had from five to thirty-five students and one to two teachers per summer, depending on funding	Approximately $25,000 in direct costs for student wages, plus $1,600 from Office of Diversity for postage, copying, orientation meeting, and exit awards dinner

Program	Timing	Description	Office of Diversity Role		Notes
Medical Scholars Early Acceptance Program (MSEAP)	One month during the summer, followed by the fall quarter	Prospective minority medical students are tracked for future School of Medicine faculty positions after completing MD and Ph.D. degrees	Office of Diversity works closely with the School of Medicine	The MSEAP program is new; therefore, the Office of Diversity will continue its liaison role. Also responsible for the spiritual and social areas	Depending on the number of students per year, Office of Diversity cost varies. We provide a social outing, several meals, etc.
Mentor-for-a-Day	March or April	Minority academy students are matched LLU minority students for a day of activity	Office of Diversity in the past has drawn students from Los Angeles, San Bernardino, and Riverside as a source of students for this program. Assists in recruiting	Academy students are brought on campus for one day and paired with an LLU student, depending on the academy students' career interest. The academy student will shadow the LLU student during classes; they eat together and then attend a workshop, finishing with a Q&A session	A refreshments time and luncheon are provided. Approximate cost: $300

Table Continued

Program/Event	Date	Audience	Contact Persons	Process MAP	Funding
BHPSA (Black Health Professional Student Association)	Term of office for BHPSA officers is one year.	All black LLU students	Office of Diversity and BHPSA officers work closely together to provide an excellent program	The success of this club depends on the commitment and leadership of the BHPSA president and officers	Office of Diversity assists BHPSA financially throughout the year, depending on their requests
ALAS (Association of Latin-American Students)	Term of office for ALAS officers is one year.	All Hispanic LLU students	Office of Diversity and ALAS officers work closely together to provide an excellent program.	The success of this club depends on the commitment and leadership of the ALAS president and officers	Office of Diversity assists ALAS financially throughout the year, depending on their requests
Black Faculty Forum	Term of office for BFF officers is two years.	All black LLU faculty	Office of Diversity works closely with the BFF	The extent of faculty involvement depends on the commitment and timely planning on the part of the officers	Office of Diversity assisted the BFF with $100 initially, and they are to raise their own funding for further programming

Diversity Training Program (DTP)	Ongoing diversity training program	Targeted to administrators and faculty	Office of Diversity has established six diversity modules—the "Six Sides of Diversity." Each module is coordinated by a team of instructors. The teams developed the materials and are ready to go to the six schools and give the training sessions. The Office of Diversity coordinates the training schedules with the schools	Each team presents their module before further training takes place	Office of Diversity does all the copying, provides all the workshop binders, and pays all expenses incurred in purchasing materials for the workshop (i.e., videos, special materials, etc.)
Diversity Awareness Sabbaths	Selected dates at interdenominational houses of worship	Community members, LLU faculty, LLU students	Local religious leaders	Invites community to participate in diversity efforts	Funded by Office of Diversity

Table Continued

Program/Event	Date	Audience	Contact persons	Process MAP	Funding
Diversity Outreach Teams	Occurs during October and February.	High school students in the San Bernardino school systems.	ALAS, BHPSA and APSA	First effort reaped $300 income for Office of Diversity	Funded by Office of Diversity
Asian Pacific Islanders Student Association (APSA)	Cultural Heritage Day in May at Drayson Center	LLU community; organized by Office of Diversity in January 1998	Offices of APSA	The students do the planning	Self-funded
Minority Introduction to the Health Sciences (MITHS)	Held annually for three weeks in July.	High school students	Black Alumni of Loma Linda University	Assists high school students with college career choices	Minority Alumni of LLU
Diversity Satellite Education	December and March	LLU faculty and staff	Office of Diversity	Appeals to faculty and Diversity Chairs	Office of Diversity
Caribbean Island Festival	April	LLU faculty, staff, and students	Office of Diversity/BHPSA	Students plan this annual cultural festival	Office of Diversity/BHPSA
Cinco De Mayo Celebration	May	LLU faculty, staff, and students	Office of Diversity/ALAS	Students plan this annual cultural festival	Office of Diversity/ALAS

Event	Timing	Audience		Logistics	
Diversity Resource Library	Purchases materials year-round	LLU faculty and staff	Office of Diversity	Administrative Assistant manages	Office of Diversity
ALAS Officers Planning Luncheon	January	ALAS Officers and club sponsors	Office of Diversity	Planned by the Office of Diversity and held at faculty residence	Office of Diversity
BHPSA Planning Luncheon	February	BHPSA Officers and club sponsors	Office of Diversity	Planned by the Office of Diversity and held at faculty residence	Office of Diversity
BALL Planning Luncheon	May	BALL Officers	Office of Diversity	Planned by the Office of Diversity and held at faculty residence	Office of Diversity
HALL Planning Luncheon	March	HALL Officers	Office of Diversity	Planned by the Office of Diversity and held at faculty residence	Office of Diversity
LLU Diversity Conference	October	LLU students, . faculty, and staff	Office of Diversity	Planned by the Office of Diversity and Diversity Planning Committee	

- equips administrators, directors, and supervisors with the skills necessary to effectively manage diversity.
- ensures fair treatment in the workplace."

This initiative sets up goals for the shaping of objectives and strategies. It reflects appreciation for the role that employees and students play in creating an inclusive community of scholarship and learning.

Foundation 3: Institutional Objectives and Strategies

Another component of effective diversity in campus environments is the establishment of institutional objectives and strategies. These targets provide measurement criteria by which the effectiveness of the institution's diversity activity may be evaluated. Samples from the LLU Office of Diversity are the following:

OBJECTIVE   The proportion of faculty and staff from underrepresented minorities and women will be progressively increased in the schools, administration, and service departments of LLU, as needed, to reflect as far as possible the composition of the United States population by the year 2005.

OBJECTIVE   The proportion of students who are African-American, Hispanic, or Native American will be increased to reflect as far as possible the composition of the United States population by the year 2005.

OBJECTIVE   The proportion of staff from underrepresented groups will progressively increase in the academic and service departments of the university to reflect as far as possible the ethnic composition of the United States by the year 2005.

OBJECTIVE   LLU will formalize partnership agreements with minority-serving institutions as a means of attracting diverse students.

Each objective will have action steps and timelines that enable its realization.

Foundation 4: Institutional Programs and Activities

Another element of creating a campus environment that respects and supports the needs of faculty, staff, and students of color on campus are real-time programs that affirm and validate their presence in the academic community. Such programming is a critical part of institution's efforts to create an inclusive residential culture. The table below represents a display of selected diversity programs and activities currently operated by the LLU Office of Diversity and/or the school-based diversity committee infrastructure.

Foundation 5: Institutional Finance

Finally, institutions where diversity is valued reflect that valuation in adequate budgeting for diversity activities. Such budgeting validates the role that diversity plays in the institution as well as providing the financial resources for personnel and programming vital to the success of the institution's commitment.

Conclusion

This article could not detail all of the factors that influence whether racial diversity will work in higher education during the 21st century. We did not detail or describe the need for academic and social support, same-race and cross-racial mentorship from teaching faculty, or a host of other programmatic practices that benefit minority students. However, there is no question that without the five foundations mentioned above, in whatever form the particular higher educational context elicits, diversity efforts will fail.

Notes

1. Cultural "otherness" is a factor in the adjustment of minority students to majority white institutions. See Chalmer E. Thompson and Bruce R. Fretz, "Predicting the Adjustment of Black Students at Predominantly White Institutions," *The Journal of Higher Education*, Vol. 62, No. 4 (July/August 1991): 437. Chalmer and Fretz note, "Findings from a cross section of research studies suggest that black students who attend predominantly white colleges and universities expect greater difficulty in achieving levels of congruence than their white counterparts. Black students perceive greater

racial tension and hostility in their environment, express lower levels of satisfaction, and greater levels of isolation, and feel less identified with the institution than white students." Such detachment make the creation of an affirming campus environment a necessity if majority white institutions will maintain their attractiveness to black students.

2. See Sylvia Hurtado, "The Campus Racial Climate: Contexts of Conflict," *The Journal of Higher Education,* Vol. 63, No. 5 (September October 1992): pp. 539–564. On 561, 562 Hurtado observes, "Minorities are more aware of racial tension both for historical reasons and because they, unlike white students who are a numerical majority, must depend on constant interracial contact in social, learning, and work spheres on predominantly white campuses."

3. On some of the issues faced by faculty of color in majority institutions, see Caroline Sotello Viernes Turner, Samuel L. Myers, Jr., and John W. Creswell, "Exploring Underrepresentation: The Case of Faculty of Color in the Midwest," *The Journal of Higher Education,* Vol. 70, No. 1 (January/February 1999): pp. 27–57.

4. On the decisional issues faced by minority students, see Laura Walter Perna "Differences in the Decision to Attend College Among African-American, Hispanics, and Whites," *The Journal of Higher Education* Vol. 71, No. 2 (March/April 2000): pp. 117–139.

5. For an intriguing approach to variations in teachers' expectations student performance based on race, See Mica Pollock "How the Question We Ask Most About Race in Education is the Very Question We Most Suppress," *Educational Researcher,* Vol. 30, No. 9: pp. 2–12. Although this ethnographic research was conducted in school districts, it has implications for leaders in higher education. Pollock asserts on page 10, "To disarm educators' understandable defensiveness about their racialized expectations, for example, we might first acknowledge that it is a widespread American habit—not simply a teacherly habit—to expect racialized achievement from racialized children."

6. Institutional leadership is central to setting a positive organizational climate for diversity. For further discussion of how the college or university as an organizational entity must also be a unit of analysis if diversity is to work in higher education, see Richard C. Richardson, Jr., and Elizabeth Fisk Skinner, "Adapting to Diversity: Organizational Influences on Student Achievement," *The Journal of Higher Education,* Vol. 61, No. 5 (September/October 1999): pp. 485–504. They write, "Most of the interventions aimed at improving participation and achievement rates have been designed to change students or to buffer them from the impact of environments perceived by many as cold, hostile, or even racist. The idea that institutions might also need to change in fundamental ways has been largely missing, in part because our society has historically treated minority populations as inferior."

7. See the results of Harvard Study described in "Diverse Populations Can Enhance Learning, New Harvard Report Shows" in American Council on Education's Higher Education and National Affairs (9 August 1999). The Harvard report examined the responses of 1,820 students who participated in the study. In response to the question "What should be done about the admissions policy at your law school seeking a student body which includes more underrepresented minorities?" 80.6 percent of the Harvard students indicated that the policy should be strengthened (47.2%) or maintained (33.4%). The study found, "White students, in particular, are enriched by interactions with other races and ethnic groups because they are more likely than others not to have much interaction with nonwhites prior to college."

8. See Elizabeth Whilt, Marcia I. Edison, Ernest T. Pascarella, Patrick T. Terenzini, Amauty Nora, "Influences on Students Openness to Diversity and Challenge in the Second and Third Years of College," *The Journal of Higher Education*, Vol. 72, No. 2 (March/April 2001): pp. 172–201.

William B. Harvey

WILLIAM B. HARVEY assumed his position as Vice President and Director of the Office of Minorities in Higher Education at the American Council on Education in August 2000. Prior to joining ACE, Dr. Harvey was Dean of the School of Education, Deputy Chancellor for Education Partnerships, and Professor of Educational Policy and Community Studies at the University of Wisconsin–Milwaukee. During his 30-year career in higher education, he has also held faculty and administrative appointments at North Carolina State University, State University of New York at Stony Brook, University of Pennsylvania, Richard Stockton College (NJ), Earlham College (IN), and Brookdale Community College (NJ). Dr. Harvey has worked in the areas of academic affairs, research administration, student affairs, and academic support services, with a special focus on interdisciplinary instruction and international programs.

The focus of his research and scholarly activity has been on the cultural and social factors that affect under-served populations, with particular emphasis on college and university settings. His latest book is *Grass Roots and Glass Ceilings: African American Administrators in Predominantly White Universities* (1999). He is also co-author of *Affirmative Rhetoric, Negative Action,* and co-editor of *New Directions for Community Colleges: Recruiting and Retaining Minority Faculty.* He has published extensively articles in professional journals and popular publications. He is a member of the Editorial Board for the *Review of Higher Education* and the *Negro Education Review,* and a Consulting Editor for *Change: The Magazine for Higher Learning.*

Dr. Harvey's service activities have included chairing the Higher Education Committee for Equity 2000, a national initiative sponsored by the College Board to raise the level of math and science instruction in K–12 systems, and chairing the Governmental Relations Committee of the Association of Deans of Colleges of Education at Land Grant Universities. He has also been a member of the Committee on Governmental Relations of the American Association of Colleges for Teacher Education, and a member of the steering committee of the Council of Great City Colleges of Education.

18

DEANS AS DIVERSITY LEADERS

MODIFYING ATTITUDES BY TAKING BOLD ACTIONS—LEARNING LESSONS AND CHANGING CULTURES

Change doesn't occur easily in the academy. Postsecondary institutions are rooted in tradition, and the comfortable and rather self-serving notion of being in an "ivory tower" has allowed academicians to be detached from the social considerations that existed outside the campus gates—in the environment that nonacademicians refer to as the "real world." But the academy is also quite real—cloistered and parochial perhaps, but real nonetheless, and rather influential to boot. Colleges and universities, quietly but very efficiently, have been the places that separate those who will be leaders from those who will be led. The individuals who shape and mold those future leaders are the members of the faculty. Faculty members inspire, mentor, challenge, and motivate their young—and increasingly, not so young—charges to better themselves, their society, and their world. What's missing from this picture are faculty members of color.

In my travels around and through the academic landscape over a period of three decades, I have been aggravated and saddened by the tacit resistance that so many members of the academic community have manifested to making college and university faculties more racially and culturally diverse. The burden of facilitating diversity still rests heavily on individuals who are minority group members even though they are often the most marginalized persons on the campuses. So, until the white members of the professoriate step forward to carry their share of the responsibility to bring about much needed change in colleges and universities, the senior administrators must exercise leadership and demonstrate vision by making increased racial diversity a demonstrated outcome of their own job performance.

Certainly we expect that the top institutional leaders—Presidents and Chancellors—can and will provide enlightened leadership to increase the representation of people of color on their faculties. Similarly, the chief academic officer at a college or university can play a key role in facilitating faculty diversity, just as he or she catalyzes progress toward other institutional goals.

But other university administrators also have tremendous opportunities and leverage to move colleges and universities forward so that the institutions are more diverse and reflective of the American population. My experiences in academic administration, particularly those I had as a Dean, helped make me aware of the various ways in which administrative officers, especially those at the cabinet level, can help their institutions to recognize the importance and value of having curricula, faculty, and administrative staff, as well as student bodies that reflect the vibrant racial and cultural diversity of the American society—a diversity that will become even more pronounced as the nation moves further into the 21st century.

When I decided to trade in the reasonably comfortable life of a tenured full professor for the somewhat more hectic existence of a university dean, I did so with the presumption and expectation that taking such a position would provide me with the latitude to have a strong impact on the makeup of the organizational unit that I was responsible for. I also expected to have some influence on the other areas of the university through my participation in policy discussions and university governance bodies. In retrospect, I learned some important lessons that might be helpful to others, particularly senior administrators who want to increase faculty diversity at their institutions.

Assuming the Deanship of a School of Education left me feeling reasonably confident that I could identify candidates of color for various faculty positions as they became available. After all, education has been the academic discipline that has produced the largest proportion of Ph.D. recipients of color, though truth be told, their representation among university faculty in most predominantly white institutions still falls below their percentage of terminal degree recipients. Having spent my entire academic career in predominantly white colleges and universities, I was not particularly anxious about the fact that the faculty that I would be working with was overwhelmingly white. In fact, with nine faculty of color out of a total of sixty-five, five of them holding tenure and two of them at the full professor rank, we were already above the national average in terms of representation. Still, one of my most urgent goals as a Dean was to dramatically increase the numbers of faculty of color in our school.

As is the case with almost all colleges and universities, my institution had committed itself in writing to pursuing diversity among the faculty and administrative staff. In its promotional materials the institution touted its urban location as a positive factor to potential candidates and also identified the mission as being urban-focused. The university was located in a city in which nearly half of the residents were African-American and Latino. But like most institutions, even those in communities where the vast majority of the population are people of color, non-white faculty members were a rare breed. I was heartened by the fact that as part of the annual review process, each of the Deans was scheduled to sit down with the President and Provost to discuss what progress, if any, had occurred to increase the diversity of the faculty and staff during the year.

When it was time to initiate the annual process of recruiting and hiring new faculty for the next year in my school, we were fortunate enough to be able to search for six positions. I called the chairs of the search committees together to explain that we needed to have a more diverse faculty and that they should communicate this message to their respective committees as an important signal about the direction that we wanted to move in, both as a school and as a university. I was quite precise, or at least, I thought I was, and having delivered the charge I then turned my attention to other duties.

So, when one after another the various search committees sent forward short lists of prospective final candidates for me to review and there were no candidates of color who were being recommended to be interviewed for any of the positions, I remember experiencing a range of emotions: first surprise, then disappointment, and finally puzzlement. There were two ways that I could interpret the situation. Either the search committees didn't know how to conduct the search processes in a way to include candidates of color, or they didn't share my concern about having a more diverse faculty. I chose to presume that the former statement was the correct one, which left me with two possible responses: to accept the short lists as an indication that the committees didn't know how to carry out my charge to them, or to return the short lists to the committees with instructions to continue the searches until they included some candidates of color.

As a new Dean, if I had chosen the first response, it would have been a dramatic statement of my principle, but it also would have implicitly questioned the integrity of the faculty. Remembering the old adage that sometimes discretion is the better part of valor, I decided in the future to make my message more compelling and my actions more proactive, which led to my first lesson:

Lesson 1:
Just because a dean articulates a message, even an important one, doesn't mean that the faculty 'gets it.' When the message is about faculty diversity, without active engagement, the customary habits and practices are likely to prevail.

As the first year on the job came to a close, I surmised that I needed to develop much closer contacts with the faculty. Going into my second year, I acted on the realization of how important it is to have allies by engaging key faculty members in formal and informal conversations and interactions. I continued the practice that I had started in year one of inviting the faculty and staff in each of the departments in the school to my home for dinner, but in the second year, I expanded the guest lists to include notable figures from the local corporate and civic communities. My remarks to the assembled groups at each one of the gatherings were brief—I offered my thanks for the warmth and congeniality with which I had been welcomed into the community, and I stated my confidence that the school would effectively serve its mission of providing leadership and service to the diverse urban environment that we were a part of. Knowing the isolation in which most faculty members work, I made a point of introducing certain key figures to prominent local personalities, such as city council members or corporate executives, and praising the research that they were conducting. The non-educators were people that I had met as a result of agreeing to serve on several civic boards in the city, and the faculty basked in the glow of describing their work to some of the eminent persons in the community.

One particularly noteworthy gathering occurred when one of the evening's dinner guests was the popular anchorperson of the most heavily watched nightly news program in the city, whom I had met at a recent charity event. As it turned out, his father had once been the local superintendent of schools, and later was the Dean of the School of Education at one of the Big Ten universities. Not only was he personable and charming, but what really surprised and delighted the faculty as I introduced him to them individually was that he was genuinely interested in the work that they did. Obviously it is impossible to say in any definitive way whether this event, or any of the others that I hosted, actually caused any faculty member to become more amenable to my agenda, which meant enhancing their diversity consciousness, but I think what the activities did accomplish was to show the faculty that their Dean knew about and appreciated their achievements and that I was willing to make them known to others.

I continued to cultivate influential faculty members during the next year, both publicly and in private. We initiated a monthly breakfast series to acquaint members of the public with policy issues related to education, and at each session I would ask faculty to stand and be recognized. I also invited the senior members of each department to small dinners at my home, and at every opportunity I stressed the key point—our faculty had to become more diverse. The composition of our faculty was the most salient way for us to demonstrate to the community and serve as an example for the rest of the university the importance that we accorded to our urban mission and focus. I think that the crucial connection for any administrator who wants to promote diversity is to get senior white faculty to accept ownership of the necessity of bringing faculty of color on board as colleagues. The importance of gaining allies among the faculty can't be overstated. I was quite fortunate because, as things turned out, I found my strongest and most influential ally in the person of the only faculty member in the School of Education who held the title of Distinguished Professor. Having the assistance of the most accomplished person in the unit, with a 30-year history of achievement, an international reputation, and a former term of office in the Deanship to boot was an incredible asset.

When it was time for the search process to be initiated in my second year, I again met with the committee chairs and stressed the importance of diversity. I also pointed each committee to possible sources for candidates, either individuals or organizations, that might help them identify some good prospects of color. In the end, my efforts paid off. Of the seven new faculty that we hired that year, four were people of color. I felt that the search committees were much more receptive than they had been in the previous year, and this outcome led me to recognize Lesson No. 2:

Lesson 2:

Find allies in the faculty so that they can carry the diversity banner, not just in formal searches, but in all of the departmental formal and informal discussions that occur—the kinds of discussions that deans aren't invited to participate in, and usually don't even know are taking place.

Fortunately, as time passed, the school and the university were expanding, but each department wanted new faculty lines, either for new programs or to maintain and enhance ones that were already in place. To facilitate the allocation of new faculty lines, I organized the Dean's Council into a review panel in which each department chair was asked to rate the importance of the position requests made by the other chairs to the needs of the school as a whole. This process essentially amounted to a kind of peer review of the various position requests, and since there were always more requests being made in a given year than there were lines available to fill them, it generated some measure of consensus around priority appointments. I was especially concerned about one of our programs in which there were no faculty of color even though, ironically, this particular area was the one in which, at the national level, the largest number of African-Americans had historically received doctoral degrees.

The department was made up of two discrete programs, and in a conversation with the department chair, who was African-American, I explained that from the standpoint of the student–faculty ratio and the credit hours delivered by the program, an additional faculty line was difficult to justify. I told him that the only way I would support an additional line was with the understanding that it would be targeted to bring in someone who would bring diversity to the area. Such an appointment would be highly significant because this program was involved in the development of administrators for our local school system, which enrolled a student population that was nearly 80 percent African-American and Hispanic. Since he harbored some doubt about the concurrence of the program faculty for this approach, I informed him that I would make the position more appealing by allowing it to be advertised at the Associate or Assistant Professor level, which meant that the successful applicant could be able to come into the university with tenure.

To avoid any appearance of special treatment for the department, I explained that the position request would still have to be presented in the usual review process, but that given the emphasis that I had placed on diversity, I felt certain that the other chairs would support it. Once he had secured the agreement of the program faculty, the department chair presented the proposal for a new position to the Dean's cabinet, where it received unanimous support. A search committee was organized with a senior faculty member serving as chair, someone who had been a previous and unsuccessful aspirant for the Deanship. Unlike my first year, when I didn't check on the deliberations of search committees after I had given them their charge, at the regular bimonthly meetings of the Dean's cabinet I regularly inquired about their progress. I was encouraged by the fact that every time I was given an update on the search in the diversity-resistant program, the chair reassured me that things were going according to plan. This particular search was the last of eleven to be concluded, five of which resulted in the hiring of people of color. However, when the short list of candidates was forwarded to me, it consisted of two white women and one white male. I immediately called the chair into my office and asked him to explain the situation.

He responded by saying that in a departmental meeting held just prior to sending me the list, his colleagues had communicated to him that these were the candidates they thought could best help the department achieve its goals. When I asked his thoughts, as chair of the department, about how this list was in direct contradiction to the school and university goals of having a more racially and culturally diverse faculty, his answer was that, as the person who was elected to be the leader of the department, he felt a responsibility to support the judgment of the senior faculty. The whole situation had taken on a surreal quality, but in fact it was all too real. With tremendous effort, I was able to control my aggravation as I said to him—in as measured and even a tone that I could muster—that in my position as Dean it was my responsibility to support the goals and objectives of the university senior administration, and as a result I was shutting down the search because the short list of candidates was not acceptable. He looked at me in amazement for a minute, and then said, "You can't do that. The faculty will be livid." I practiced my most beguiling smile as I told him, "Of course I can do it—in fact, it's done." Lesson No. 3:

Lesson 3:

Shut it down: When a search has been conducted and it turns out that diversity considerations have been ignored or overlooked, close the search and start again.

My action brought the expected fusillade of memos from the aggrieved faculty members, filled with accusations that I had exceeded my authority, intruded into faculty prerogatives, and demonstrated a dogmatic approach to management, and they were not only written to me, but also to the Provost and the Chancellor. My written response to their bombastic communiqués was short and direct. I offered to meet with the entire department to explain my position and indicated that in this meeting, I would address any and all points that they chose to discuss. I also made it clear that I was not about to engage in a "memo war," drafting point-by-point rebuttals or explanations to the objections they had raised.

The meeting was scheduled at the soonest mutually agreeable time, and to be certain that there were no erroneous interpretations of any statements that I made, one of the Associate Deans accompanied me to take notes of the discussion. When we arrived, we were both surprised to find out that though my invitation had been extended to meet with everyone in the department, only the tenured faculty members were present. The chair apparently noticed our surprise because he hastened to say that the senior faculty members had discussed the matter in an executive committee meeting and determined that it was appropriate to restrict the matters under discussion to those persons who were tenured. The Associate Dean and I later surmised that the reason the junior faculty were excluded was because they were not supportive of the outcome of the search. Everyone who was untenured in the department had been hired within the past two years, since the time that I had assumed the Deanship, and we believed—from the interviews that we conducted with them when they were candidates and subsequent conversations with them since they had joined the faculty—that they also felt that it was important for the department to become more racially and culturally diverse. On the other hand, the senior faculty were all long-timers in the department and they seemed quite content with the composition of the department as it stood. While not specifically articulating this position, their perspective seemed to be that not only did they have an African-American in the ranks, they had even elected him as the chair. And that, is seemed, was as much diversity as they were interested in having.

Ignoring the tension in the air, I politely asked how they would like to proceed—whether they would like to offer their comments first and have me respond, or vice-versa. They indicated that they would like to begin by expressing their extreme dissatisfaction with my action of closing the search, and then each of the tenured faculty members, in turn, proceeded to present information about the department's history, mission, objectives, and standing in the academic community. The final admonition was presented by the individual who had held the rank of full professor the longest, who it turns out had also been the chair of the search committee. Prior to my arrival, she had served as Interim Dean, and she emphasized the point that under no circumstances would she as Dean have ever overruled the wisdom and insight of a search committee that was composed of experts in the field regarding the selection of a candidate who they felt was the most qualified.

I listened quietly and respectfully and told them, first of all, that I appreciated the time and energy that they had put into conducting the search and the background information that they had provided me about the department and its respective programs. I then explained that the history of the department was important, but that even more important was the future of the department, and the school, and the university for that matter. The Chancellor had explained quite clearly that our future was one of engagement, of connecting and relating to the community that we were pledged to serve. What we did in our school was particularly important, I said, because by recognizing and responding to the needs of the students, parents, teachers, and administrators who were involved in schools in the city, we could demonstrate clearly that we intended to be a good partner to the citizens of the community. Being a good partner, I emphasized, meant reflecting the needs, and to the degree possible, the composition of the city's population.

The point on which I concluded was that I would be remiss in carrying out my responsibilities by letting the search go forward, and I made it clear that my decision would not change. While I didn't really expect to change the minds or the hearts of these malcontents, as the Dean I did want to take the high road. So, I announced that if they felt that as the result of my decision some class offerings would have to be cancelled, I would entertain a written proposal for a one-year adjunct appointment to be made to the department. After all, I hastened to add, I felt certain that none of us wanted the students to suffer because of *our* difference of opinion. As far as the full-time position was concerned, I explained that the department would be welcome to make another request in the next hiring cycle. On my way out of the room, I glanced at the department chair, who had remained mostly silent during the meeting. Our eyes failed to meet since he was staring down at the table in front of him. Later I realized that I must have been involuntarily shaking my head as I wondered what could have been going through his mind.

It's incredibly important to know who can be trusted to actively and earnestly campaign for increased diversity. Faculty culture, with its emphasis on tradition, personal connections, and relationships, and its inclination to look backwards rather than forward stands as one of the main reasons why there are so few faculty of color. It would be wonderful if academicians didn't fall victim to the prevalent cultural values of racial and ethnic discrimination that are omnipresent in the American fabric, but they do.

Because of the sense of marginality that the academy often imposes upon us, on occasion some faculty of color behave in a way that frustrates diversity rather than advances it—a hard lesson to accept. While

I feel comfortable in saying that faculty of color can usually be counted on as supporters of faculty diversity, my experiences in this particular situation impressed upon me that even in the academy, it's important to know who you are dealing with and what they are all about. It took an unnerving experience for me to come to this realization, but it was a lesson that was crucial for me to learn.

Lesson 4:
Know whom to trust: Not everyone who looks like you is necessarily your friend or shares your values. Hopefully, not everyone who looks different from you is necessarily your enemy either or stands opposed to having more faculty of color among their ranks.

While adding promising junior faculty of color to an institution's professorial ranks is important and beneficial, that approach alone is not nearly so significant as bringing in tenured faculty of color, particularly at the full professor rank. I was fortunate to have a position opening for a full professor, which was not committed to a particular department. I desperately wanted to fill this position with a person of color who would be dedicated to our institutional mission of urban education, and we advertised this opening for two years while we sought the right person for the job. In addition to placing advertisements in all the usual outlets, I was privately contacting several nationally known scholars whom I thought might be interested in joining us.

Finally, during the third year of searching, I was made aware of the fact that a highly distinguished scholar in a nearby city was leaving his position as the holder of an endowed chair at one of the most outstanding universities in the country because of an administrative reorganization that was taking place there. I immediately contacted him to inquire whether he would be interested in the position that we were holding, and I was very gratified when he responded positively. We talked at greater length over the succeeding weeks and even arranged for him to have an informal visit to the campus when as expected, he wowed everyone who met him. Even though the situation looked like a great fit, to ensure transparency in the hiring process, I readvertised the position, and surprisingly, in addition to the individual that we were cultivating, the respondents included another person of color who was very prominent in his field and who had not previously been on our radar screen.

What this fortuitous circumstance presented was a possible opportunity to get two outstanding scholars rather than just one. I made an immediate call on the Provost to brief him on the situation and to make my best pitch for increasing the university's scholarly reputation and its diversity profile at the same time. Fortunately for me, and to his credit, he understood both the value and the significance of bringing both of these outstanding academicians into the institution. He did backpedal a bit when I suggested to him that since he thought it was an important step to take his office should provide the salary for the second position. However, we ultimately worked out a 50–50 salary sharing arrangement as a demonstration to other academic units on campus that the financial costs of bringing in senior minority scholars was something to which the administration was prepared to commit resources.

With the financial issues resolved, we went on to interview, offer positions to, and successfully hire the two African-American Full Professors within days of each other. To put this situation into context, when I arrived at the university there were two African Americans in the School of Education who were Full Professors. While I feel comfortable in saying that faculty of color can usually be counted on as supporters of faculty diversity, my experiences in this particular situation impressed upon me that even in the academy, it's important to know who you are dealing with and what they are all about. It took an unnerving experience for me to come to this realization, but it was a lesson that was critical for me to learn. Following my arrival, we had promoted another person to this rank and now had five people at this level. In fact, the total number of faculty of color in full professor positions was equal to the combined count of the other nine schools and colleges.

There is a saying in the military that "rank has its privileges," and this holds true in the academic community as well. Our new Full Professors were able to lend their impact both overtly and discreetly in many ways and on many different occasions. Because of their reputations, they were accorded a certain amount of respect and even deference, and they provided invaluable assistance and support to me in the netherworld of academic politics. It was wonderful to observe as they

served as guides and mentors, not just to junior faculty, but in racially
sensitive matters to several of their senior colleagues as well.

Lesson 5:

*Get some stars. It's wonderful to have young faculty members
of color who are filled with potential and promise, but it's even
better to have some seasoned, experienced, and accomplished
senior faculty who can and will address issues of inequity and
injustice, and not have to worry whether doing so will result in
an unfavorable review of their performance and/or the enmity
of their colleagues.*

Conclusion

The historical pattern of participation for the few and exclusion of the
many has closely paralleled national attitudes and patterns of dominance
and submission along race, class, and gender lines. And though some of
the barriers that have historically excluded those individuals with the
least social, economic, and political clout have begun to be pushed aside,
especially where race and ethnicity are concerned, America's colleges
and universities continue to be embarrassingly unrepresentative of the
nation's population.

Relying exclusively on faculty of color to be the advocates for
increased faculty diversity is both unrealistic and inappropriate. It is
crucial for white faculty to take ownership of the responsibility for
bringing faculty of color into the academy. Rather than being allowed
to shirk this duty, they must be challenged, encouraged, and assisted to
carry it out. Being able to rely on the key players among the faculty
provides both greater opportunity and flexibility to the administrative
officials to press for the realization of this important objective from
their vantage points.

Using the approaches identified here (and applying the lessons
learned) we were able to increase the representation of faculty of color
by 100 percent over a period of five years. I don't claim to have done
this by myself—fortunately I had the support and encouragement of
the administrators at the highest levels of the university, as well as
the assistance and cooperation of a number of my faculty colleagues.

Further, I don't presume that these specific methods would work in every situation—there is too much environmental variation in the nation's colleges and universities to believe that is the case. But, at the risk of seeming naive, I believe that it is possible to increase faculty diversity at any institution if the individuals who truly want this to happen organize and energize themselves and are prepared to press the case. Particularly in the academic community, the people who know and understand the culture must be the ones to transform it.

Chancellors and Presidents should take the lead in this effort but, unfortunately, sometimes they don't. Deans can use their positions, their influence, and their budgets to begin this transformation within their own units. When they exert themselves in pursuit of diversity, some of their faculty will follow, and through their combined efforts and energies, they *can* recruit and retain people of color. Those of us who have been fortunate enough to get into such positions owe it to ourselves, to the sacrifices made by those who came before us, and to the potential of those who will come after us to diversify the American professoriate so that it more accurately reflects the demographic makeup of the American society. We must use any and all means that are available to us to make this happen.

APPENDIX

HALE'S INVENTORY FOR ASSESSING AN INSTITUTION'S COMMITMENT TO MULTICULTURAL PROGRAMMING

Introduction

There is documented evidence that improving educational opportunities for students, faculty, and personnel of color in higher education achieves improved educational results. In an attempt to fill the great gaps that exist between most Americans of color and white Americans, a number of institutions of higher education are making efforts to remove the barriers that have made it difficult for students, faculty, and staff of color to have access to and experience the high-quality education available to other campus constituents.

The inventory included here is provided to assist institutional personnel and units (faculty, administrators, departments, colleges, and universities) to evaluate various aspects of the institution (traditions, policies, practices, and goals) to determine their effectiveness in providing a dynamic pluralistic environment on their campuses. The inventory is divided into eight areas: Administrative Leadership, Admissions and Recruitment, Financial Assistance, Student Support Services, Curriculum, Campus Environment, Graduate and Professional Programs, and Multicultural Hiring.

The inventory should be useful in promoting discussions on how best an institution can develop and implement strategies to facilitate multicultural programming and affirmative action throughout the fabric of the organization as well as within individual units.

Summary

This inventory spans a comprehensive schematic for assessing, implementing, and improving the environment for diversity on a college or university campus. The assessment may be done by administrators, faculty, or students. All three approaches could be helpful in obtaining a comprehensive view of how the campus community feels about the institution's commitment to diversity.

While administrators and faculty are key figures in promoting a positive climate for diversity, students and staff bear no small share of responsibility in creating a climate that fosters a commitment to equal opportunity and social justice. Some positive initiatives that have been documented and that should be encouraged are:

- formulating a forthright vision and commitment to diversity by the president and his/her administrative staff;

- developing a team of deans, departmental chairs, faculty, staff, and student leaders who are jointly committed to achieving diversity;

- creating a climate for discussion, dialogue, and debate on issues of diversity;

- setting admission criteria that include factors other than quantitative ones for admissibility;

- providing priorty consideration and financial support that traditionally has been underfunded;

- placing a high value on establishing retention strategies that will enable members of underrepresented groups to persist and graduate;

- recognizing the unique experiences and contributions of people of color by establishing the principles of justice and multiculturalism to be reflected in the institution's curricula and its invitation of scholars and artists of color to participate in campus events;

- encouraging the social bonding of students from a common culture in affirming their right to be drawn to each other and to have some campus space set aside where they can engage in social and educational exchanges;

- developing strategies to identify capable undergraduates as prospective graduate students, so as to provide them with funding support and mentoring opportunities that will ensure their success as students and as future family members;

- hiring faculty of color and establishing mentoring programs for junior faculty to facilitate their requirements for promotion and tenure.

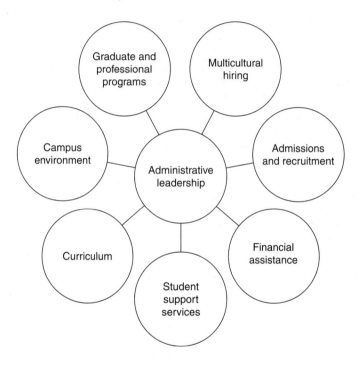

I. Institutional Commitment Begins with Administrative Leadership

	Very often	Often	Occasionally	Rarely	Never
1. The administration makes a serious effort to develop and implement policies to increase the representation of people of color.	☐	☐	☐	☐	☐
2. The campus community is apprised of the short and long-range goals designed to promote cultural diversity.	☐	☐	☐	☐	☐
3. The level of multicultural programming is prominent within each unit throughout the institution.	☐	☐	☐	☐	☐
4. A cumulative record of information on faculty and staff of color is collected and distributed throughout the institution annually.	☐	☐	☐	☐	☐
5. Staff development seminars and workshops are conducted to acquaint institutional personnel with the goals and procedures for creating a more diverse community on campus.	☐	☐	☐	☐	☐
6. Special links are developed between the institution and the local community (schools, parents, churches, and organizations) to promote early planning for children to attend college.	☐	☐	☐	☐	☐
7. Articulation agreements are developed to promote and encourage the transfer of students of color from community colleges to the institution.	☐	☐	☐	☐	☐
8. The institution provides special incentives and rewards to personnel and units for being effective in making ethnic cultural diversity a high priority.	☐	☐	☐	☐	☐
9. Multicultural programming is supported, for the most part, by institutional funding.	☐	☐	☐	☐	☐
10. The institution develops and enforces policies against discrimination, racial harassment, and "stonewalling."	☐	☐	☐	☐	☐

Comments _____

_____

_____

II. Admissions and Recruitment

	Very often	Often	Occasionally	Rarely	Never
1. The institution offers an optional thirteenth-year program.	☐	☐	☐	☐	☐
2. Institutional programs are targeted involving high school counselors in the recruitment of students of color.	☐	☐	☐	☐	☐
3. A systematic effort is under way to involve institutional alumni in the recruitment of students of color.	☐	☐	☐	☐	☐
4. Offices are set up at high school sites to ensure that these students are aware of college entrance requirements.	☐	☐	☐	☐	☐
5. The cooperation of the media (radio, TV, newspapers, etc.) is used to promote the institution.	☐	☐	☐	☐	☐
6. Parents are engaged in a meaningful way, on or off campus, in the recruitment process.	☐	☐	☐	☐	☐
7. Students already enrolled are used to recruit other students, targeting the high schools from which they were graduated.	☐	☐	☐	☐	☐
8. The institution uses tests as diagnostic indicators rather than as selective indicators.	☐	☐	☐	☐	☐
9. Admissions criteria are flexible.	☐	☐	☐	☐	☐
10. Ethnic-focused brochures are used in recruiting.	☐	☐	☐	☐	☐
11. Ethnic student representation adequately reflects their proportion in the general population.	☐	☐	☐	☐	☐

Comments _____

_____

_____

III. Financial Assistance

	Very often	Often	Occa-sionally	Rarely	Never
1. The institution uses internal funds to supplement federal dollars.	☐	☐	☐	☐	☐
2. Money is set aside from a restricted general fund to provide grants.	☐	☐	☐	☐	☐
3. Workshops are conducted on budgeting, money management, and alternative financial aid sources for students and parents.	☐	☐	☐	☐	☐
4. The institution makes a conscious effort to minimize the loan debt of low-income students through creative strategies such as in-house loans and parent loan programs at low interest rates.	☐	☐	☐	☐	☐
5. Special scholarships are available to high-ranking students of color.	☐	☐	☐	☐	☐
6. The institution offers an extended payment plan for low-income students.	☐	☐	☐	☐	☐
7. Special fundraising programs and campaigns are conducted to secure funds for students of color.	☐	☐	☐	☐	☐
8. Students are assisted in securing employment both on and off campus.	☐	☐	☐	☐	☐
9. Discretionary funds are available to students in emergency situations.	☐	☐	☐	☐	☐
10. The institution conducts exit interviews to determine the impact of the financial aid factor on the student's departure.	☐	☐	☐	☐	☐

Comments _____

_____

_____

IV. Student Support Services

	Very often	Often	Occa-sionally	Rarely	Never
1. The institution sponsors workshops to help students of color assess their personal goals.	☐	☐	☐	☐	☐
2. Programs are offered to help new culturally different students become active in the campus community.	☐	☐	☐	☐	☐
3. Students of color make use of the counseling center.	☐	☐	☐	☐	☐
4. Students are enlisted as peer advisors to assist the faculty with the advising program.	☐	☐	☐	☐	☐
5. The placement and career center attracts students of color.	☐	☐	☐	☐	☐
6. Students of color are active in student organizations.	☐	☐	☐	☐	☐
7. A structured procedure has been developed to assess the strengths and skills of disadvantaged students.	☐	☐	☐	☐	☐
8. Special mechanisms are used to assess and screen potential counselors for their ability to work with diverse populations.	☐	☐	☐	☐	☐
9. The institution provides mentors for all students who need special help.	☐	☐	☐	☐	☐
10. Input is sought from constituents of color before programs that affect them are put in place.	☐	☐	☐	☐	☐
11. Support services for students of color have a funding base that promotes stability.	☐	☐	☐	☐	☐
12. Tutoring is available on a walk-in basis.	☐	☐	☐	☐	☐

Comments _____

_____

_____

V. Curriculum

	Very often	Often	Occasionally	Rarely	Never
1. Textbooks are selected that reflect the contributions of persons of various ethnic cultures.	☐	☐	☐	☐	☐
2. Curriculum reform measures have been established to create courses that will expose students to new knowledge about ethnic minorities.	☐	☐	☐	☐	☐
3. Majority students are encouraged to enroll in ethnic-focused courses.	☐	☐	☐	☐	☐
4. Teaching throughout the institution is sensitive to multicultural issues and concerns.	☐	☐	☐	☐	☐
5. The institution promotes the use of educational television as a mechanism for helping students learn more about pluralism.	☐	☐	☐	☐	☐
6. Holdings in the library and bookstore reflect expanding support for multicultural curricula.	☐	☐	☐	☐	☐
7. Ethnic study courses are a part of the required core curriculum.	☐	☐	☐	☐	☐
8. Workshops are conducted to train faculty how to expand and strengthen their courses to reflect a multicultural perspective.	☐	☐	☐	☐	☐
9. Mechanisms have been put in place to assess the diversity of institutional curricula on a regular basis.	☐	☐	☐	☐	☐
10. The institution encourages research (term papers, essays, etc.) on multicultural issues.	☐	☐	☐	☐	☐

Comments _____

_____

_____

VI. Campus Environment

	Very often	Often	Occa-sionally	Rarely	Never
1. Administrators meet with faculty and students of color to learn of their interests and concerns.	☐	☐	☐	☐	☐
2. Administrators and faculty set aside time to attend multicultural events.	☐	☐	☐	☐	☐
3. The institution expects students of color to succeed and develops strategies to help them do so.	☐	☐	☐	☐	☐
4. Institutional initiatives are developed and implemented topromote racial awareness and sensitivity to multicultural issues.	☐	☐	☐	☐	☐
5. A conscious effort is made to involve college personnel in ethnic minority community organizations.	☐	☐	☐	☐	☐
6. Weekend programs and projects are established to involve local (off-campus) youth of color and to acquaint them with college resources.	☐	☐	☐	☐	☐
7. Students of color have a center or "family room" area where they can feel comfortable and share common interests and concerns.	☐	☐	☐	☐	☐
8. The institution recognizes eminent leaders and alumni of color by naming buildings, scholarships and lectureships in their honor and by awarding them honorary degrees.	☐	☐	☐	☐	☐
9. Scholars and artists of color are invited to the campus to participate in campus events.	☐	☐	☐	☐	☐
10. Students of color are encouraged to participate in campus organizations.	☐	☐	☐	☐	☐
11. Students are encouraged to form their own support groups to provide opportunities for educational and social interaction.	☐	☐	☐	☐	☐

Comments _____

_____

_____

VII. Graduate and Professional Programs

	Very often	Often	Occa-sionally	Rarely	Never
1. Textbooks are selected that reflect the contributions of persons of various ethnic cultures.	☐	☐	☐	☐	☐
1. The institution uses qualifying test scores (GRE, GMAT, LSAT, MCAT, etc.) as major instruments of selection.	☐	☐	☐	☐	☐
2. The institution includes non-cognitive factors in considering the admissibility of students of color.	☐	☐	☐	☐	☐
3. Links between the institution and historical institutions of color are established to assist in recruiting students of color.	☐	☐	☐	☐	☐
4. Faculty and graduates of color are used to recruit prospective graduates and professional students of color.	☐	☐	☐	☐	☐
5. A mechanism is in place to target undergraduate students of color within the institution and make them aware of graduate opportunities available on campus.	☐	☐	☐	☐	☐
6. Fellowships and assistantships have been designated for students of color.	☐	☐	☐	☐	☐
7. Visitation programs are a part of the institution's graduate and professional recruitment efforts.	☐	☐	☐	☐	☐
8. Faculty are trained to be aware of multicultural issues and to serve as mentors for students of color.	☐	☐	☐	☐	☐
9. Students of color are advised to form interest groups in the area of their academic concentration for peer support.	☐	☐	☐	☐	☐
10. Special incentives are available to departments that have innovative projects to recruit and retain people of color.	☐	☐	☐	☐	☐

Comments _____

_____

_____

VIII. Multicultural Hiring

	Very often	Often	Occa- sionally	Rarely	Never
1. A system of incentives has been provided to attract and retain teachers of color.	☐	☐	☐	☐	☐
2. The institution makes time for teachers of color to pursue research beyond the requirements of the classroom.	☐	☐	☐	☐	☐
3. A "grow your own" strategy is underway to identify bright graduate students of color and fund them for doctorial work before assigning them teaching responsibilities.	☐	☐	☐	☐	☐
4. There is a strong effort to seek employment for the spouse of a faculty member who has been hired by the institution.	☐	☐	☐	☐	☐
5. Faculty and/or staff of color are involved in searches.	☐	☐	☐	☐	☐
6. Senior faculty are assigned as mentors to junior faculty of color.	☐	☐	☐	☐	☐
7. Special funds are available to faculty of color for professional development.	☐	☐	☐	☐	☐
8. The institution recognizes and gives credit to faculty and staff of color who, beyond their required duties, serve students of color.	☐	☐	☐	☐	☐
9. Administrative internships are available to personnel of color who wish to gain skills that will prepare them for administrative opportunities.	☐	☐	☐	☐	☐
10. Employee education programs are available to help adult employees of color gain academic skills, pursue college work, and ultimately graduate.	☐	☐	☐	☐	☐

Comments _____

_____

_____

INDEX